EDCO
MATHS
REVISE WISE

JUNIOR CERTIFICATE ORDINARY LEVEL

Brian Brophy and Tony Daly

Edco
The Educational Company of Ireland

The Educational Company of Ireland
Ballymount Road
Walkinstown
Dublin 12
A member of the Smurfit Kappa Group

© Brian Brophy, Tony Daly, 2006

Editor: Kristin Jensen

Cover design: Combined Media

Cover photo: istockphoto

Interior design: DTP Workshop

Printed in the Republic of Ireland by: ColourBooks Ltd

1 2 3 4 5 6 7 8 9.

Contents

Introduction	iv	
Examination Section	v	

Paper 1

1 Sets	1	☐
2 Arithmetic	17	☐
3 Arithmetic 2	28	☐
4 Algebra	44	☐
5 Algebra 2	57	☐
6 Functions	73	☐

Revised

Paper 2

7 Two-Dimensional and Three-Dimensional Figures	87	☐
8 Geometry	119	☐
9 Co-ordinate Geometry	169	☐
10 Trigonometry	190	☐
11 Statistics	212	☐
Glossary	230	☐
Study Plan	234	

Revised

Introduction

This book has been written as a revision aid for the Junior Certificate Ordinary Level Maths course. The aim of this book is to present the material in a clear, logical fashion and to prepare the student for the Junior Certificate Ordinary Level Examination. While not designed as a substitute for a textbook, a well-motivated student could use this book as a self-contained work.

The chapter sequencing follows the order in which the topics appear in the Junior Certificate Examination. Chapters 1 to 6 deal with the Paper 1 material, while chapters 7 to 11 deal with the Paper 2 material.

The authors have presented the material using a simple, clear approach to each topic. Each chapter begins with a set of learning objectives, which highlight the sections and set out the aims of the chapter. Each individual section has bullet point information necessary for solving the problems. This information is supplemented by top tips where appropriate. Each section ends with a self-test exercise, which should be attempted before checking the solutions at the end of the chapter. Each chapter ends with a set of key points that summarise the important information contained within, followed by relevant questions from two recent Junior Certificate Examinations.

Finally, a glossary is included, explaining the terminology used in the text.

Examination Section

Junior Certificate Ordinary Level Maths Commonly Asked Questions

What can and should I bring to the exam centre?
(a) Mathematical instruments, e.g. ruler, compass.
(b) A calculator you know how to use.
(c) Pens, pencils, an eraser and a sharpener.

What can I get from the superintendent in the exam centre?
Maths tables, graph paper and additional paper on which to write if you need it.

What is the first thing I should do when I get the exam paper?
Ask for a copy of the maths tables if there is not already a copy on your desk. You need the maths tables because it contains formulae for answering questions on area and volume. Note that formulae for co-ordinate geometry are given on Paper 2.

Do I write in pen or pencil?
Write in blue or black pen. The person who will mark your paper may find writing in pencil difficult to read. However, pencils are very useful for graphs, diagrams and rough work.

Do I have to start at question 1?
No. You can start with whatever question or part of a question you are most comfortable with.

Do I have to attempt every question on the paper?
Yes. There is no choice on Paper 1 or Paper 2, so you have to attempt every question.

If I decide that a solution I have written down is wrong, what should I do?
Do not use Tippex or cross it out. Simply draw a line through your work and start again. If you attempt the same part of a question more than once, each attempt is marked and the highest of the marks gained in the various attempts is the final mark awarded.

Is 'rough work' of any value?

Yes. All work handed in will be marked. Candidates often gain marks for rough work, so do not erase it. Sometimes it also helps the examiner decide how you arrived at a solution. Rough work can be done on extra sheets of paper obtained from the superintendent.

Using a calculator, should I show the steps in the calculation or give the final answer only?

Show all the steps that you can by writing down each stage of the calculation as you progress through the problem. A wrong answer on its own, without any work shown, will get zero marks.

Are diagrams important?

In geometry, they are essential. In topics such as co-ordinate geometry and trigonometry, diagrams can be extremely helpful. However, do remember that distances, angles and the like must be calculated and not measured from a diagram unless the question specifically states to measure from the diagram.

What about graph paper?

Graphs in statistics and function (quadratic and straight line graphs) questions should be done on graph paper, which is included as part of the question in the booklet. You may need to read answers from your graph and this can only be done reasonably accurately if using graph paper. Graph paper can also be used to advantage in co-ordinate geometry questions to suggest whether answers you obtain by calculation are correct or not.

How long should I spend on each question?

You should spend five to ten minutes at the start looking through the paper and reading the questions carefully. Some questions take more time than others to complete, so the best advice is that if you find yourself getting stuck on a question, leave it and move on to another one. Make sure to leave time at the end to try a question or part of a question again and to check over your answers.

What should I do at the end of the exam?

Check the front cover of your booklet to make sure that you have written your exam number and the make and model of your calculator in the boxes indicated. Also, include any extra graph paper or rough work paper that you have used.

Attempt every question and good luck!

CHAPTER 1
Sets

Learning Objectives
- What is a set?
- Use of Venn diagrams.
- Important symbols in sets.
- Set operations — union, intersection, set difference, complement.
- Solve difficult problems using Venn diagrams.

What is a set?

A **set** is a collection of well-defined objects, and each object of a set is called an **element**. The following are sets:

1) All the students in your class who are 15 years of age.
2) The 32 counties of Ireland.

But 'all the good programmes on TV' is not a set because the objects/elements are not well defined, that is, we cannot say for certain whether a particular programme is good or not.

Use of Venn diagrams

- We use capital letters to name sets and small letters or numbers to name elements.
- An element is included in a set only once.
- Sets are illustrated by Venn diagrams.
- The capital letter U represents the universal set, the set of all elements under discussion.

Example 1

$U = \{a, b, c, d, e, f\}$, $K = \{a, b, c\}$,
$S = \{b, c, d\}$

Fill all the elements into the Venn diagram.

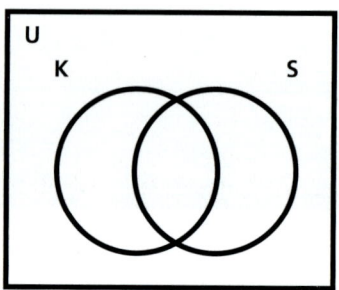

Solution

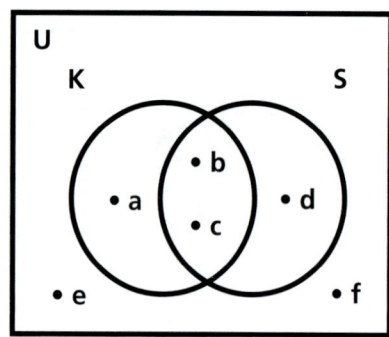

Top Tips

• Fill in the elements b and c first that belong to both sets K and S.

Example 2

$U = \{1, 2, 3, 4, 5, 6, 7, 8, 9\}$,
$P = \{1, 2, 3, 5, 6\}$,
$Q = \{2, 3, 4, 7\}$,
$R = \{1, 3, 5, 7, 8\}$

Fill all the elements into the Venn diagram.

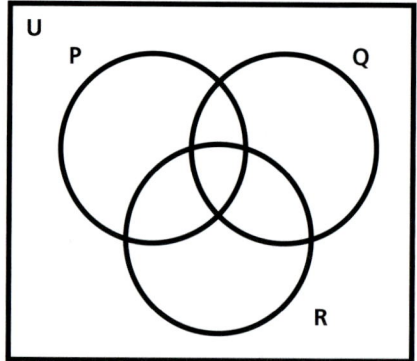

Solution

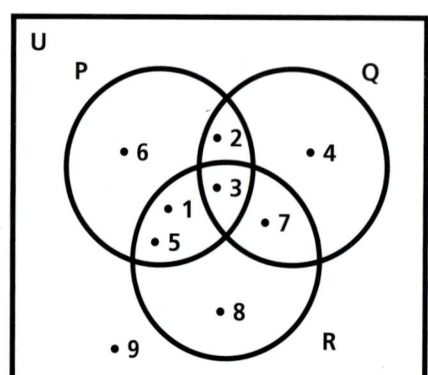

Top Tips

• Fill in the element 3 first that belongs to all three sets, P, Q and R.

Self-test 1

1. $A = \{1, 2, 3, 4, 5\}$, $B = \{2, 4, 6, 7\}$

   Fill all the elements into the Venn diagram.

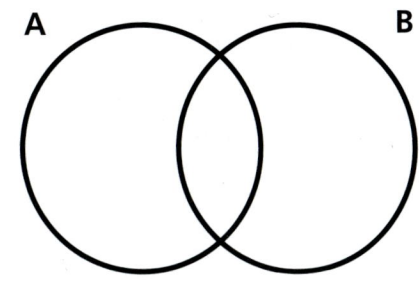

2. $U = \{a, b, c, d, e, f\}$, $M = \{a, b, c, d\}$, $N = \{c, d, e\}$

   Fill all the elements into the Venn diagram.

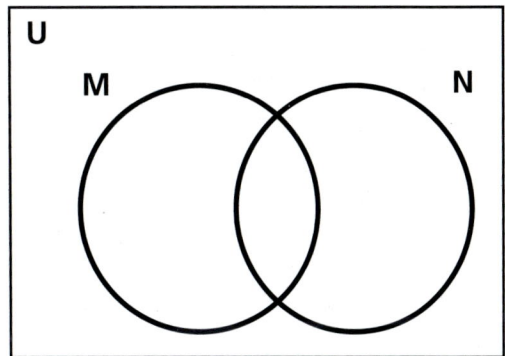

3. $U = \{1, 2, 3, 4, 5, 6, 7, 9, 10, 12\}$, $X = \{2, 3, 6, 7\}$, $Y = \{2, 5, 7, 12\}$, $Z = \{3, 5, 7, 9\}$

   Fill all the elements into the Venn diagram.

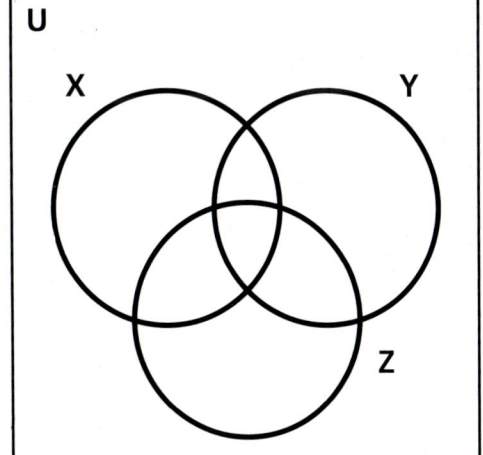

Important symbols in sets

- $\in$ means 'is an element of' and $\notin$ means 'is not an element of', e.g. $2 \in \{1, 2, 3, 4\}$ but $6 \notin \{1, 2, 3, 4\}$.
- $\{\ \}$ or ϕ means the 'empty set' or 'null set'.
- # means the 'cardinal number of a set', that is, the number of elements in a set, e.g. $K = \{a, c, d\}$, then $\#(K) = 3$.
- $\subset$ means 'is a subset of' and $\not\subset$ means 'is not a subset of', e.g. $A = \{1, 2, 3\}$, $B = \{1, 2, 3, 4, 5, 6\}$, then $A \subset B$ but $B \not\subset A$.

Example 1

S = {3, 5, 7}, D = {a, b, d, g}

(a) What is the cardinal number of S?
(b) Write out all the subsets of S.
(c) What is the cardinal number of D?
(d) Write out any three subsets of D.

> **Top Tips**
> - Every set is a subset of itself,
>   e.g. if $A = \{2, 5, 7, 9\}$, then $A \subset A$.
> - The empty set is a subset of every set,
>   e.g. if $A = \{2, 5, 7, 9\}$, then $\phi \subset A$.

Solution
(a) $\#(S) = 3$
(b) $\phi, \{3\}, \{5\}, \{7\}, \{3, 5\}, \{3, 7\}, \{5, 7\}, \{3, 5, 7\}$
(c) $\#(D) = 4$
(d) {a}, {a, b}, {a, b, d}

Self-test 2

1. **Write down** the cardinal number of each of the following sets.
   (a) $M = \{3, 6, 9\}$
   (b) $N = \{a, b, c, d, e\}$
   (c) $P = \{\ \}$
   (d) $Q = \{0, 2, 5, 8\}$

2. **Write down** all the subsets of $K = \{x, y, z\}$.

Set operations

- ∪ means the union of sets, i.e. all the elements in two or more sets, counting each element once.

Example 1

$A = \{1, 2, 3\}, B = \{3, 4, 5\}$

$\Rightarrow A \cup B = \{1, 2, 3, 4, 5\}$

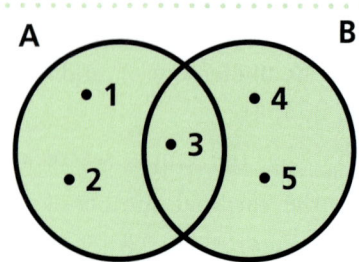

- ∩ means the **intersection of sets**, i.e. all the elements common to two or more sets, counting each element once.

> **Top Tips**
>
> - Always use dots for elements in a Venn diagram.

Example 2

$A = \{1, 2, 3\}, B = \{3, 4, 5\}$

$\Rightarrow A \cap B = \{3\}$

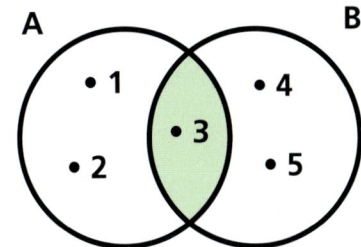

- \ means **set difference**, i.e. all the elements in one set that are not in another set.

Example 3

$A = \{1, 2, 3\}, B = \{3, 4, 5\}$

$\Rightarrow A \backslash B = \{1, 2\}$

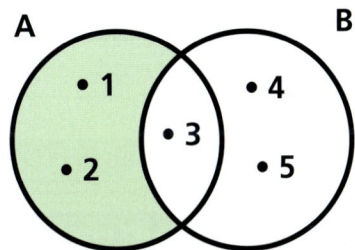

- ′ means the **complement of a set**, i.e. all the elements that are not in a set.

Example 4

$U = \{1, 2, 3, 4, 5\}, A = \{1, 2, 3\}$

$\Rightarrow A' = \{4, 5\}$ or $U \backslash A = \{4, 5\}$

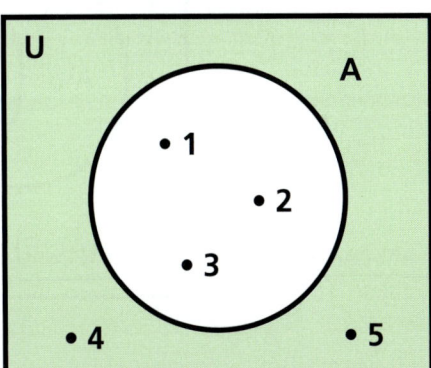

Example 5

U is the universal set.

$A = \{7, 6, 3, 2\}, B = \{8, 5, 3, 1\}$

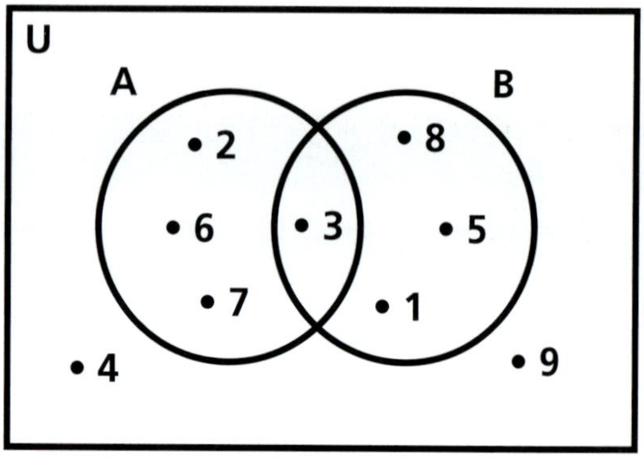

Given the Venn diagram, list the elements of:

(a) $A \cup B$

(b) $A \backslash B$

(c) $A \cap B$

(d) B'

Solution

(a) $A \cup B = \{1, 2, 3, 5, 6, 7, 8,\}$

(b) $A \backslash B = \{2, 6, 7\}$

(c) $A \cap B = \{3\}$

(d) $B' = \{2, 4, 6, 7, 9\}$

Top Tips

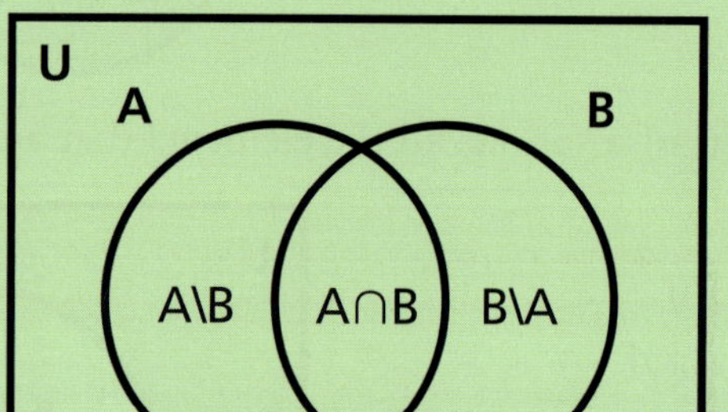

$A \backslash B$ $A \cap B$ $B \backslash A$

$(A \cup B)'$ or $U \backslash (A \cup B)$

Also:

- $A \cup B$ = all the elements in A or B or both.
- B' = all the elements outside of B.
- A' = all the elements outside of A.

Example 6

U is the universal set.

$A = \{1, 2, 3, 5, 6\}$,
$B = \{2, 3, 4, 5, 7\}$,
$C = \{3, 4, 5, 6, 8\}$

Given the Venn diagram, list the elements of:

(a) $A \cup B$

(b) $A \cap B \cap C$

(c) $B \backslash C$

(d) C'

(e) $A \backslash (B \cup C)$

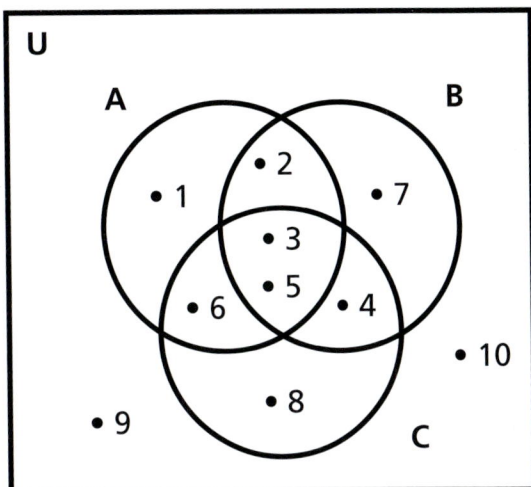

Solution (a) $A \cup B = \{1, 2, 3, 4, 5, 6, 7\}$

(b) $A \cap B \cap C = \{3, 5\}$

(c) $B \backslash C = \{2, 7\}$

(d) $C' = \{1, 2, 7, 9, 10\}$

(e) $A \backslash (B \cup C) = \{1\}$

Note
- $B \cup C = \{2, 3, 4, 5, 6, 7, 8\}$, then $A \backslash (B \cup C) = \{1\}$

Top Tips

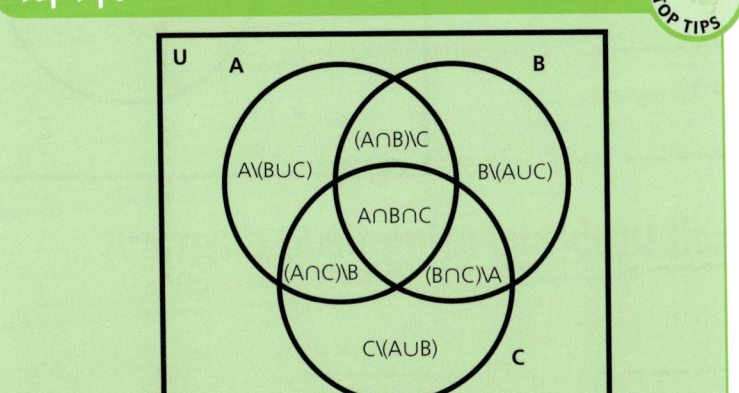

Also:

- $A \cup B \cup C =$ all the elements in A or B or C.

- $B \backslash C =$ all the elements in B but not in C.

- $C' =$ all the elements outside of C.

Self-test 3

1. $U = \{a, b, c, d, e, f\}$,
   $P = \{a, b, c, d\}$,
   $Q = \{b, c, e\}$

   List the elements of:

   (a) $P \cap Q$

   (b) $P \cup Q$

   (c) $P \backslash Q$

   (d) P'

   (e) $(P \cup Q)'$

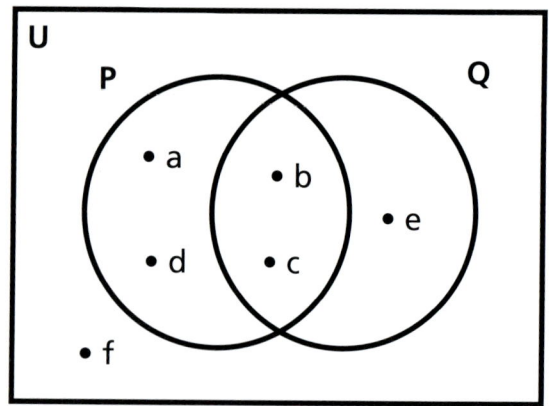

2. U is the universal set
   $X = \{3, 5, 6, 7, 8, 9\}$,
   $Y = \{2, 3, 4, 7, 9, 10\}$,
   $Z = \{1, 2, 3, 5, 6\}$

   List the elements of:

   (a) $X \cup Y$

   (b) $(X \cup Y) \backslash Z$

   (c) $(X \cap Y) \cap Z$

   (d) $(Y \cup Z)'$

   (e) $Z \backslash (X \cup Y)$

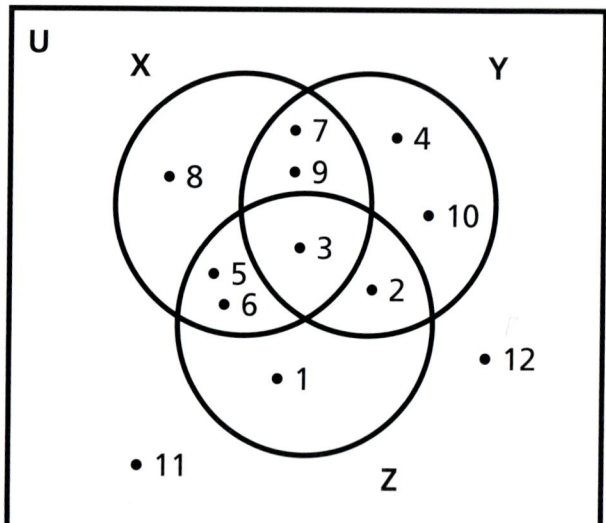

Solve difficult problems using Venn diagrams

Example 1

In a class of 38 boys, 25 play basketball (B), 16 play soccer (S) and 3 play neither sport.

Using a Venn diagram, or otherwise, **answer** the following questions.

(a) How many boys play both basketball and soccer?

(b) How many boys play soccer but not basketball?

(c) How many boys play basketball but not soccer?

(d) How many boys play exactly one of the two sports?

CHAPTER 1: SETS

Top Tips

- Always try to fill in the information given by starting from the centre of the Venn diagram.
- Always use block brackets [ ] for a cardinal number in a Venn diagram.

Solution

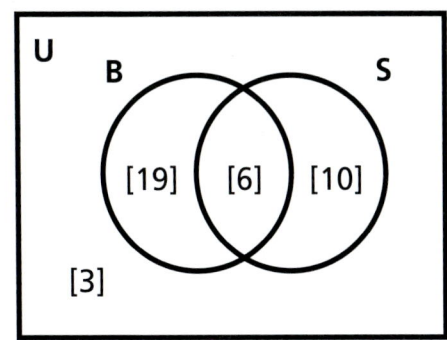

(a) How many boys play both basketball and soccer?

  Solution $38 - 3 = 35$ and $25 + 16 = 41$

  So, $41 - 35 = 6$ boys

(b) How many boys play soccer but not basketball?

  Solution $16 - 6 = 10$ boys

(c) How many boys play basketball but not soccer?

  Solution $25 - 6 = 19$ boys

(d) How many boys play exactly one of the two sports?

  Solution $19 + 10 = 29$ boys

Help

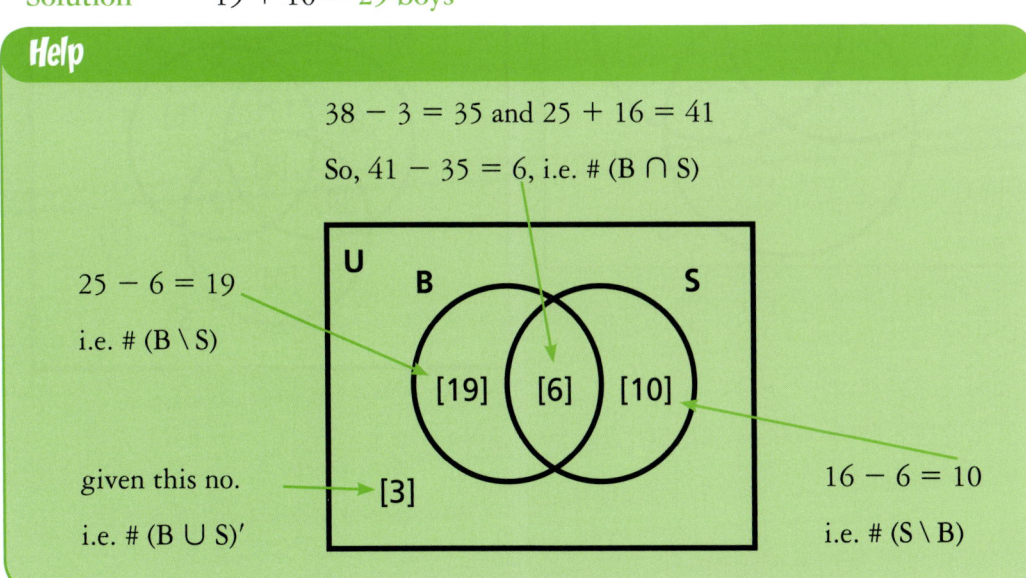

9

Example 2

In a class of 30 students, 14 passed Maths (M), 13 passed Irish (I), 10 passed Science (S), 5 passed Maths and Irish, 3 passed Maths and Science, 4 passed Irish and Science and 2 passed all three subjects.

Using a Venn diagram, or otherwise, answer the following questions:

(a) How many passed Maths only?

  Solution   8 students

(b) How many passed one subject only?

  Solution $8 + 6 + 5 = 19$ students

(c) How many passed Irish and Science only?

  Solution   2 students

(d) How many passed none of these subjects?

  Solution   3 students

(e) How many passed at least two subjects?

  Solution $1 + 3 + 2 + 2 = 8$ students

Solution

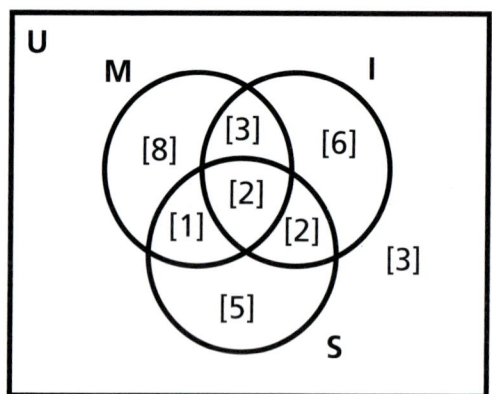

Help

This Venn diagram explains what each region stands for.

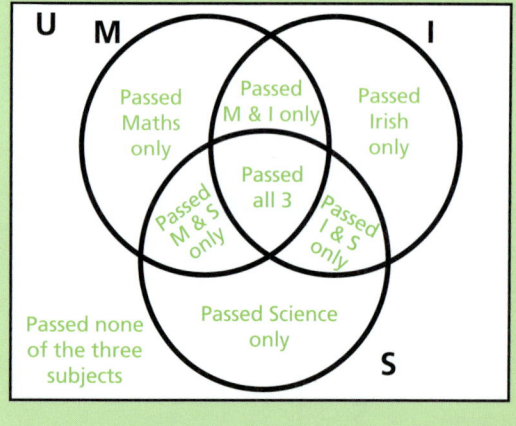

How to calculate the no. for each region

$14 - (1 + 2 + 3)$
$= 14 - 6$
$= 8$

$5 - 2$
$= 3$

given
2

$13 - (3 + 2 + 2)$
$= 13 - 7$
$= 6$

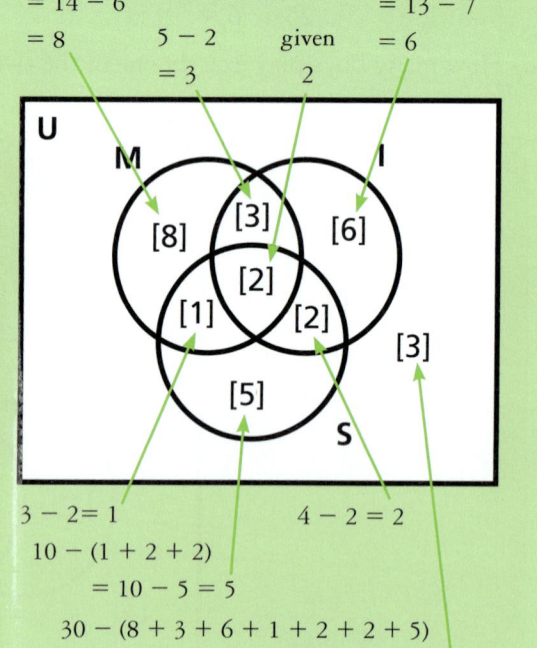

$3 - 2 = 1$

$4 - 2 = 2$

$10 - (1 + 2 + 2)$
$= 10 - 5 = 5$

$30 - (8 + 3 + 6 + 1 + 2 + 2 + 5)$
$= 30 - 27 = 3$

Self-test 4

1. In a survey of 35 teenagers, 15 liked music (M), 22 liked sport (S) and 6 liked both music and sport.

   Complete the Venn diagram and **answer** the following questions.

   (a) How many liked music only?

   (b) How many liked sport only?

   (c) How many liked neither sport nor music?

   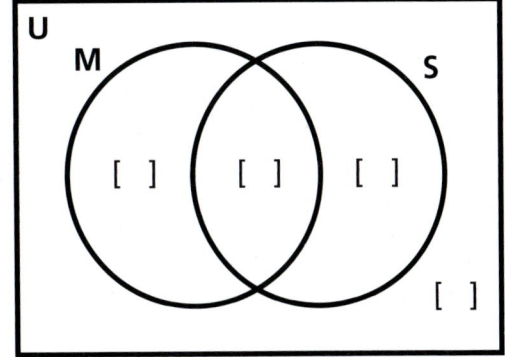

2. A group of 36 pupils was asked if they buy tea (T), coffee (C) or milk (M). The following are the results: 19 buy tea, 21 buy coffee, 14 buy milk, 6 buy tea and milk, 4 buy all three, 5 buy milk only and 10 buy tea and coffee.

   Complete the Venn diagram below and **answer** the following questions.

   (a) How many buy tea and coffee only?

   (b) How many buy none of these drinks?

   (c) How many buy one drink only?

   (d) How many buy two drinks only?

   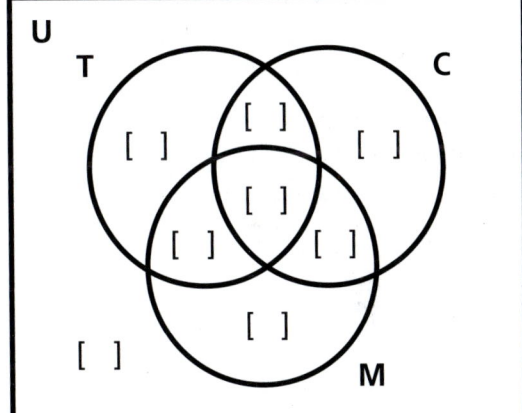

Self-test answers

Self-test 1

1.
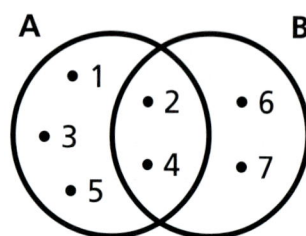

2.
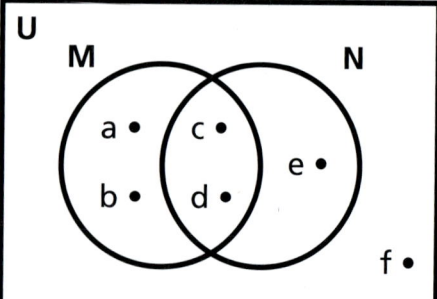

3.
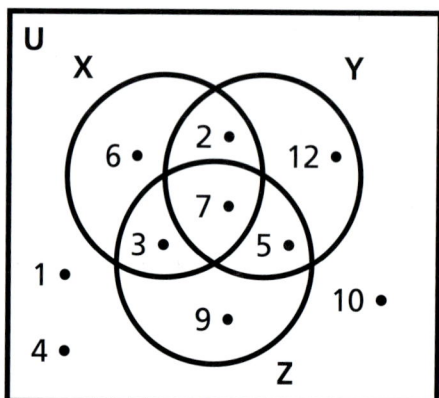

Self-test 2

1. (a) #(M) = 3
   (b) #(N) = 5
   (c) #(P) = 0
   (d) #(Q) = 4

2. { }, {x}, {y}, {z}, {x, y}, {x, z}, {y, z}, {x, y, z}

Self-test 3

1. (a) $P \cap Q$ = {b, c}
   (b) $P \cup Q$ = {a, b, c, d, e}
   (c) P\Q = {a, d}
   (d) P' = {e, f}
   (e) $(P \cup Q)'$ = {f}

2. (a) $X \cup Y$ = {2, 3, 4, 5, 6, 7, 8, 9, 10}
   (b) $(X \cup Y)\backslash Z$ = {4, 7, 8, 9, 10}
   (c) $(X \cap Y) \cap Z$ = {3}
   (d) $(Y \cup Z)'$ = {8, 11, 12}
   (e) $Z\backslash(X \cup Y)$ = {1}

Self-test 4

1. (a) 9
   (b) 16
   (c) 4

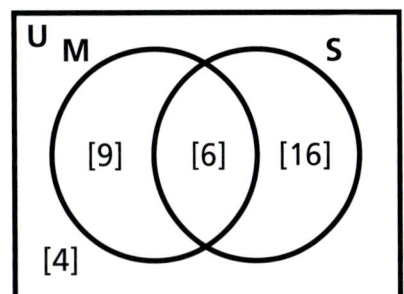

2. (a) 6
   (b) 1
   (c) 7 + 8 + 5 = 20
   (d) 6 + 2 + 3 = 11

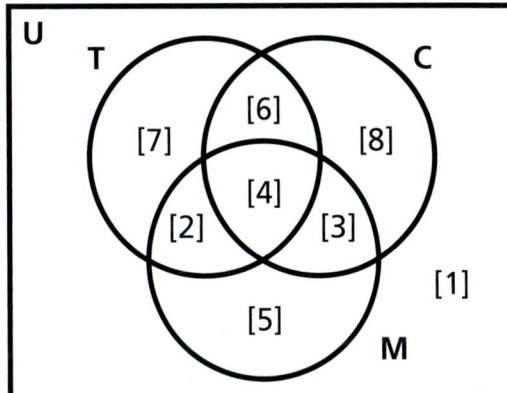

Key Points

- An **element** is included in a set only once.
- The symbol U represents the universal set and is illustrated by a rectangle.
- The important symbols are $\cup$ for **union**, $\cap$ for **intersection**, $\setminus$ for **set difference**, $'$ for **complement**.
- $A \cup B = B \cup A$, $A \cap B = B \cap A$, but $A \setminus B \neq B \setminus A$.
- When filling elements into a Venn diagram, use **dots**, but when filling cardinal numbers into a Venn diagram, use **block brackets**.

Junior Certificate Examination 2004

Paper 1, Q1

1. (a) i. Using the Venn diagram below, shade in the region that represents $P \cap Q$.

   Solution

   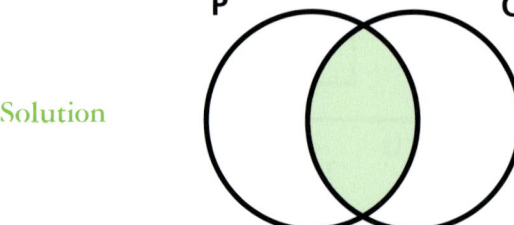

   ii. Using the Venn diagram below, shade in the region that represents $P \cup Q$.

   Solution

   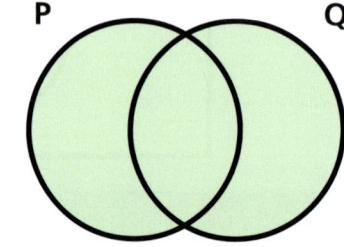

   (b) U is the universal set.
   $A = \{3, 8, 9\}$
   $B = \{1, 2, 6, 8, 9\}$
   $C = \{1, 2, 4, 5, 8\}$

   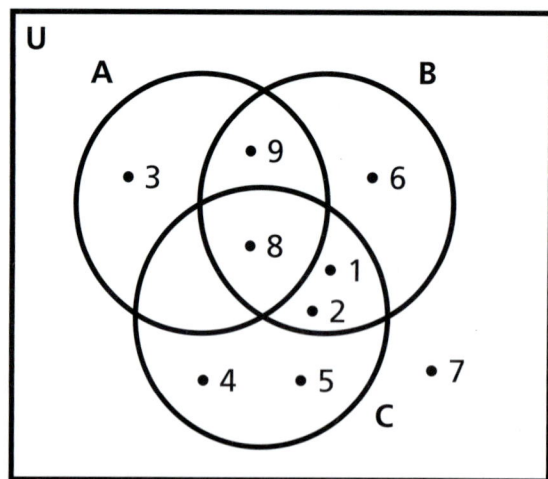

List the elements of:

i. $A \cup B$
   Solution   {1, 2, 3, 6, 8, 9}

ii. $B \backslash C$
   Solution   {6, 9}

iii. A'
   Solution   {1, 2, 4, 5, 6, 7}

iv. $A \cup (B \backslash C)$
   Solution   {3, 6, 8, 9}

(c) i. P is the set of prime numbers between 1 and 12. List the elements of the set P.
   Solution $P = \{2, 3, 5, 7, 11\}$

ii. $Q = \{1, 3, 5, 7, 9, 11\}$.
   Write down #(Q).
   Solution   #(Q) = 6

iii. $T = \{2, 4, 6, 8, 10, 12\}$
   Write down the elements of T that are multiples of 3.
   Solution   {6, 12}

iv. Express 12 as the product of three prime numbers.
   Solution $12 = 2 \times 2 \times 3$

Help

- See Chapter 3: Prime numbers, multiples, factors, HCF and LCM section.

Junior Certificate Examination 2005

Paper 1, Q1

1. (a) $P = \{x, y, w\}$

   i. Write down a subset of P that has one element.
      Solution   {x} or {y} or {w}

   ii. Write down a subset of P that has two elements.
      Solution   {x, y} or {x, w} or {y, w}

(b) U is the universal set.

   $A = \{1, 2, 4, 8\}$ the set of divisors of 8.

   $B = \{1, 2, 3, 4, 6, 12\}$ the set of divisors of 12.

   $C = \{1, 2, 4, 5, 10, 20\}$ the set of divisors of 20.

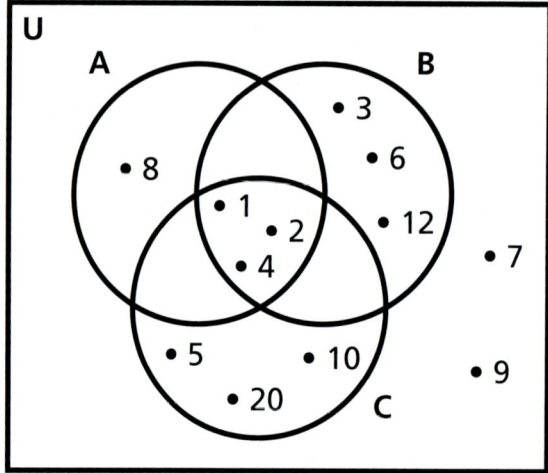

i. List the elements of $A \cap C$.
Solution {1, 2, 4}

ii. List the elements of B', the complement of the set B.
Solution {5, 7, 8, 9, 10, 20}

iii. List the elements of $C \setminus (A \cap B)$.
Solution {5, 10, 20}

iv. Using the Venn diagram above, or otherwise, find the highest common factor (HCF) of 8, 12 and 20.
Solution $A \cap B \cap C = \{1, 2, 4\}$
So, HCF = 4
or
Divs. of 8 = {1, 2, 4, 8}
Divs. of 12 = {1, 2, 3, 4, 6, 12}
Divs. of 20 = {1, 2, 4, 5, 10, 20}
So, HCF = 4

Help
- See Chapter 3: Prime numbers, multiples, factors, HCF and LCM section.

(c) M is the set of natural numbers from 1 to 20, inclusive.

i. List the elements of M that are multiples of 3.
Solution {3, 6, 9, 12, 15, 18}

ii. List the elements of M that are multiples of 5.
Solution {5, 10, 15, 20}

iii. Write down the lowest common multiple (LCM) of 3 and 5.
Solution LCM = 15

iv. Express 10 as the sum of three prime numbers.
Solution 10 = 2 + 3 + 5

CHAPTER 2
Arithmetic 1

Learning Objectives

- Ratio.
- Proportion – direct proportion and inverse proportion.
- Foreign exchange (currency conversion).
- Percentages.
- Value added tax (VAT).
- Annual interest and compound interest.
- Income tax.

Ratio

A comparison of one number to another is a *ratio*, e.g. 5:2.

Example 1

€350 is shared between Joe and Ann in the ratio 3:4. How much does each receive?

Solution

$3 + 4 = 7$ shares
1 share = €350 ÷ 7 = €50
Joe: 3 shares = 3 × €50 = **€150**
Ann: 4 shares = 4 × €50 = **€200**

Help

- Step 1: Addition of numbers in ratio = number of shares.
- Step 2: Sum of money ÷ number of shares = value of 1 share.
- Step 3: Number of shares each receives × value of 1 share = answer.

Example 2

Divide 240 kg amongst *A*, *B* and *C* in the ratio 5:2:1.

Solution
$5 + 2 + 1 = 8$ shares
1 share $= 240$ kg $\div 8 = 30$ kg
A: 5 shares $= 5 \times 30$ kg $= 150$ kg
B: 2 shares $= 2 \times 30$ kg $= 60$ kg
C: 1 share $= 1 \times 30$ kg $= 30$ kg

Example 3

€1040 was divided in the ratio 6:7. The larger amount was given to charity. **How much** was this?

Solution
$6 + 7 = 13$ shares

1 share $=$ €1040 $\div 13 =$ €80

Larger amount $= 7$ shares $= 7 \times$ €80 $=$ €560

Self-test 1

1. Two numbers are in the ratio 4:5. If the sum of the numbers is 162, **what are** the numbers?
2. **Divide** €750 amongst three people in the ratio 3:2:1.
3. A prize fund is divided between Bill and Jill in the ratio 5:7. If Bill gets €125, **how much** does Jill get?

Help
- Divide €125 by 5 and multiply by 7.

Proportion – direct proportion and inverse proportion

Direct proportion

- As first quantity rises, second quantity rises.
- As first quantity falls, second quantity falls.

Top Tips
- Put whatever quantity you know most about on the left-hand side in your equation.

Example 1

If 5 tickets cost €120, find the cost of 8 tickets.

Solution

$$5 \text{ tickets} = €120$$
$$\Rightarrow 1 \text{ ticket} = \frac{€120}{5} \leftarrow \text{Divide}$$
$$\Rightarrow 8 \text{ tickets} = \frac{€120 \times 8}{5} = €192$$

Help

- We know most about 'tickets', so put 'tickets' on the left-hand side and solve.

Inverse proportion

- As first quantity rises, second quantity falls.
- As first quantity falls, second quantity rises.

Example 2

If 5 men can build a house in 120 days, how long will it take 8 men to build a house?

Solution

$$5 \text{ men} = 120 \text{ days}$$
$$\Rightarrow 1 \text{ man} = 120 \times 5 \leftarrow \text{Multiply}$$
$$\Rightarrow 8 \text{ men} = \frac{120 \times 5}{8} = 75 \text{ days}$$

Help

- We know most about 'men', so put 'men' on the left-hand side and solve.

Self-test 2

1. A car travels 150 km on 20 litres of petrol. How far will the car travel on 36 litres of petrol?
2. 15 people share a prize and each gets €100. If 10 people share the prize, how much will each get?

Foreign exchange (currency conversion)

Example 1

1 euro = 140 Japanese yen
Change €120 into yen.
Solution
$$€1 = ¥140$$
$$\Rightarrow €120 = 120 \times 140 \quad \leftarrow \text{Multiply}$$
$$\Rightarrow €120 = ¥16\,800$$

Top Tips

- When converting from your currency to another currency, **multiply**.
- When converting from another currency back to your currency, **divide**.

Example 2

1 euro = US$1.35
Change US$405 into euro.
Solution
$$\$1.35 = €1$$
$$\Rightarrow \$1 = \frac{1}{1.35} \quad \leftarrow \text{Divide}$$
$$\Rightarrow \$405 = \frac{1 \times 405}{1.35} = €300$$

Self-test 3

1. If 1 euro = US$1.40

    (a) How many dollars would you get for €250?

    (b) How many euro would you get for $175?

2. If 1 euro = Stg. £0.70

    (a) Change €320 into Sterling

    (b) Change £175 pounds Sterling into euro.

Percentages

Example 1

Find 30% of €150.

Solution
$$30\% \text{ of } €150.$$
$$= \frac{30 \times 150}{100}$$
$$= €45$$

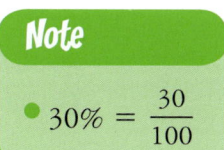

Note
- $30\% = \frac{30}{100}$

Example 2

A man bought a car for €5000 (CP) and sold it for €6000 (SP). **Calculate** the profit as a percentage of the cost price (CP).

Solution
$$\text{Profit} = €6000 - €5000 = €1000$$
$$\% \text{ profit} = \frac{1000 \times 100}{5000} = 20\%$$

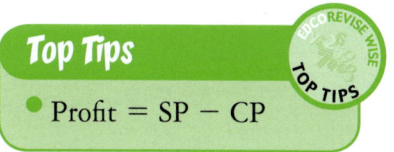

Top Tips
- Profit = SP − CP

Example 3

A TV purchased for €480 (CP) was sold for €360 (SP). **Calculate** the loss as a percentage of the selling price (SP).

Solution
$$\text{Loss} = €480 - €360 = €120$$
$$\% \text{ loss} = \frac{120 \times 100}{360} = 33\tfrac{1}{3}\%$$

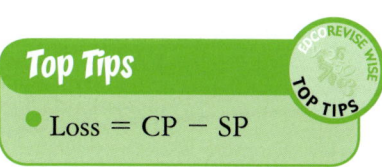

Top Tips
- Loss = CP − SP

Example 4

When a camera is sold for €147, a profit of 5% is made. Find the cost price (CP).

Solution CP + profit = 100% + 5% = 105%
So, 105% = €147
$\Rightarrow$ 1% = $\frac{147}{105}$

$\Rightarrow$ 100% = $\frac{147 \times 100}{105}$ = €140

Self-test 4

1. Find 10% of €132.
2. If a student buys a book for €28 and sells it for €35, calculate the percentage profit on the cost price (CP).

Value added tax (VAT)

Top Tips
- VAT is a tax **added** to the price of a good or service.

Example 1

Calculate the VAT at 15% added to a CD that costs €10.

Solution VAT = 15% × €10

$\Rightarrow$ VAT = $\frac{15 \times 10}{100}$ = €1.50

Note
- 15% = $\frac{15}{100}$

Example 2

Find the total cost of an ESB bill of €240 plus VAT at 13.5%.

Solution VAT = 13.5% × €240

$\Rightarrow$ VAT = $\frac{13.5 \times 240}{100}$ = $\frac{3240}{100}$ = €32.40

So, total bill = €240 + €32.40 = €272.40

Example 3

The cost of a holiday plus VAT at 10% is €440. **Find** the cost of the holiday before VAT is added on.

Solution Cost + VAT = 100% + 10% = 110%

So, 110% = €440

$\Rightarrow$ 1% = $\dfrac{440}{110}$

$\Rightarrow$ 100% = $\dfrac{440 \times 100}{110}$ = €400

Self-test 5

1. VAT at 15% is added to a bill of €44.40. **Calculate** the total bill.
2. 5 tickets cost €30 each + VAT at 21%. **Find** the total cost of the tickets.

Annual interest and compound interest

Example 1

Calculate the interest on €3500 for one year at 6%.

Solution Interest = 6% × 3500

$\Rightarrow$ Interest = $\dfrac{6 \times 3500}{100}$ = €210

Example 2

What sum of money will earn €91 interest after one year at 7% p.a. (per annum)?

Solution 7% = €91

$\Rightarrow$ 1% = $\dfrac{91}{7}$

$\Rightarrow$ 100% = $\dfrac{91 \times 100}{7}$ = €1300

Example 3

(a) €2000 is invested at 3% p.a. What is the amount of the investment at the end of one year?

Solution

	€
Principal for first year =	2000
Interest for first year =	60
Amount at end of first year =	€2060

Work-out: how to calculate interest for year 1:

$3\% \times €2000$

$= \dfrac{3 \times 2000}{100} = €60$

(b) €360 is withdrawn from this amount at the beginning of the second year. The interest rate for the second year is 2.4% p.a. What is the amount of the investment at the end of that year?

Solution

	€
Amount at end of first year =	2060.00
Withdrawal at end of first year =	360.00
Principal for second year =	1700.00
Interest for second year =	40.80
Amount at end of second year =	1740.80

Work-out: how to calculate interest for year 2:

$2.4\% \times €1700 = \dfrac{2.4 \times 1700}{100}$

$= €40.80$

Example 4

Calculate the compound interest on €4000 after two years at 5% p.a.

Solution

	€
Principal for first year =	4000.00
Interest for first year =	200.00
Principal for second year =	4200.00
Interest for second year =	210.00
Amount after two years =	4410.00
Principal for first year =	4000.00
Compound interest =	410.00

Note

- Compound interest = amount − principal (1st year)

Top Tips

- **Principal** is the sum of money invested/saved or borrowed.
- **Interest** is money paid to a saver or by a borrower.
- **Amount** = principal + interest.
- **Compound interest** means earning interest on interest.

Self-test 6

1. **Calculate** the interest on €875 for one year at 8%.
2. **Calculate** the compound interest on €2500 after two years at 4% p.a.

Income tax

Example 1

Gary's gross pay is €30 000. His tax credit is €2600. He pays income tax at the rate of 20%. **Calculate** his take-home pay.

Solution

$$\boxed{\text{tax} = \frac{20 \times 30\,000}{100} = €6000}$$ →

$$\boxed{\text{tax credit} = \text{tax refunded}}$$ →

		€
Gross pay	=	30 000
Tax @ 20%	=	6 000 ← Subtract
Pay after tax	=	24 000
Tax credit	=	2 600 ← Add
Net pay	=	26 600

Top Tips

- **Tax credit** = tax refunded = tax paid but given back.
- **SRCOP** = standard rate cut-off point = maximum amount of pay at standard rate of tax.
- **Net tax** = gross tax − tax credit.
- **Net pay** = take-home pay.

Example 2

Niamh has an annual salary of €45 000. Her tax credit is €3500 and her standard rate cut-off point is €31 000. If the rates of tax are 20% standard rate and 42% higher rate, **calculate** the amount of tax she pays.

Solution

		€	Tax:		€
Annual salary	=	45 000			
SRCOP	=	31 000	→ €31 000 @ 20% =		6200
Balance	=	14 000	→ €14 000 @ 42% =		5880 ← Add
			Gross tax	=	12 080
			Tax credit	=	3500 ← Subtract
			Net tax	=	8580

Self-test 7

1. Brian earns €280 per week. He has a weekly tax credit of €30. He pays income tax at the rate of 25%. **What is** his take-home pay?
2. Connor's annual pay is €50 000. His tax credit is €2600 and his standard rate cut-off point is €29 000. If the standard rate of tax is 20% and the higher rate of tax is 42%, **calculate** his net pay.

Self-test answers

Self-test 1
1. 72, 90
2. €375:€250:€125
3. €175

Self-test 2
1. 270 km
2. €150

Self-test 3
1. (a) US$350
   (b) €125
2. (a) Stg. £224
   (b) €250

Self-test 4
1. €13.20
2. 25%

Self-test 5
1. €51.06
2. €181.50

Self-test 6
1. €70
2. €204

Self-test 7
1. €240
2. €37 980

Key Points

- A **ratio** may be written in the form 6:7 or $\frac{6}{7}$.
- **Direct proportion** means that as first quantity rises, second quantity rises; and as first quantity falls, second quantity falls.
- **Inverse proportion** means that as first quantity rises, second quantity falls; and as first quantity falls, second quantity rises.
- To convert the euro into a foreign currency, **multiply**, and to convert a foreign currency into the euro, **divide**.
- Gross tax − tax credit = **net tax**.

CHAPTER 3
Arithmetic 2

Learning Objectives

- Indices.
- Scientific notation (standard form).
- Estimation (approximation) and the calculator.
- Household bills.
- Distance/time/speed.
- Metric system.
- Prime numbers, factors, multiples, HCF and LCM.

Indices

Rules of indices

Rule 1 $a^m \cdot a^n = a^{m+n}$ e.g. $a^2 \cdot a^7 = a^{2+7} = a^9$
                                           e.g. $5^2 \cdot 5^7 = 5^{2+7} = 5^9$

Rule 2 $a^m \div a^n = a^{m-n}$ e.g. $a^8 \div a^3 = a^{8-3} = a^5$
                                           e.g. $3^8 \div 3^3 = 3^{8-3} = 3^5$

Rule 3 $(a^m)^n = a^{mn}$ e.g. $(a^2)^3 = a^{2.3} = a^6$
                                     e.g. $(7^2)^3 = 7^{2.3} = 7^6$

Example 1

Simplify $\dfrac{a^9 \times a^3}{a^5 \times a^2}$, giving your answer in the form a^n, where $n \in \mathbb{N}$.

Solution $\dfrac{a^9 \times a^3}{a^5 \times a^2} = \dfrac{a^{9+3}}{a^{5+2}} = \dfrac{a^{12}}{a^7} = a^{12-7} = a^5$

Note
- We use Rule 1 followed by Rule 2.

Example 2

Simplify $(a^7 \times a^2)^3$, giving your answer in the form a^n, where $n \in \mathbb{N}$.

Solution $(a^7 \times a^2)^3 = (a^{7+2})^3 = (a^9)^3 = a^{27}$

Note
- We use Rule 1 followed by Rule 3.

Example 3

If $3^k = 9^{½}$, **solve** for $k \in \mathbb{N}$.

Solution $3^k = 9^{½} \Rightarrow 3^k = (3^2)^{½} \Rightarrow 3^k = 3^1 \Rightarrow k = 1$

Note
- $\sqrt{9} = 9^{½}$ and $3 = 3^1$

Self-test 1

1. **Simplify** each of the following, giving your answer in the form a^n, where $n \in \mathbb{N}$.

   (a) $\dfrac{a^3 \times a^4 \times a^2}{a^5 \times a}$ (b) $(a^5 \times a^3)^2$

2. **Simplify** each of the following, giving your answer in the form 3^n, where $n \in \mathbb{N}$.

   (a) $\dfrac{3^5 \times 3^6}{(3^2)^4}$ (b) $(3^8 \times 3) \div 3^2$

3. If $5^k = 25^{½}$, **solve** for $k \in \mathbb{N}$.

Scientific notation (standard form)

We use scientific notation to rewrite numbers in the form

$$a \times 10^n \text{ where } 1 \leq a < 10, n \in N.$$

Top Tips

- There must be a whole number between 1–9 inclusive in front of the decimal point.

Example 1

Express the numbers (a) 24 500 (b) 245 in the form $a \times 10^n$ where $1 \leq a < 10, n \in N$.

Solution (a) $24\,500 = 2.45 \times 10\,000 = 2.45 \times 10^4$
(b) $245 = 2.45 \times 100 = 2.45 \times 10^2$

Top Tips

- To convert an ordinary number into scientific notation, locate the decimal point, e.g. $24\,500 = 24\,500.0$, and move the decimal point four places to the left to give 2.45×10^4.

Example 2

Multiply 480 by 0.3 and express your answer in the form $a \times 10^n$ where $1 \leq a < 10, n \in N$.

Solution $480 \times 0.3 = 144 = 1.44 \times 10^2$

Example 3

Express $62.1 \times 10^3 + 1.9 \times 10^2$ in the form $a \times 10^n$ where $1 \leq a < 10, n \in N$.

Solution $62.1 \times 10^3 + 1.9 \times 10^2$
$= 62\,100 + 190$
$= 62\,290$
$= 6.229 \times 10^4$

Help

- Step 1: Convert both values back to whole numbers.
- Step 2: Add both whole numbers.
- Step 3: Convert the answer into the form $a \times 10^n$.

Top Tips

- To convert from scientific notation back to ordinary numbers, move the decimal point the number of places the power indicates, e.g. 1.9×10^2, move the decimal point two places to the right to give 190.

Example 4

Express $2.4 \times 10^4 \times 5 \times 10^2$ in the form $a \times 10^n$ where $1 \leq a < 10$, $n \in N$.

Solution
$$2.4 \times 10^4 \times 5 \times 10^2$$
$$= 2.4 \times 5 \times 10^4 \times 10^2$$
$$= 12.0 \times 10^{4+2}$$
$$= 12.0 \times 10^6$$
$$= 1.2 \times 10^1 \times 10^6$$
$$= 1.2 \times 10^7$$

Self-test 2

1. **Express** the numbers (a) 462 (b) 50 160 in the form $a \times 10^n$ where $1 \leq a < 10$, $n \in N$.
2. **Multiply** 3700 by 0.2 and express your answer in the form $a \times 10^n$ where $1 \leq a < 10$, $n \in N$.
3. **Express** the following in the form $a \times 10^n$ where $1 \leq a < 10$, $n \in N$.
   (a) $6.34 \times 10^4 - 12.4 \times 10^2$
   (b) $42.3 \times 10^2 \times 5.4 \times 10$

Estimation (approximation) and the calculator

Top Tips

- The symbol for approximation is $\approx$.

- 5 or more **round up** and less than 5 **round down**.
  Example: $7.63 \approx 8$, but $7.43 \approx 7$.

Example 1

(a) By **rounding** each of these numbers to the nearest whole number, **estimate** the value of $\frac{47.98 + 24.24}{7.85}$.

Solution $\frac{47.98 + 24.24}{7.85}$

$\approx \frac{48 + 24}{8} = \frac{72}{8} = 9$

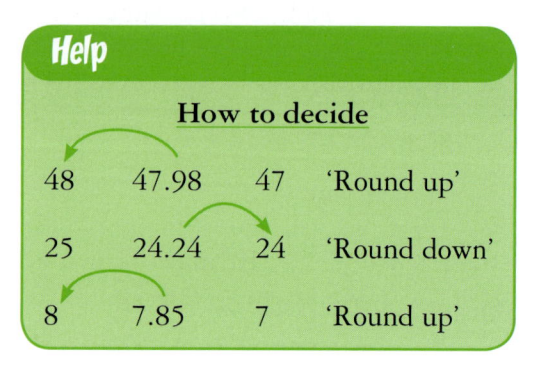

Help

How to decide

48	47.98	47	'Round up'
25	24.24	24	'Round down'
8	7.85	7	'Round up'

(b) Using a **calculator**, or otherwise, **find** the exact value of $\frac{47.98 + 24.24}{7.85}$.

Method: Key in

(47.98 + 24.24) ÷ 7.85 =

Solution $= \frac{72.22}{7.85} = 9.2$

Example 2

Evaluate and give your answer correct to two decimal places.

$(4.65)^2 \times \sqrt{70.56} - \frac{1}{2.56}$

Method: Key in

4.65 x^2 × (√ 70.56) − (2.56 $\frac{1}{x}$) =

Solution $= 21.6225 \times 8.4 - 0.390625$
$= 181.629 - 0.390625$
$= 181.238375$
≈ 181.24

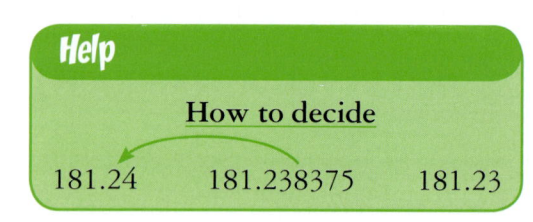

Help

How to decide

181.24   181.238375   181.23

Self-test 3

1. (a) By **rounding** each of these numbers to the nearest whole number, **estimate** the value of $\frac{17.25 \times 6.4}{1.875}$.

   (b) Using a **calculator**, or otherwise, **find** the exact value of $\frac{17.25 \times 6.4}{1.875}$.

2. **Evaluate** and give your answer correct to two decimal places:

   $\sqrt{13.69} + \frac{1}{4.23} \times (7.13)^2$

Household bills

Example 1

Bronwen bought three books. Each book cost €13.50. **How much** change did she get from a €50 note?

Solution   3 × €13.50 = €40.50
              €50 − €40.50 = **€9.50**

Example 2

Calculate the total cost in euro of:

5 litres of milk   @ 97c per litre
4 boxes of cereal   @ €2.99 per box
2 bags of sugar   @ €1.33 per bag

Solution   5 × 97c   =   €4.85
              4 × €2.99   =   €11.96
              2 × €1.33   =   €2.66
              ─────────────────────
              Total cost =   **€19.47**

> **Note**
> • 100 cent = €1
> • 485 cent = €4.85

Self-test 4

1. Eimear purchased four chocolate bars at 65c each. How much change did she get from a €10 note?
2. Margaret bought five cups at 90c each, three plates at €2.50 each and seven spoons at 75c each. Calculate the total cost.
3. On Monday, a meter reading was 12 475 units, and on Friday it was 12 710.

   (a) Calculate the number of units used.

   (b) Find the total cost of the units used at 13c per unit.

Distance/time/speed

Top Tips

- distance = speed × time
- speed = distance ÷ time
- time = distance ÷ speed

Dad's silly triangle.

Top Tips

- Division by a fraction becomes multiplication by the fraction turned upside down.

  e.g. $120 \div \frac{1}{4} = 120 \times \frac{4}{1} = 480$.

Example 1

On Friday, a train left Sligo at 14.10 and arrived in Dublin at 17.55.

(a) **How many** hours and minutes did the journey take?

   Solution   Time = 17.55 − 14.10 = 3 hours 45 minutes

(b) The distance travelled was 210 km.

   Calculate the average speed of the journey in km/h.

   Solution   speed = distance ÷ time

   $\Rightarrow$ speed = $210 \div 3\frac{3}{4}$

   $\Rightarrow$ speed = $210 \div \frac{15}{4}$ Or $210 \div 3.75 = 56$ km/h

   $\Rightarrow$ speed = $\frac{210 \times 4}{15}$

   $\Rightarrow$ speed = $\frac{840}{15}$ = 56 km/h

Example 2

If the average speed is 50 km/h and the time is $3\frac{1}{2}$ hours, **find** the distance.

   Solution   distance = speed × time

   $\Rightarrow$ distance = $50 \times 3\frac{1}{2}$ = 175 km

Example 3

If the average speed is 60 km/h and the distance is 150 km, **find** the time.

   Solution   time = distance ÷ speed

   $\Rightarrow$ time = $150 \div 60 = 2\frac{1}{2}$ hours

Self-test 5

1. A bus leaves Galway at 17.15 hours and arrives in Athlone 57 minutes later. At **what time** did the bus arrive in Athlone?

2. (a) Speed = 40 km/h and time = $2\frac{1}{2}$ hours. **Find** distance.
   (b) Distance = 200 km and time = 4 hours. **Find** speed.
   (c) Distance = 900 km and speed = 300 km/h. **Find** time.

Metric system

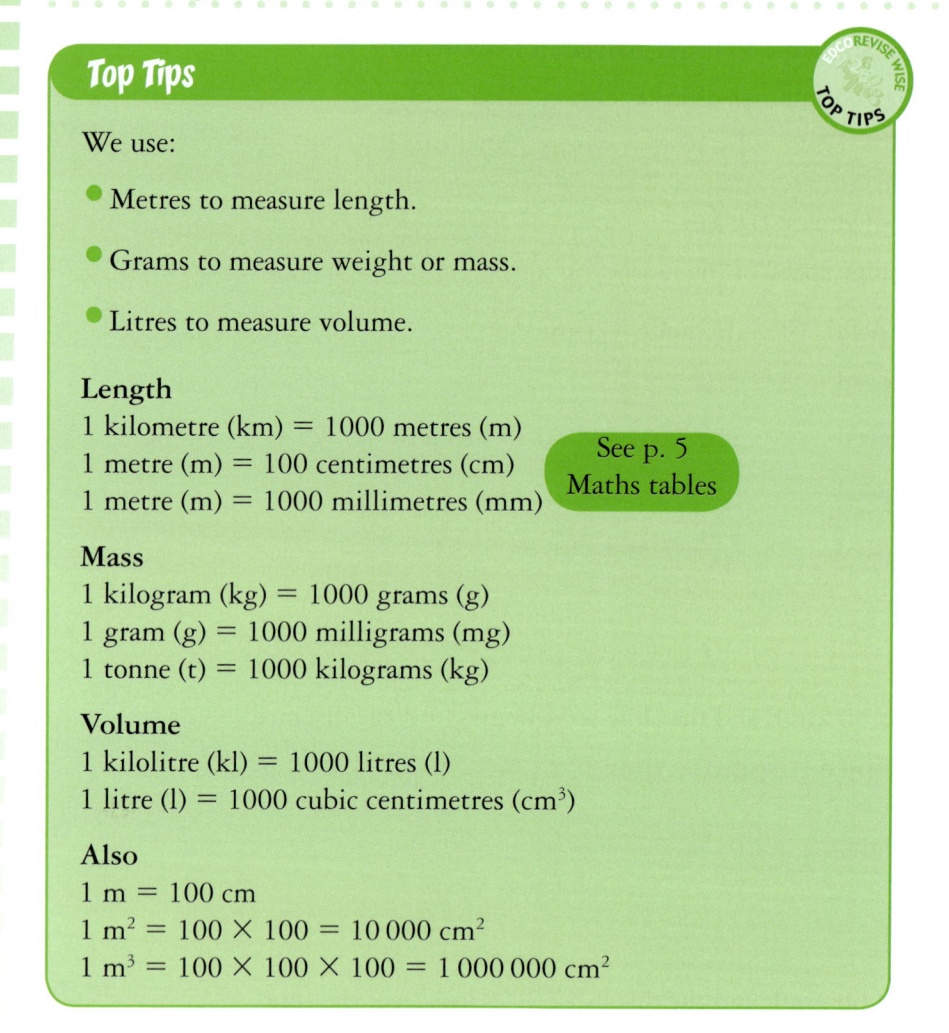

Top Tips

We use:
- Metres to measure length.
- Grams to measure weight or mass.
- Litres to measure volume.

Length
1 kilometre (km) = 1000 metres (m)
1 metre (m) = 100 centimetres (cm)
1 metre (m) = 1000 millimetres (mm)

See p. 5 Maths tables

Mass
1 kilogram (kg) = 1000 grams (g)
1 gram (g) = 1000 milligrams (mg)
1 tonne (t) = 1000 kilograms (kg)

Volume
1 kilolitre (kl) = 1000 litres (l)
1 litre (l) = 1000 cubic centimetres (cm^3)

Also
1 m = 100 cm
$1 \, m^2 = 100 \times 100 = 10\,000 \, cm^2$
$1 \, m^3 = 100 \times 100 \times 100 = 1\,000\,000 \, cm^2$

Prime numbers, multiples, factors, HCF and LCM

A **prime number** is a number with two and only two divisors, i.e. the number itself and one. 7 is a typical prime number, as it has only two divisors, 7 and 1.

Example 1

List all the prime numbers between 10 and 30.

Solution   {11, 13, 17, 19, 23, 29}

A **multiple** of a number *K* is either the number *K* itself or a larger number into which the original number *K* divides evenly.

Example 2

List all the multiples of 3 between 1 and 20.

Solution   Multiples of 3 = {3, 6, 9, 12, 15, 18}

A **factor (divisor)** of a number *K* is either the number *K* itself or a smaller number that divides evenly into the number *K*.

Example 3

List all the factors (divisors) of 20.

Solution   Divisors of 20 = {1, 2, 4, 5, 10, 20}

HCF (highest common factor) is the largest number that divides evenly into two or more other numbers.

Example 4

Find the HCF of 12 and 18.

Solution   Divisors of 12 = {1, 2, 3, 4, ⑥, 12}

Divisors of 18 = {1, 2, 3, ⑥, 9, 18}

So, HCF = 6

LCM (lowest common multiple) is the smallest number that two or more other numbers will divide into evenly.

Example 5

Find the LCM of 12 and 18.

Solution   Multiples of 12 = {12, 24, ㊱, 48, 60 ...}

Multiples of 18 = {18, ㊱, 54, 72, 90 ...}

So, LCM = 36

> **Top Tips**
>
> HCF 6 ← 12, 18 → 36 LCM

Self-test 6

1. List all the prime numbers between 4 and 18.
2. List all the multiples of 7 between 10 and 40.
3. List all the factors (divisors) of 24.
4. Find the HCF of 21 and 35.
5. Find the LCM of 8 and 9.

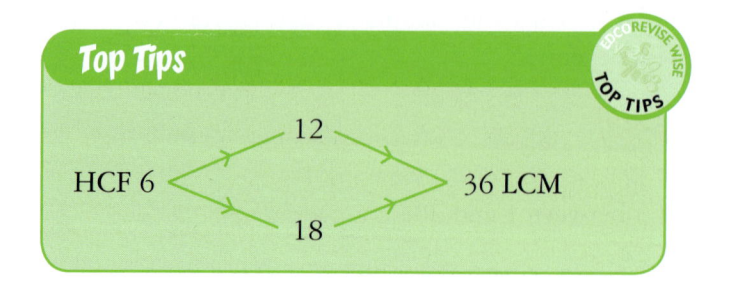

Self-test answers

Self-test 1

1. (a) a^3 (b) a^{16}
2. (a) 3^3 (b) 3^7
3. $k = 1$

Self-test 2

1. (a) 4.62×10^2
   (b) 5.016×10^4
2. $740; 7.4 \times 10^2$
3. (a) 6.216×10^4
   (b) 2.2842×10^5

Self-test 3

1. (a) 51
   (b) 58.88
2. 15.72

Self-test 4

1. €7.40
2. €17.25
3. (a) 235 units
   (b) €30.55

Self-test 5

1. 18.12 hours
2. (a) 100 km
   (b) 50 km/h
   (c) 3 hours

Self-test 6

1. {5, 7, 11, 13, 17}
2. {14, 21, 28, 35}
3. {1, 2, 3, 4, 6, 8, 12, 24}
4. 7
5. 72

CHAPTER 3: ARITHMETIC 2

Key Points

- A number raised to the power of $\frac{1}{2}$ means the **square root** of the number, e.g. $9^{1/2} = \sqrt{9} = 3$.

- A number or a variable raised to the power of zero is equal to 1, e.g. $6^0 = 1$, $x^0 = 1$.

- For **scientific notation** use $a \times 10^n$ where $1 \leq a < 10$, $n \in N$.

- The symbol for **estimation/approximation** is $\approx$.

- For **distance/time/speed**, use 'dad's silly triangle'.

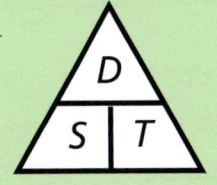

- In estimation/approximation: 5 or more round up, less than 5 round down.

- HCF = highest common factor.

- LCM = lowest common multiple.

Junior Certificate Examination 2004

Paper 1, Q2

2. (a) €400 is shared between Mary and Tom in the ratio 7:3. How much does each receive?

   Solution $7 + 3 = 10$ shares
   €400 ÷ 10 = €40
   Mary: $7 \times €40 = €280$
   Tom: $3 \times €40 = €120$
   Mary = €280, Tom = €120

   (b) i. Simplify $\dfrac{a^7 \times a^4}{a^3 \times a^2}$, giving your answer in the form a^n, where $n \in N$.

   Solution $\dfrac{a^7 \times a^4}{a^3 \times a^2} = \dfrac{a^{7+4}}{a^{3+2}} = \dfrac{a^{11}}{a^5} = a^{11-5} = a^6$

ii. By rounding each of these numbers to the nearest whole number, estimate the value of $\dfrac{66.88 - 27.36}{7.6}$.

Solution $\dfrac{66.88 - 27.36}{7.6}$ is approximately equal to:

$$\dfrac{67 - 27}{8} = \dfrac{40}{8} = 5$$

iii. Using a calculator, or otherwise, find the exact value of $\dfrac{66.88 - 27.36}{7.6}$.

Solution $\dfrac{66.88 - 27.36}{7.6} = \dfrac{39.52}{7.6} = 5.2$

(c) Using a calculator, or otherwise, find the exact value of:

i. $9^{½}$
Solution $9^{½} = \sqrt{9} = 3$

ii. $(5.32)^2$
Solution $(5.32)^2 = 28.3024$

iii. Hence, evaluate $9^{½} + (5.32)^2 \times \dfrac{1}{0.625}$ and give your answer correct to two decimal places.

Solution $9^{½} + (5.32)^2 \times \dfrac{1}{0.625}$

$= 3 + 28.3024 \times 1.6$
$= 3 + 45.28384$
$= 48.28384$
≈ 48.28

Junior Certificate Examination 2005

Paper 1, Q2

2. (a) If 12 m² of carpet cost €504, find the cost of 15 m² of the same carpet.

Solution $12 m^2 = €504$
$\Rightarrow 1 m^2 = 504 \div 12$

$\Rightarrow 15 m^2 = \dfrac{504 \times 15}{12} = €630$

(b) *i.* Simplify $\dfrac{a^9 \times a^5}{a^6 \times a^2}$, giving your answer in the form a^n, where $n \in \mathbb{N}$.

Solution $\dfrac{a^9 \times a^5}{a^6 \times a^2} = \dfrac{a^{9+5}}{a^{6+2}} = \dfrac{a^{14}}{a^8} = a^{14-8} = a^6$

ii. By rounding each of these numbers to the nearest whole number, estimate the value of $\frac{56.214}{2.31 + 5.79}$.

> Solution $\frac{56.214}{2.31 + 5.79}$ is approximately equal to:
> $$\frac{56}{2+6} = \frac{56}{8} = 7$$

iii. Using a calculator, or otherwise, find the exact value of $\frac{56.214}{2.31 + 5.79}$.

> Solution $\frac{56.214}{2.31 + 5.79} = \frac{56.214}{8.1} = 6.94$

(c) Using a calculator, or otherwise, find the exact value of:

i. $49^{½}$

> Solution $49^{½} = \sqrt{49} = 7$

ii. $\frac{1}{6.4}$

> Solution $\frac{1}{6.4} = 0.15625$

iii. Using a calculator, or otherwise, evaluate $\sqrt{65.61} \times \frac{3.14}{0.47} - (2.42)^2$. Give your answer correct to two decimal places.

> Solution $\sqrt{65.61} \times \frac{3.14}{0.47} - (2.42)^2$
> $= 8.1 \times 6.68085 - 5.8564$
> $= 54.114885 - 5.8564$
> $= 48.258485$
> ≈ 48.26

Junior Certificate Examination 2004

Paper 1, Q3

3. (a) Ann bought two cans of cola. Each can cost 80c. How much change did she get from a €10 note?

   Solution 2 cans @ 80c = €1.60
   €10 − €1.60 = **€8.40**

   (b) i. John's gross pay is €21 000. His tax credit is €2369. He pays income tax at the rate of 22%. What is his take-home pay?

   Solution Gross pay   €21 000   Work out: Tax @ 22% = $\dfrac{€21\,000 \times 22}{100}$ = €4620
   Tax @ 22%   €4620   €4620 − €2369 = €2251
   Tax credit   €2369   €21 000 − €2251 = €18 749
   Tax due   €2251
   Take-home pay   **€18 749**

   ii. VAT at 15% is added to a bill of €84.60. Calculate the total bill.

   Solution VAT @ 15% = $\dfrac{€84.60 \times 15}{100}$ = €12.69

   So, total bill = €84.60 + €12.69 = **€97.29**

   (c) i. €3000 is invested at 4% per annum. What is the amount of the investment at the end of one year?

   Solution Principal for first year   =   €3000
   Interest for first year   =   €120
   Amount at end of first year   =   **€3120**
   Interest = $\dfrac{3000 \times 4}{100}$ =   €120

   ii. €500 is withdrawn from this amount at the beginning of the second year. The interest rate for the second year is 3.6% per annum. What is the amount of the investment at the end of that year?

   Solution Amount at end of first year   =   €3120.00
   Withdrawal at beginning of second year =   €500.00
   Principal for second year   =   €2620.00
   Interest for second year   =   €94.32
   Amount at end of second year   =   **€2714.32**

Junior Certificate Examination 2005

Paper 1, Q3

3. (a) Aoife bought three compact discs at €16.50 each and two magazines at €4.20 each. How much did she pay altogether?

   Solution

3 discs @ €16.50 each	=	€49.50
2 magazines @ €4.20 each	=	€8.40
Total cost	=	**€57.90**

   (b) i. Patrick bought a car for €14 080 and sold it for €16 000. Calculate his profit as a percentage of the selling price.

   Solution **Profit:** €16 000 − €14 080 = €1920

   $$\% \text{ profit} = \frac{1920 \times 100}{16\,000}$$

   $$= \mathbf{12\%}$$

   ii. €6000 is invested at 5% per annum. What is the amount of the investment at the end of one year?

   Solution

Principal for first year	=	€6000
Interest for first year	=	€300
Amount at end of first year	=	**€6300**
Interest $= \frac{6000 \times 5}{100}$	=	€300

   (c) Helen's weekly wage is €850. She pays income tax at the rate of 20% on the first €600 of her wage and income tax at the rate of 42% on the remainder of her wage. Helen has a weekly tax credit of €54.

   i. Calculate the tax payable at the rate of 20% on the first €600 of her wage.

   Solution   Tax @ 20% $= \frac{600 \times 20}{100} = $ **€120**

   ii. Calculate the tax payable at the rate of 42% on the remainder of her wage.

   Solution   €850 − €600 = €250

   So, tax @ 42% $= \frac{250 \times 42}{100} = $ **€105**

   iii. Hence calculate Helen's gross tax.

   Solution   Gross tax = €120 + €105 = **€225**

   iv. Calculate the tax payable by Helen.

   Solution   Gross tax − tax credit
   = €225 − €54 = **€171**

CHAPTER 4
Algebra 1

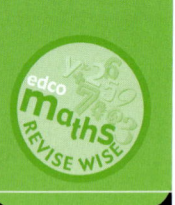

Learning Objectives
- Definitions.
- Evaluate expressions.
- Simplify expressions.
- Solve simple equations.
- Form and solve simple equations.
- Methods of factorisation.
- Use factors to simplify a fraction.
- Inequalities — solve and graph.

Definitions

- A variable is any letter, e.g. a, b, x, y.
- A constant is any number, e.g. $5, -6, \frac{1}{2}$.
- A term is any letter or number or a product of both, e.g. $2, y, 3x$.
- An expression is a term or a group of terms, e.g. $4x, 3x + 2y$.
- A coefficient is a number that stands in front of a variable, e.g. $3k, -2x$.
- An equation is a term or a group of terms made equal to some value, e.g. $3x = 6$, $x + 3y = 7$.
- An inequality is a term or a group of terms $<, \leq, >, \geq$ to some value, e.g. $3x \leq 9$, $4x - 5 > 11$.

Evaluate expressions

Example 1

If $a = 2$ and $b = 5$, find the value of $3a + 4b$.

Solution
$$\begin{aligned} 3a + 4b &= 3(2) + 4(5) \\ &= 6 + 20 \\ &= 26 \end{aligned}$$

Example 2

If $x = 3$, find the value of $x^2 - 4x + 11$.

Solution
$$\begin{aligned} x^2 - 4x + 11 &= (3)^2 - 4(3) + 11 \\ &= 9 - 12 + 11 \\ &= 8 \end{aligned}$$

Example 3

If $a = 4$, $b = 1$ and $c = -5$, find the value of $\dfrac{6a + 4bc}{3c}$.

Solution
$$\begin{aligned} \dfrac{6a + 4bc}{3c} &= \dfrac{6(4) + 4(1)(-5)}{3(-5)} \\ &= \dfrac{24 + (-20)}{-15} \\ &= \dfrac{24 - 20}{-15} \\ &= \dfrac{4}{-15} \\ &= -\dfrac{4}{15} \end{aligned}$$

Top Tips

- **Substitution** is the method used in examples 1, 2, 3. Remove each variable and replace with the value given.

Simplify expressions

Addition and subtraction

Example 1

Simplify $(3a + 4b) + (5a - b)$.

Solution
$$\begin{aligned} (3a + 4b) + (5a - b) &= 3a + 4b + 5a - b \\ &= 3a + 5a + 4b - b \\ &= 8a + 3b \end{aligned}$$

Example 2

Simplify $4xy + 2z - 3xy + 7z$.

Solution
$$\begin{aligned} 4xy + 2z - 3xy + 7z &= 4xy - 3xy + 2z + 7z \\ &= xy + 9z \end{aligned}$$

Top Tips

- We can only add or subtract 'like' terms, i.e. with the same variable.
  Ex: $3a + 5a + 4b - b$ $3a$ and $5a$ are 'like' terms, and
  $= 8a + 3b$ $4b$ and $-b$ are 'like' terms.

Removing brackets

Example 3

Simplify $4(3a + 2b)$.

Solution $4(3a + 2b)$
$= 12a + 8b$

Example 4

Simplify $5(2x - y + 3)$.

Solution $5(2x - y + 3)$
$= 10x - 5y + 15$

Top Tips

- Multiply each term inside the brackets by the value outside the brackets, Ex: $4(3a + 2b)$.

Multiplication

Example 5

Simplify $(2y + 3)(y - 4)$.

Solution $\quad(2y + 3)(y - 4)$
$= 2y^2 - 8y + 3y - 12$
$= 2y^2 - 5y - 12$

Example 6

Simplify $(2x - 3)(3x^2 + x - 4)$.

Solution $\quad(2x - 3)(3x^2 + x - 4)$
$= 6x^3 + 2x^2 - 8x - 9x^2 - 3x + 12$
$= 6x^3 - 7x^2 - 11x + 12$

Example 7

Simplify $(a + b)(a^2 + ab)$.

Solution $\quad(a + b)(a^2 + ab)$
$= a^3 + a^2b + a^2b + ab^2$
$= a^3 + 2a^2b + ab^2$

Top Tips

- Multiply each term inside the first pair of brackets by each term inside the second pair of brackets.

  Ex: $(2y + 3)(y - 4)$

Self-test 1

1. If $x = 4$ and $y = -9$, find the value of $5x + 2y$.
2. Simplify each of the following.
   (a) $(11a + 7b) + (6a - b)$
   (b) $(9c + 5d) - (8c + 3d)$
   (c) $(x + 2y)(x^2 - 3y)$

Solve simple equations

Example 1

Solve $3x = 15$.

Solution $\quad 3x = 15$.
$\Rightarrow x = 5$

Example 2

Solve $4x + 3 = 11$.

Solution $\quad 4x + 3 = 11$
$\Rightarrow \quad 4x = 11 - 3$
$\Rightarrow \quad 4x = 8$
$\Rightarrow \quad x = 2$

Top Tips

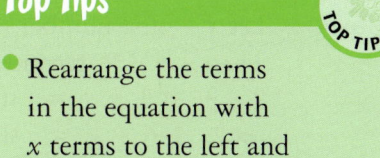

- Rearrange the terms in the equation with x terms to the left and numbers to the right of $=$.
- Divide across by the number in front of x to solve for x.

Example 3

Solve $3k - 9 = k + 7$.

Solution $\quad 3k - 9 = k + 7$
Rearrange terms
$\Rightarrow \quad 3k - k = 7 + 9$
$\Rightarrow \quad 2k = 16$
$\Rightarrow \quad k = 8$

Example 4

Solve $5(3x - 1) = 40$.

Solution $\quad 5(3x - 1) = 40$
$\Rightarrow \quad 15x - 5 = 40$
$\Rightarrow \quad 15x = 40 + 5$
$\Rightarrow \quad 15x = 45$
$\Rightarrow \quad x = 3$

Form and solve simple equations

Example 1

If 5 is added to a certain number, the result is 19. What is the number?

Solution $\quad$ Let $x =$ the number.
Then $x + 5 = 19$
$\Rightarrow x = 19 - 5$
$\Rightarrow x = 14$

Help

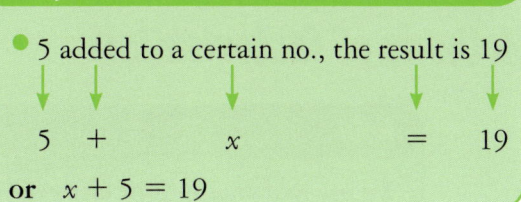

- 5 added to a certain no., the result is 19

$\quad 5 \quad + \quad x \quad = \quad 19$

or $\quad x + 5 = 19$

Example 2

One number is 3 greater than another number. If twice the larger number is added to the smaller number, the result is 30. **Find** the numbers.

Solution Let x = first number.
Then $x + 3$ = second number.
$2(x + 3) + x = 30$
$\Rightarrow 2x + 6 + x = 30$
$\Rightarrow 2x + x = 30 - 6$
$\Rightarrow 3x = 24$
$\Rightarrow x = 8$
and, $x + 3 = 8 + 3 = 11$

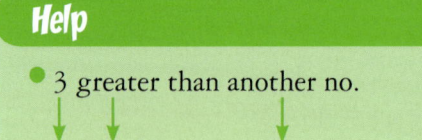

Help

- 3 greater than another no.

  $3 \quad + \quad x$ or $x + 3$

- Twice (larger no.) added to smaller no. gives result 30

  $2 \quad (x + 3) \quad + \quad x \quad = \quad 30$

Self-test 2

1. **Solve** the equation $3(4x + 1) = 27$.
2. When -6 is subtracted from a certain number, the answer is -12. **Find** the number.
3. Una is 7 years older than Maeve. If the sum of their ages is 29, **find** both of their ages.
4. If a number is multiplied by 4 and then 7 is added, the result is 43. **Find** the number.

Methods of factorisation

Note

We use four methods of factorisation: **taking out the common factor, grouping to get the common factor, quadratic trinomials and the difference of two squares.**

Taking out the common factor

Example 1

Factorise $2xy + 6xz$.

Solution $\quad 2xy + 6xz$
$\qquad = 2x(y + 3z)$

Example 2

Factorise $3a^2 + ab + ac$.

Solution $\quad 3a^2 + ab + ac$
$\qquad = a(3a + b + c)$

Top Tips

- Find the HCF.
  Ex: $2x$ is the HCF of $2xy$ and $6xz$.

- Divide the HCF into each term.

Grouping to get the common factors

Example 3

Factorise $ax + by + ay + bx$.
Solution $\quad ax + by + ay + bx$
$\qquad = (ax + ay) + (bx + by)$
$\qquad = a(x + y) + b(x + y)$
$\qquad = (x + y)(a + b)$

Example 4

Factorise $xy - 2xz + 3y - 6z$.
Solution $\quad xy - 2xz + 3y - 6z$
$\qquad = (xy - 2xz) + (3y - 6z)$
$\qquad = x(y - 2z) + 3(y - 2z)$
$\qquad = (y - 2z)(x + 3)$

Top Tips

- Rearrange the four terms into two groups of two.

- Find the HCF of each group.

- Divide each group by its HCF.

- We must get the same common factor inside both sets of brackets
  Ex: $a(x + y) + b(x + y)$.

- Take out the common factor.

Example 5

Factorise $10a^2 - 2ab - 15ad + 3bd$.

Solution
$$10a^2 - 2ab - 15ad + 3bd$$
$$= (10a^2 - 2ab) - (15ad - 3bd)$$
$$= 2a(5a - b) - 3d(5a - b)$$
$$= (5a - b)(2a - 3d)$$

Top Tips

- If there is to be a minus sign outside the brackets, then change the sign inside.
  Ex: $-15ad + 3bd = -(15ad - 3bd)$.

Quadratic trinomials

Example 6

Factorise $x^2 + 5x + 6$.

Solution $x^2 + 5x + 6$

x^2	x	$+3$	6
$= x.x$	x	$+2$	$= 2.3$

$$= (x + 3)(x + 2)$$

check: $x.2 = 2x$
and $x.3 = 3x$
$3x + 2x = 5x$

Top Tips

- In examples 6, 7 and 8, cross-multiply and add to check the middle term.
- Read off factors horizontally.

Example 7

Factorise $k^2 - 2k - 24$.
Solution $k^2 - 2k - 24$

$k \quad -6$
$k \quad +4$

$= (k - 6)(k + 4)$

Help

- Factors of 24

  24 by 1

  12 by 2

  8 by 3

  ✓ 6 by 4

Example 8

Factorise $m^2 + 2m - 8$.
Solution $m^2 + 2m - 8$

$m \quad +4$
$m \quad -2$

$= (m + 4)(m - 2)$

Difference of two squares

Example 9

Factorise $x^2 - 25$.

Solution
$$x^2 - 25$$
$$= (x)^2 - (5)^2$$
$$= (x - 5)(x + 5)$$

Example 10

Factorise $9 - p^2$.

Solution
$$9 - p^2$$
$$= (3)^2 - (p)^2$$
$$= (3 - p)(3 + p)$$

Example 11

Factorise $1 - a^2$.

Solution
$$1 - a^2$$
$$= (1)^2 - (a)^2$$
$$= (1 - a)(1 + a)$$

Example 12

Factorise $x^2 - y^2$.

Solution
$$x^2 - y^2$$
$$= (x)^2 - (y)^2$$
$$= (x - y)(x + y)$$

Top Tips

- Express each term as a 'perfect square'. Ex: $x^2 = (x)^2$ and $25 = (5)^2$.
- Write out the factors in the form $(? - ?)(? + ?)$, Ex: $(x - 5)(x + 5)$.

Self-test 3

1. Factorise each of the following.
   (a) $x^2 + 3x$
   (b) $ab^2 + a^2b$

2. Factorise each of the following.
   (a) $2ac - 4ad + bc - 2bd$
   (b) $x^2 + xy - 5x - 5y$

3. Factorise each of the following.
   (a) $x^2 - 7x + 12$
   (b) $x^2 + 2x - 35$

4. Factorise each of the following.
   (a) $k^2 - 1$
   (b) $49 - m^2$

Use factors to simplify a fraction

Example 1

Simplify $\dfrac{6x + 6y}{2x + 2y}$.

Solution
$$\dfrac{6x + 6y}{2x + 2y}$$
$$= \dfrac{6(x + y)}{2(x + y)}$$
$$= \dfrac{6}{2}$$
$$= 3$$

Example 2

Simplify $\dfrac{x^2 + 7x + 12}{x + 3}$.

Solution
$$\dfrac{x^2 + 7x + 12}{x + 3}$$
$$= \dfrac{(x + 4)(x + 3)}{x + 3}$$
$$= x + 4$$

Take $x^2 + 7x + 12$

$= (x + 4)(x + 3)$

Top Tips

- Factorise the top of the fraction (the numerator)
  Ex: $6x + 6y = 6(x + y)$
  and the bottom of the fraction (the denominator)
  Ex: $2x + 2y = 2(x + y)$

- Cancel the common factors
  Ex: $\dfrac{6(x + y)}{2(x + y)} = \dfrac{6}{2} = 3$

Example 3

Simplify $\dfrac{x^2 - 1}{x + 1}$.

Solution
$$\dfrac{x^2 - 1}{x + 1}$$
$$= \dfrac{(x - 1)(x + 1)}{x + 1}$$
$$= x - 1$$

Take $x^2 - 1$
$= (x)^2 - (1)^2$
$= (x - 1)(x + 1)$

Self-test 4

Q. Using factors, **simplify** each of the following:

(a) $\dfrac{x^2 - y^2}{x + y}$

(b) $\dfrac{x^2 - x - 42}{x + 6}$

(c) $\dfrac{7x - 14y}{6x - 12y}$

Inequalities

> **Top Tips**
>
> - Inequality symbols:
>   - $<$ less than
>   - $\leq$ less than or equal to
>   - $>$ greater than
>   - $\geq$ greater than or equal to

Example 1

Find the values of x for which $2x + 8 \leq 10$, $x \in N$.

Solution $2x + 8 \leq 10$
$\Rightarrow 2x \leq 10 - 8$
$\Rightarrow 2x \leq 2$
$\Rightarrow x \leq 1$
So, $x = 0$ or $x = 1$

> **Top Tips**
>
> - Rearrange the terms in the inequality with x terms to the left and numbers to the right of the symbol.
>
> - Divide across by the number in front of x to solve for x.

Example 2

Solve for x the inequality $4x + 11 > 6x - 5$, $x \in R$.

Solution $4x + 11 > 6x - 5$
$\Rightarrow 4x - 6x > -5 - 11$
$\Rightarrow -2x > -16$
$\Rightarrow -x > -8$
$\Rightarrow x < 8$

> **Top Tips**
>
> - When changing the sign ($+$ or $-$) on both sides of an inequality, make sure to reverse the symbol, e.g. $>$ to $<$ or $\geq$ to $\leq$ or $<$ to $>$ or $\leq$ to $\geq$, as in Example 2.

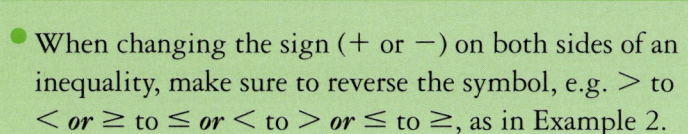

Example 3

Graph on the number line the solution set of $7x - 3 < 32$, $x \in N$.

Solution
$$7x - 3 < 32$$
$$\Rightarrow 7x < 32 + 3$$
$$\Rightarrow 7x < 35$$
$$\Rightarrow x < 5$$
So, $x \in \{0, 1, 2, 3, 4\}$

Top Tips

- N = Natural numbers
  = Positive whole numbers

- Z = Integers
  = Positive and negative whole numbers

- R = Real numbers
  = Positive and negative whole numbers, fractions, decimals.

Top Tips

- When $x \in N$ or $x \in Z$, highlight each value of x with a **dot** on the number line, as in Example 3.

Example 4

Graph on the number line the solution set of $2(x + 3) \geq 14$, $x \in R$.

Solution
$$2(x + 3) \geq 14$$
$$\Rightarrow 2x + 6 \geq 14$$
$$\Rightarrow 2x \geq 14 - 6$$
$$\Rightarrow 2x \geq 8$$
$$\Rightarrow x \geq 4$$

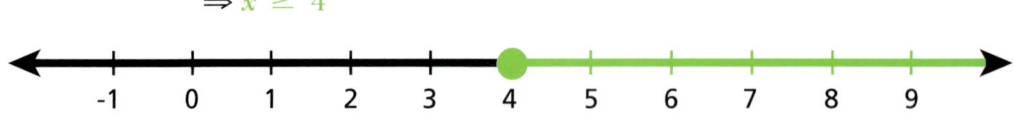

Top Tips

- When $x \in R$, highlight the values of x with a shaded line on the number line, as in Example 4.
- For $x \geq$ or $x \leq$, use a closed disc (circle) to indicate that the endpoint is included.
- For $x >$ or $x <$, use an open disc (circle) to indicate that the endpoint is excluded.

Self-test 5

1. Find the values of x for which $3x + 1 < 16$, $x \in N$.
2. Find the set of values of x for which $5x - 2 > 2x + 10$, $x \in R$.
3. Graph on the number line the solution set of $3(x - 2) \leq 0$, $x \in N$.
4. Graph on the number line the solution set of $4(x + 5) > 28$, $x \in R$.

Self-test answers

Self-test 1

1. 2
2. (a) $17a + 6b$
   (b) $c + 2d$
   (c) $x^3 - 3xy + 2x^2y - 6y^2$

Self-test 3

1. (a) $x(x + 3)$
   (b) $ab(b + a)$
2. (a) $(c - 2d)(2a + b)$
   (b) $(x + y)(x - 5)$
3. (a) $(x - 4)(x - 3)$
   (b) $(x + 7)(x - 5)$
4. (a) $(k + 1)(k - 1)$
   (b) $(7 - m)(7 + m)$

Self-test 2

1. 2
2. -18
3. Maeve: 11 years; Una: 18 years
4. 9

Self-test 4

(a) $x - y$
(b) $x - 7$
(c) $\dfrac{7}{6}$

Self-test 5

1. 0, 1, 2, 3, 4
2. $x > 4$
3. $x \in \{0, 1, 2\}$

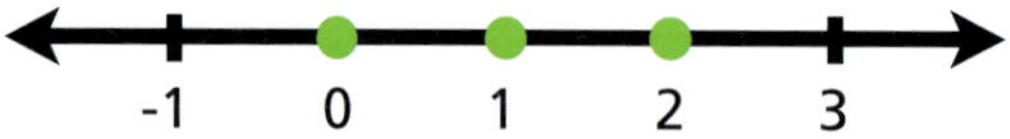

4. $\{x \mid x > 2, x \in R\}$

Key Points

- Multiply or divide before you add or subtract, except where brackets are involved.
- When multiplied or divided, like signs always give +, but unlike signs always give −.
- There are four different methods of factorisation.
- The inequality symbols are $<, \leq, >, \geq$.
- When graphing the solution set on a number line, use dots for sets N and Z and a continuous line for set R.
- Inequality (special case) if $-3x \leq 12$
  $\Rightarrow 3x \geq -12$
  $\Rightarrow x \geq -4$
- To change signs on both sides of an inequality involves reversing the symbol in the centre to the opposite symbol, e.g. $\leq$ becomes $\geq$.

CHAPTER 5
Algebra 2

Learning Objectives

- Add and subtract algebraic fractions.
- Solve algebraic equations involving fractions.
- Solve problems involving algebraic fractions.
- Multiply and divide algebraic fractions.
- Solve quadratic equations.
- Solve problems involving quadratic equations.
- Solve simultaneous equations.
- Solve simultaneous equations using graphs.
- Solve problems involving simultaneous equations.

Add and subtract algebraic fractions

Example 1

Simplify $\dfrac{3x}{4} - \dfrac{2x}{5}$.

Solution $\dfrac{3x}{4} - \dfrac{2x}{5}$

LCM of 4, 5 = 20

$= \dfrac{5(3x) - 4(2x)}{20}$

$= \dfrac{15x - 8x}{20}$

$= \dfrac{7x}{20}$

Example 2

Simplify $\dfrac{x+7}{5} + \dfrac{x-2}{3}$.

Solution $\dfrac{x+7}{5} + \dfrac{x-2}{3}$

LCM of 5, 3 = 15

$= \dfrac{3(x+7) + 5(x-2)}{15}$

$= \dfrac{3x + 21 + 5x - 10}{15}$

$= \dfrac{8x + 11}{15}$

Top Tips

- To add and subtract fractions, use lowest common multiple (LCM).

> **Top Tips**
>
> - When simplifying an expression (as above), use LCM and hold onto it.
> - When solving an equation (as below), use LCM and throw it away.

Solve algebraic equations involving fractions

Example 1

Solve $\dfrac{2x}{3} = 4$.

Solution $\dfrac{2x}{3} = \dfrac{4}{1}$

LCM of 3, 1 = 3

$\Rightarrow \dfrac{3(2x)}{3} = \dfrac{3(4)}{1}$

$\Rightarrow 2x = 12$

$\Rightarrow x = 6$

Example 2

Solve $\dfrac{3x}{4} - \dfrac{2x}{3} = \dfrac{1}{6}$.

Solution $\dfrac{3x}{4} - \dfrac{2x}{3} = \dfrac{1}{6}$

LCM of 4, 3, 6 = 12

$\Rightarrow \dfrac{12(3x)}{4} - \dfrac{12(2x)}{3} = \dfrac{12(1)}{6}$

$\Rightarrow 3(3x) - 4(2x) = 2(1)$

$\Rightarrow 9x - 8x = 2$

$\Rightarrow x = 2$

Example 3

Solve $\dfrac{3x-1}{4} = \dfrac{2x-3}{2}$.

Solution $\dfrac{3x-1}{4} = \dfrac{2x-3}{2}$

LCM of 4, 2 = 4

$\dfrac{4(3x-1)}{4} = \dfrac{4(2x-3)}{2}$

$\Rightarrow 1(3x-1) = 2(2x-3)$

$\Rightarrow 3x - 1 = 4x - 6$

$\Rightarrow 3x - 4x = -6 + 1$

$\Rightarrow -x = -5$

$\Rightarrow x = 5$

> **Help**
>
> - Example 1 has LCM = 3 so, multiply both sides by 3.
>   Example 2 has LCM = 12 so, multiply both sides by 12.
>   Example 3 has LCM = 4 so, multiply both sides by 4.
>
> - After multiplying both sides we are left with no fractions.

Solve problems involving algebraic fractions

Example 1

The sum of half a number and a quarter of the same number is 6. Find the number.

Solution   Let $x =$ the number.
Then $\frac{x}{2} + \frac{x}{4} = 6$
LCM $= 4$
$\Rightarrow \quad 2x + x = 24$
$\Rightarrow \quad 3x = 24$
$\Rightarrow \quad x = 8$

Example 2

When half of a certain number is taken from two-thirds of the same number, the result is 5. Find the number.

Solution   Let $x =$ the number.
Then $\frac{2x}{3} - \frac{x}{2} = 5$
LCM $= 6$
$\Rightarrow 2(2x) - 3(x) = 6(5)$
$\Rightarrow \quad 4x - 3x = 30$
$\Rightarrow \quad x = 30$

Help

- If we let $x =$ the number, then half of the number $= \frac{1}{2}(x) = \frac{x}{2}$, and a quarter of the number $= \frac{1}{4}(x) = \frac{x}{4}$.

Multiply and divide algebraic fractions

Example 1

Multiply $\frac{6ab}{5c}$ by $\frac{15c^2}{2}$.

Solution $\frac{6ab}{5c} \cdot \frac{15c^2}{2}$

$= \frac{\overset{3}{6ab}}{\underset{}{5c}} \cdot \frac{\overset{3}{15c^{2^{c}}}}{2}$ ← Cancel

$= 3\,ab \cdot 3 \cdot c$

$= 9abc$

Example 2

Divide $\frac{15x^2}{2y}$ by $\frac{5x}{8y^2}$.

Solution $\frac{15x^2}{2y} \div \frac{5x}{8y^2}$

$= \frac{\overset{3}{15x^{2^{x}}}}{2y} \cdot \frac{\overset{4}{8y^{2^{y}}}}{5x}$ ← Cancel

$= 3 \cdot x \cdot 4 \cdot y$

$= 12xy$

Top Tips

- To divide one fraction by another fraction, keep the fraction on the left the way it is but turn the fraction on the right upside down and change the operation from divide to multiply.

$$\text{Ex: } \frac{15x^2}{2y} \div \frac{5x}{8y^2} = \frac{15x^2}{2y} \cdot \frac{8y^2}{5x}$$

Self-test 1

1. Express $\dfrac{5x+1}{3} - \dfrac{x}{2}$ as a single fraction.

2. Solve for x: $\dfrac{x-3}{2} - \dfrac{x}{5} = 3$.

3. If three-quarters of a number is added to two-thirds of the same number, the result is 51. Find the number.

4. (a) Multiply $\dfrac{4a^2}{7b}$ by $\dfrac{14b^2}{a}$.

   (b) Divide $\dfrac{16x^2}{3y}$ by $\dfrac{8x}{9y^2}$.

Solve quadratic equations

Example 1

Solve $2x^2 - 10x = 0$.
Solution
$$2x^2 - 10x = 0$$
$$\Rightarrow 2x(x-5) = 0$$
$$\Rightarrow 2x = 0,\ x - 5 = 0$$
$$\Rightarrow x = 0,\ x = 5$$

Example 2

Solve $x^2 - 81 = 0$.
Solution
$$x^2 - 81 = 0$$
$$\Rightarrow (x)^2 - (9)^2 = 0$$
$$\Rightarrow (x-9)(x+9) = 0$$
$$\Rightarrow x - 9 = 0,\ x + 9 = 0$$
$$\Rightarrow x = 9,\ x = -9$$

Example 3

Solve $x^2 - 5x + 6 = 0$.
Solution
$$x^2 - 5x + 6 = 0$$

x ⟶ -3
x ⟶ -2

$$\Rightarrow (x-3)(x-2) = 0$$
$$\Rightarrow x - 3 = 0,\ x - 2 = 0$$
$$\Rightarrow x = 3,\ x = 2$$

Top Tips

- Make sure that every term is on the left-hand side of $= 0$.

- Factorise the left-hand side by the proper method:
  Ex. 1: 'Taking out the common factor', i.e. use HCF.
  Ex. 2: 'Difference of two squares', i.e. make each term a perfect square.
  Ex. 3: 'Quadratic trinomial'.

- Make each factor equal to zero and solve for x.

Help

- Cross-multiply and add to check the middle term.

- Read off factors horizontally.

Solve problems involving quadratic equations

Example 1

The sum of a positive number and its square is 56. **Find** the number.

Solution   Let $x =$ the number.
Then $x + x^2 = 56$
$\Rightarrow x^2 + x - 56 = 0$

$x + 8$
$x - 7$

$\Rightarrow (x + 8)(x - 7) = 0$
$\Rightarrow x - 7 = 0$
$\Rightarrow x = 7$

Help

- 'The sum of a positive number and its square is 56'
  is the same as
  'A positive number added to its square is 56'

  $x + x^2 = 56$

  So, $x + x^2 = 56$

Take this factor to get the positive answer.

Example 2

When three times a positive number is added to its square, the result is 40. **Find** the number.

Solution   Let $x =$ the number.
Then $3x + x^2 = 40$
$\Rightarrow x^2 + 3x - 40 = 0$

$x + 8$
$x - 5$

$\Rightarrow (x + 8)(x - 5) = 0$
$\Rightarrow x - 5 = 0$
$\Rightarrow x = 5$

Help

- three → 3
- times → multiply
- positive number → x
- added to → +
- its square → x^2
- the result is → =
- 40 → 40

So, $3x + x^2 = 40$

Self-test 2

1. **Solve** the equation $x^2 - 11x + 30 = 0$.
2. **Solve** the equation $5p^2 - 20p = 0$.
3. **Solve** the equation $k^2 - 49 = 0$.
4. If 4 is added to the square of a certain number, the result is 85. **Find** the number.

Solve simultaneous equations

> **Top Tips**
> - $x + 3y = 7$ is a linear equation in two variables.
> - If an equation has two variables, then we need two such equations to solve for x and y.

Example 1

Solve for x and y: $x + y = 5$
$\qquad\qquad\qquad\quad x - y = 11$

Solution:

① $\quad x + y = 5$
② $\quad x - y = 11$
$\quad\overline{\quad 2x = 16\quad}$
$\Rightarrow\quad x = 8$

Sub. for $x = 8$

① $\quad x + y = 5$
$\Rightarrow\quad 8 + y = 5$
$\Rightarrow\quad\quad\, y = -3$

So, $x = 8, y = -3$.

> **Top Tips**
> - **To solve simultaneous equations:**
> Step 1: Keep the x terms under each other, the y terms under each other, = under = and constant under constant.
> Step 2: Cancel the x terms **or** the y terms.
> Step 3: Solve for the remaining variable.
> Step 4: Use substitution to solve for the cancelled variable.

Example 2

Solve for x and y: $2x + 3y = 5$
$\qquad\qquad\qquad\quad 5x + 4y = 2$

Solution:

① $\quad 2x + 3y = 5$
② $\quad 5x + 4y = 2$

4 by ① $\quad\;\; 8x + 12y = 20$
-3 by ② $\;\underline{-15x - 12y = -6}$
$\qquad\qquad\quad -7x = 14$
$\Rightarrow\qquad\quad\; 7x = -14$
$\Rightarrow\qquad\qquad x = -2$

Sub. for $x = -2$

① $\qquad\qquad 2x + 3y = 5$
$\Rightarrow\; 2(-2) + 3y = 5$
$\Rightarrow\quad\; -4 + 3y = 5$
$\Rightarrow\qquad\quad\;\; 3y = 9$
$\Rightarrow\qquad\qquad\; y = 3$

So, $x = -2, y = 3$

Help

- Multiply equation ① across by 4 and equation ② across by -3 to get the y terms to cancel.
- We are left with $-7x = 14$ so, solve for x.
- Substitute $x = -2$ into equation ① and solve for y.

Solve simultaneous equations using graphs

Top Tips

- To draw the graph of a linear equation, e.g. $x + y = 6$, we need two points.
- To get two points, let x or y equal any number.
- Two very useful points are where the line cuts the x-axis and y-axis, respectively.
- Let $y = 0$ to get the point where the line cuts the x-axis. Let $x = 0$ to get the point where the line cuts the y-axis.

Example 1

Solve the following simultaneous equations $x + y = 6$ and $x - y = 4$, using graphs.

Solution

$$\begin{aligned}
\text{line ①} \quad & x + y = 6 \\
\text{Let } y = 0 \Rightarrow & x + 0 = 6 \\
\Rightarrow & x = 6 \\
& \text{point } (6, 0) \\
\text{Let } x = 0 \Rightarrow & 0 + y = 6 \\
\Rightarrow & y = 6 \\
& \text{point } (0, 6)
\end{aligned}$$

$$\begin{aligned}
\text{line ②} \quad & x - y = 4 \\
\text{Let } y = 0 \Rightarrow & x - 0 = 4 \\
\Rightarrow & x = 4 \\
& \text{point } (4, 0) \\
\text{Let } x = 0 \Rightarrow & 0 - y = 4 \\
\Rightarrow & -y = 4 \\
\Rightarrow & y = -4 \\
& \text{point } (0, -4)
\end{aligned}$$

Top Tips

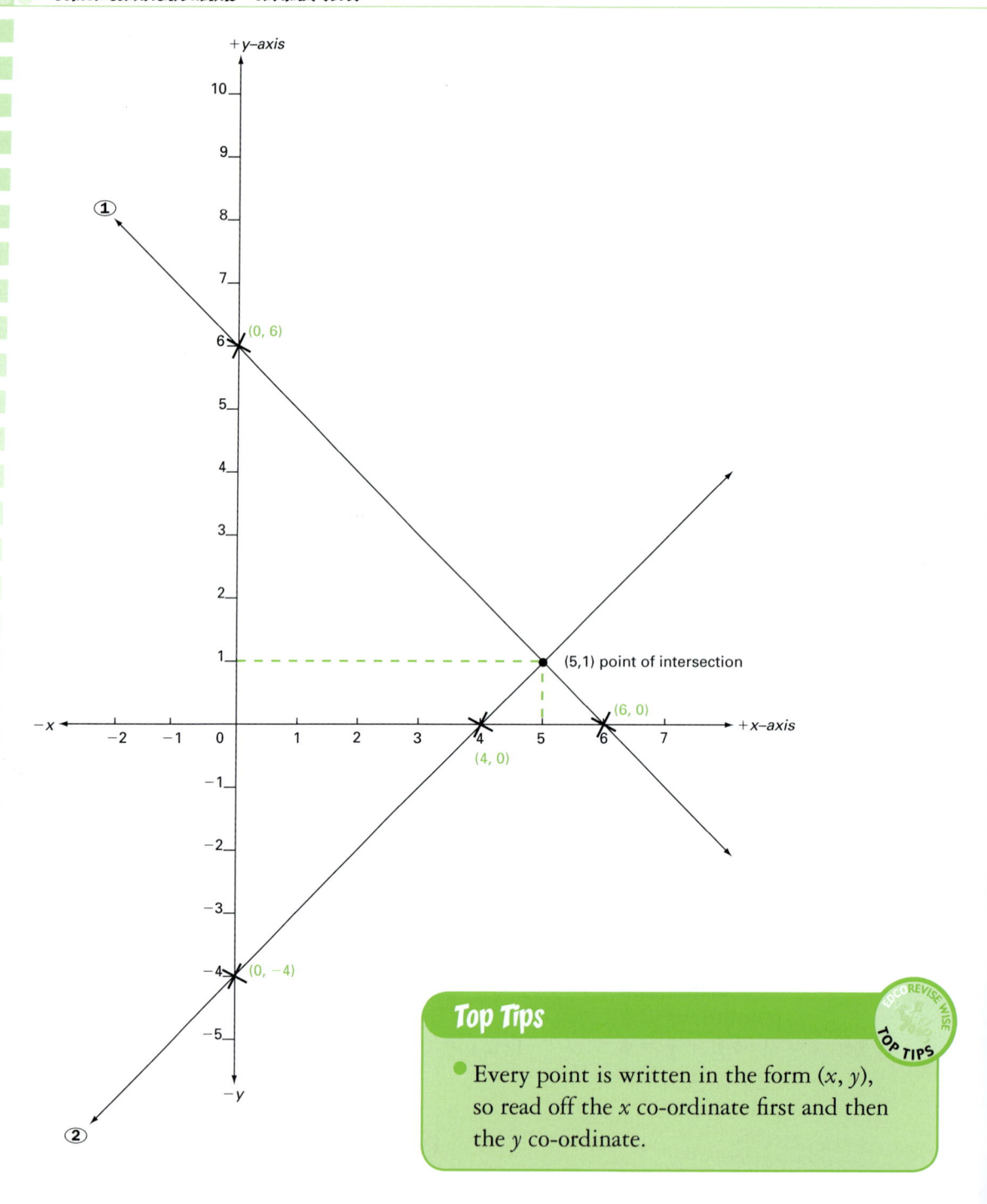

- Every point is written in the form (x, y), so read off the x co-ordinate first and then the y co-ordinate.

From graph point of intersection = (5, 1). So, $x = 5, y = 1$.

Solve problems involving simultaneous equations

Example 1

If the sum of two numbers is 37 and their difference is 21, what are the numbers?

Solution Let x = first number
Let y = second number

① $x + y = 37$
② $x - y = 21$
$2x = 58$
$\Rightarrow x = 29$

Sub. for $x = 29$
① $\quad x + y = 37$
$\Rightarrow 29 + y = 37$
$\Rightarrow \quad y = 8$

Note
- Sum = addition
- Difference = subtraction

Example 2

If two copies and three pens cost €2.35 and one copy and two pens cost €1.35, find the price of a copy and the price of a pen.

Solution Let x = price of copy.
Let y = price of pen.

① $\quad 2x + 3y = 235$
② $\quad x + 2y = 135$
① $\quad 2x + 3y = 235$
-2 by ② $\quad -2x - 4y = -270$
$\quad\quad\quad\quad -y = -35$
$\quad\quad\quad\Rightarrow y = 35$

So, price of copy = 65c
price of pen = 35c.

Sub. for $y = 35$
② $\quad x + 2y = 135$
$\Rightarrow x + 70 = 135$
$\Rightarrow x = 65$

Top Tips
- Convert euro to cents.
  €2.35 = 235c
  €1.35 = 135c

Self-test 3

1. **Solve** the following simultaneous equations:
   (a) $3x - y = 5$
   $4x + y = 9$
   (b) $6x + 5y = 35$
   $x - 2y = 3$

2. The cost of match tickets for five adults and three children is €100. The cost of match tickets for four adults and one child is €66. Let €x be the cost of a match ticket for an adult. Let €y be the cost of a match ticket for a child.
   (a) **Write** two equations, each in x and y, to represent the above information.
   (b) **Solve** these equations to find the cost of a match ticket for an adult and the cost of a match ticket for a child.

Self-test answers

Self-test 1
1. $\dfrac{7x + 2}{6}$
2. 15
3. 36
4. (a) $8ab$ (b) $6xy$

Self-test 2
1. 5, 6
2. 0, 4
3. 7, −7
4. 9

Self-test 3
1. (a) $x = 2, y = 1$
   (b) $x = 5, y = 1$
2. (a) $5x + 3y = 100$; $4x + y = 66$
   (b) Adult = €x = €14, Child = €y = €10

Key Points

- Use LCM to add or subtract algebraic fractions.

- In **simultaneous equations**, cancel one variable in order to solve for the other variable and then use substitution to solve for the cancelled variable.

- A **linear (line) function** has a highest power of x equal to 1, e.g. $y = x^1 + 3$ and the graph is a straight line.

- A **quadratic function** has a highest power of x equal to 2, e.g. $y = x^2 + 5x + 6$ and the graph is a parabola.

- A line cuts the x-axis at $y = 0$, and a line cuts the y-axis at $x = 0$.

Junior Certificate Examination 2004

Paper 1, Q4

4. (a) If $a = 2$ and $b = 7$, find the value of:

   i. Solution $2a + b$
   $= 2(2) + 7$
   $= 4 + 7$
   $= 11$

   ii. Solution $3ab + 1$
   $= 3(2)(7) + 1$
   $= 42 + 1$
   $= 43$

   (b) i. Solve the equation $5(2x + 1) = 45$.

   Solution
   $5(2x + 1) = 45$
   $\Rightarrow 10x + 5 = 45$
   $\Rightarrow 10x = 40$
   $\Rightarrow x = 4$

   ii. Write in its simplest form: $(6x - y) - 3(x - 2y + 1)$.

   Solution
   $(6x - y) - 3(x - 2y + 1)$
   $= 6x - y - 3x + 6y - 3$
   $= 6x - 3x - y + 6y - 3$
   $= 3x + 5y - 3$

   (c) The cost of five books and one magazine is €32.

   The cost of eight books and three magazines is €54.

   Let €x be the cost of a book and let €y be the cost of a magazine.

   i. Write down two equations, each in x and y, to represent the above information.
   Solution   First equation: $5x + y = 32$
   Second equation: $8x + 3y = 54$

   ii. Solve these equations to find the cost of a book and the cost of a magazine.

   Solution

   ① $\quad 5x + y = 32$ Sub for $x = 6$.
   ② $\quad 8x + 3y = 54$ ① $\quad 5x + y = 32$
   -3 by ① $\quad -15x - 3y = -96$ $\Rightarrow 30 + y = 32$
   ② $\quad 8x + 3y = 54$ $\Rightarrow y = 32 - 30$
   $\quad -7x = -42$ $\Rightarrow y = 2$
   $\Rightarrow x = 6$ So, cost of book = €6
   cost of magazine = €2

Junior Certificate Examination 2005

Paper 1, Q4

4. (a) If $x = 4$, find the value of:

   i. Solution $5x + 3$

   $= 5(4) + 3$

   $= 20 + 3$

   $= 23$

   ii. Solution $x^2 - x + 7$

   $= (4)^2 - 4 + 7$

   $= 16 - 4 + 7$

   $= 19$

(b) i. Multiply $(3x - 2)$ by $(4x + 5)$ and write your answer in its simplest form.

   Solution $(3x - 2)(4x + 5)$

   $= 12x^2 + 15x - 8x - 10$

   $= 12x^2 + 7x - 10$

   ii. Write in its simplest form: $(4x^2 - 3x + 7) + (x^2 - 2x - 8)$.

   Solution $(4x^2 - 3x + 7) + (x^2 - 2x - 8)$

   $= 4x^2 - 3x + 7 + x^2 - 2x - 8$

   $= 4x^2 + x^2 - 3x - 2x + 7 - 8$

   $= 5x^2 - 5x - 1$

(c) A rectangle has a length $(x + 6)$ cm and width x cm, as in the diagram.

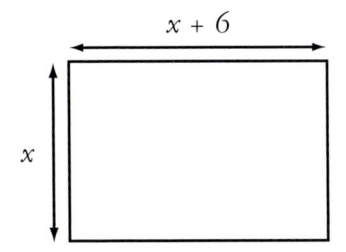

$x + 6$

x

i. Find the perimeter of this rectangle in terms of x.
   Solution Perimeter
   $= 2(x + 6) + 2(x)$
   $= 2x + 12 + 2x$
   $= (4x + 12)$ cm

ii. If the perimeter of the rectangle is 40 cm, write down an equation in x to represent this information.
   Solution $4x + 12 = 40$

iii. Solve the equation that you formed in part (ii) above, for x.
   Solution $4x + 12 = 40$
   $\Rightarrow \quad 4x = 28$
   $\Rightarrow \quad x = 7$ cm

iv. Find the area of the square with the same perimeter as the given rectangle. Give your answer in cm².
   Solution Perimeter of rectangle $= 40$ cm
   So, perimeter of square $= 40$ cm
   $\Rightarrow$ length of side of square $= 40 \div 4 = 10$ cm
   Area of square $= 10 \times 10 = 100$ cm²

Junior Certificate Examination 2004

Paper 1, Q5

5. (a) Find the values of x for which $2x + 1 \leq 7, x \in N$.

   Solution $2x + 1 \leq 7, x \in N$
   $\Rightarrow 2x \leq 7 - 1$
   $\Rightarrow 2x \leq 6$
   $\Rightarrow x \leq 3$
   So, $x \in \{0, 1, 2, 3\}$

(b) i. Factorise $3x - 3y + ax - ay$.

Solution $(3x - 3y) + (ax - ay)$
$= 3(x - y) + a(x - y)$
$= (x - y)(3 + a)$

ii. Factorise $x^2 - 25$.

Solution $x^2 - 25$
$= (x)^2 - (5)^2$
$= (x - 5)(x + 5)$

iii. Express $\frac{2}{3} - \frac{1}{9}$ as a single fraction.

Solution $\frac{2}{3} - \frac{1}{9}$

LCM $= 9$

$= \frac{3(2) - 1(1)}{9}$

$= \frac{6 - 1}{9}$

$= \frac{5}{9}$

iv. Express $\frac{x + 7}{3} - \frac{x}{9}$ as a single fraction. Give your answer in its simplest form.

Solution $\frac{x + 7}{3} - \frac{x}{9}$

LCM $= 9$

$= \frac{3(x + 7) - 1(x)}{9}$

$= \frac{3x + 21 - x}{9}$

$= \frac{2x + 21}{9}$

(c) i. Solve the equation $x^2 - 3x - 10 = 0$.

Solution $x^2 - 3x - 10 = 0$

$x \quad - 5$
$x \quad + 2$

$\Rightarrow (x - 5)(x + 2) = 0$
$\Rightarrow x - 5 = 0, x + 2 = 0$
$\Rightarrow x = 5, x = -2$

ii. Multiply $(x - 4)$ by $(x^2 + 3x - 1)$. Give your answer in its simplest form.

Solution $\quad (x - 4)(x^2 + 3x - 1)$
$$= x^3 + 3x^2 - x - 4x^2 - 12x + 4$$
$$= x^3 + 3x^2 - 4x^2 - x - 12x + 4$$
$$= x^3 - x^2 - 13x + 4$$

Junior Certificate Examination 2005

Paper 1, Q5

5. (*a*) Solve the equation $5x - 6 = 3(x + 4)$.

Solution $\quad 5x - 6 = 3(x + 4)$
$$\Rightarrow 5x - 6 = 3x + 12$$
$$\Rightarrow 5x - 3x = 12 + 6$$
$$\Rightarrow 2x = 18$$
$$\Rightarrow x = 9$$

(*b*) Factorise:

i. $4ab + 8b$

Solution $\quad 4ab + 8b$
$$= 4b(a + 2)$$

ii. $ab + 2ac + 5b + 10c$

Solution $\quad ab + 2ac + 5b + 10c$
$$= (ab + 2ac) + (5b + 10c)$$
$$= a(b + 2c) + 5(b + 2c)$$
$$= (b + 2c)(a + 5)$$

iii. $x^2 + 2x - 15$

Solution $\quad x^2 + 2x - 15$

$$= (x + 5)(x - 3)$$

iv. $x^2 - y^2$

Solution $x^2 - y^2$
$$= (x)^2 - (y)^2$$
$$= (x - y)(x + y)$$

(c) i. Express $\dfrac{x+5}{4} + \dfrac{x+2}{3}$ as a single fraction. Give your answer in its simplest form.

Solution $\dfrac{x+5}{4} + \dfrac{x+2}{3}$

LCM $= 12$

$$= \dfrac{3(x+5) + 4(x+2)}{12}$$
$$= \dfrac{3x + 15 + 4x + 8}{12}$$
$$= \dfrac{7x + 23}{12}$$

ii. Hence, or otherwise, solve the equation $\dfrac{x+5}{4} + \dfrac{x+2}{3} = \dfrac{5}{2}$.

Solution $\dfrac{x+5}{4} + \dfrac{x+2}{3} = \dfrac{5}{2}$

$\Rightarrow \dfrac{7x + 23}{12} = \dfrac{5}{2}$

LCM $= 12$

$\Rightarrow \dfrac{12(7x + 23)}{12} = \dfrac{12(5)}{2}$

$\Rightarrow 1(7x + 23) = 6(5)$

$\Rightarrow 7x + 23 = 30$

$\Rightarrow 7x = 30 - 23$

$\Rightarrow 7x = 7$

$\Rightarrow x = 1$

iii. Solve for x and for y: $3x - y = 8$.

Solution

① $3x - y = 8$
② $x + 2y = 5$
2 by ① $6x - 2y = 16$
② $x + 2y = 5$
$\overline{}$
$7x = 21$
$\Rightarrow x = 3$

Sub. for $x = 3$.
② $x + 2y = 5$
$\Rightarrow 3 + 2y = 5$
$\Rightarrow 2y = 2$
$\Rightarrow y = 1$

CHAPTER 6
Functions

Learning Objectives

- Understand relations and functions, domain and range.
- Draw graphs of linear (line) functions.
- Find the points where a line cuts the x-axis and the y-axis.
- Draw graphs of quadratic functions: minimum point parabola and maximum point parabola.

Relations and functions, domain and range

- A **couple** is also called an **ordered pair**, e.g. (x, y).
- A **relation** (R) is a set of couples, e.g. $R = \{(1, 2), (3, 4), (5, 6)\}$ or $R = \{(3, 7), (3, 5), (2, 9)\}$.
- The **domain** (Do) is the set of all first components in a relation, e.g. $R = \{(1, 2), (3, 4), (4, 5)\} \Rightarrow Do = \{1, 3, 4\}$.
- The **range** (Ra) is the set of all second components in a relation, e.g. $R = \{(1, 2), (3, 4), (5, 6)\} \Rightarrow Ra = \{2, 4, 6\}$.
- A **function** (f) is also a set of couples, but no couples have the same first components, e.g. $f = \{(1, 2), (3, 4), (5, 6)\}$, but $\{(3, 7), (3, 5), (2, 9)\}$ is **not** a function.

Example 1

$R = \{(2, 5), (3, 7), (4, 9), (5, 11)\}$.

(a) Write out the domain and range of R.

Solution $D_o = \{2, 3, 4, 5\}$
$R_a = \{5, 7, 9, 11\}$

(b) Draw an arrow-graph of R.

Solution

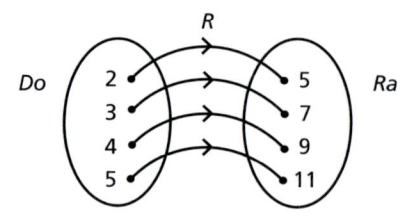

Top Tips
- R = relation.
- f = function.
- D_o = domain.
- R_a = range.

(c) Is the relation R a function? Explain.

Solution Yes, because no couples in the set have the same first component.

Example 2

$f: x \to 2x + 5$ has the domain $(D_o) = \{0, 1, 2, 3\}$. Find the range (R_a) of the function f.

Solution $f(x) = 2x + 5$

Let $x = 0 \Rightarrow f(0) = 2(0) + 5 = 0 + 5 = 5$
Let $x = 1 \Rightarrow f(1) = 2(1) + 5 = 2 + 5 = 7$
Let $x = 2 \Rightarrow f(2) = 2(2) + 5 = 4 + 5 = 9$
Let $x = 3 \Rightarrow f(3) = 2(3) + 5 = 6 + 5 = 11$

So, range $(R_a) = \{5, 7, 9, 11\}$.

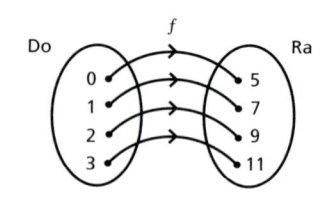

Example 3

$f(x) = 3x - 2$. Find (a) $f(1)$ (b) $f(5)$ (c) $f(-2)$.

Solution $f(x) = 3x - 2$

(a) $f(1) = 3(1) - 2 = 3 - 2 = 1$
(b) $f(5) = 3(5) - 2 = 15 - 2 = 13$
(c) $f(-2) = 3(-2) - 2 = -6 - 2 = -8$

Top Tips
- Given x, find $f(x)$.
- Use substitution, i.e. replace x with each of the values given, and then simplify.

Example 4

$g: x \rightarrow 5x^2 + 3x$. Find (a) $g(0)$ (b) $g(-1)$ (c) $g(2)$.

Solution $g(x) = 5x^2 + 3x$

(a) $g(0) = 5(0)^2 + 3(0) = 5(0) + 3(0) = 0 + 0 = 0$

(b) $g(-1) = 5(-1)^2 + 3(-1) = 5(1) + 3(-1) = 5 - 3 = 2$

(c) $g(2) = 5(2)^2 + 3(2) = 5(4) + 3(2) = 20 + 6 = 26$

Example 5

If $f(x) = 4x - 3$, solve the following equations: (a) $f(x) = 9$ (b) $f(x) = -11$.

Solution (a) $f(x) = 9$

$\Rightarrow 4x - 3 = 9$

$\Rightarrow 4x = 9 + 3$

$\Rightarrow 4x = 12$

$\Rightarrow x = 3$

Solution (b) $f(x) = -11$

$\Rightarrow 4x - 3 = -11$

$\Rightarrow 4x = -11 + 3$

$\Rightarrow 4x = -8$

$\Rightarrow x = -2$

Top Tips

- Given $f(x)$, find x.
- Use substitution, but this time, replace $f(x)$ with the expression given and then solve the equation.

Graph of linear (line) functions

Example 1

Draw the graph of the function $f(x) = 5x - 3$ in the domain $0 \leq x \leq 3$, $x \in R$.

Solution   Points

$f(x) = 5x - 3$ ↓

$x = 0 \Rightarrow f(0) = 5(0) - 3 = 0 - 3 = -3 \Rightarrow (0, -3)$

$x = 1 \Rightarrow f(1) = 5(1) - 3 = 5 - 3 = 2 \Rightarrow (1, 2)$

$x = 2 \Rightarrow f(2) = 5(2) - 3 = 10 - 3 = 7 \Rightarrow (2, 7)$

$x = 3 \Rightarrow f(3) = 5(3) - 3 = 15 - 3 = 12 \Rightarrow (3, 12)$

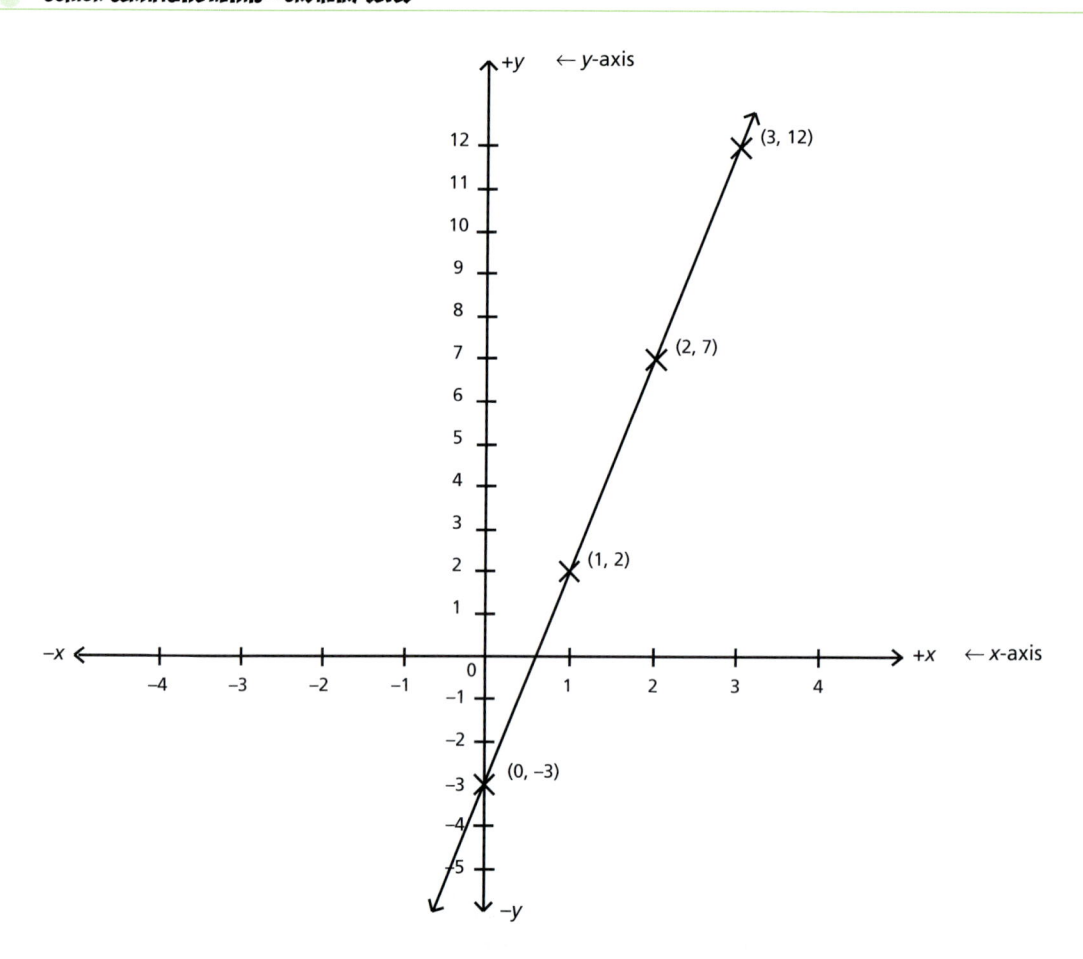

Top Tips

- **How to draw a graph**

    Step 1: Draw the *x* and *y* axes.
    Step 2: Examine the points (couples) and mark in a suitable scale on both axes.
    Step 3: Plot each point with a heavy dot or ×.
    Step 4: Join up all the points to get the graph.

CHAPTER 6: FUNCTIONS

Points where a line cuts the x-axis and y-axis

Example 1

Find the points (couples) where the line $y = x + 5$ cuts the x-axis and y-axis and draw the line.

Solution

$$y = x + 5$$

Points
↓

Let $y = 0 \Rightarrow 0 = x + 5 \Rightarrow x = -5 \Rightarrow (-5, 0)$

Let $x = 0 \Rightarrow y = 0 + 5 \Rightarrow y = 5 \Rightarrow (0, 5)$

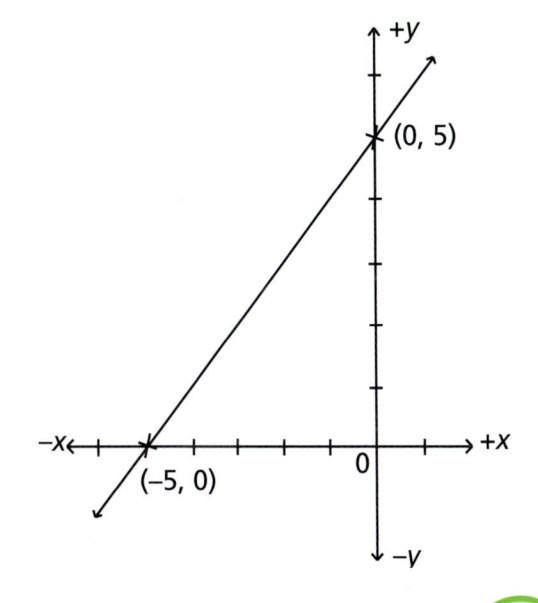

Top Tips

- A line cuts the x-axis at $y = 0$.
- A line cuts the y-axis at $x = 0$.

Graphs of quadratic functions

Example 1

Draw the graph of the function $f: x \to x^2 - 4x + 3$ in the domain $-1 \leq x \leq 5, x \in R$. Use your graph to **find** (a) the value of $f(3.5)$ (b) the values of x for which $f(x) = 0$ (c) the minimum value of $f(x)$.

Use $y = + x^2 - 4x + 3$ and $Do = \{-1, 0, 1, 2, 3, 4, 5\}$.

Top Tips

- How to construct a table

  Step 1: Number of rows (→) = number of terms in y-function + 2.
  Step 2: Number of columns (↓) = #(Do) + 1.
  Step 3: Fill in all the x values in the boxes along the top row.
  Step 4: Fill in all the terms of the function in the boxes under x in the first column.

Note

- y is the same as $f(x)$ is the same as $f: x \to$

x	-1	0	1	2	3	4	5
x^2	1	0	1	4	9	16	25
$-4x$	4	0	-4	-8	-12	-16	-20
3	3	3	3	3	3	3	3
y	8	3	0	-1	0	3	8
Points	$(-1, 8)$	$(0, 3)$	$(1, 0)$	$(2, -1)$	$(3, 0)$	$(4, 3)$	$(5, 8)$

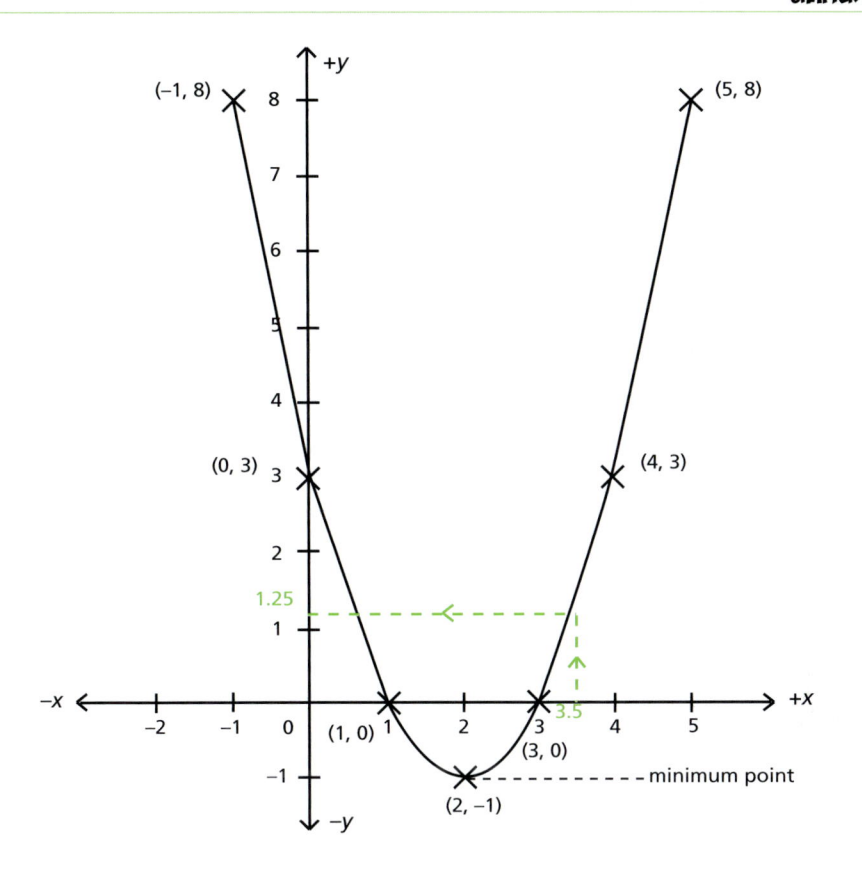

Top Tips

- $+$ in front of x^2 gives minimum point parabola.

Solution (a) $f(3.5) = 1.25$

(b) $f(x) = 0 \Rightarrow x = 1$ or $x = 3$

(c) Minimum value of $f(x) = -1$

Help

- Locate $x = 3.5$ on the x-axis. Move up to the graph and read across to get $y = 1.25$ on the y-axis.

- $f(x) = 0$, i.e. $y = 0$ along the x-axis. The graph cuts the x-axis at $x = 1$ or $x = 3$.

- Minimum value of $f(x)$, i.e. the lowest value of y on the y-axis that the graph reaches down to is -1.

Junior Certificate Maths – Ordinary Level

Example 2

Draw the graph of the function $f: x \to 2 - x - x^2$ in the domain $-3 \leq x \leq 2, x \in R$. Use your graph to **find** (*a*) the value of $f(0.5)$ (*b*) the values of x for which $f(x) = f(0) + f(2)$ and (*c*) **draw** the axis of symmetry of the graph $f(x)$.

Use $y = 2 - x - x^2$ and $D_0 = \{-3, -2, -1, 0, 1, 2\}$.

Solution

x	-3	-2	-1	0	1	2
2	2	2	2	2	2	2
$-x$	3	2	1	0	-1	-2
$-x^2$	-9	-4	-1	0	-1	-4
y	-4	0	2	2	0	-4
Points	$(-3, -4)$	$(-2, 0)$	$(-1, 2)$	$(0, 2)$	$(1, 0)$	$(2, -4)$

Top Tips

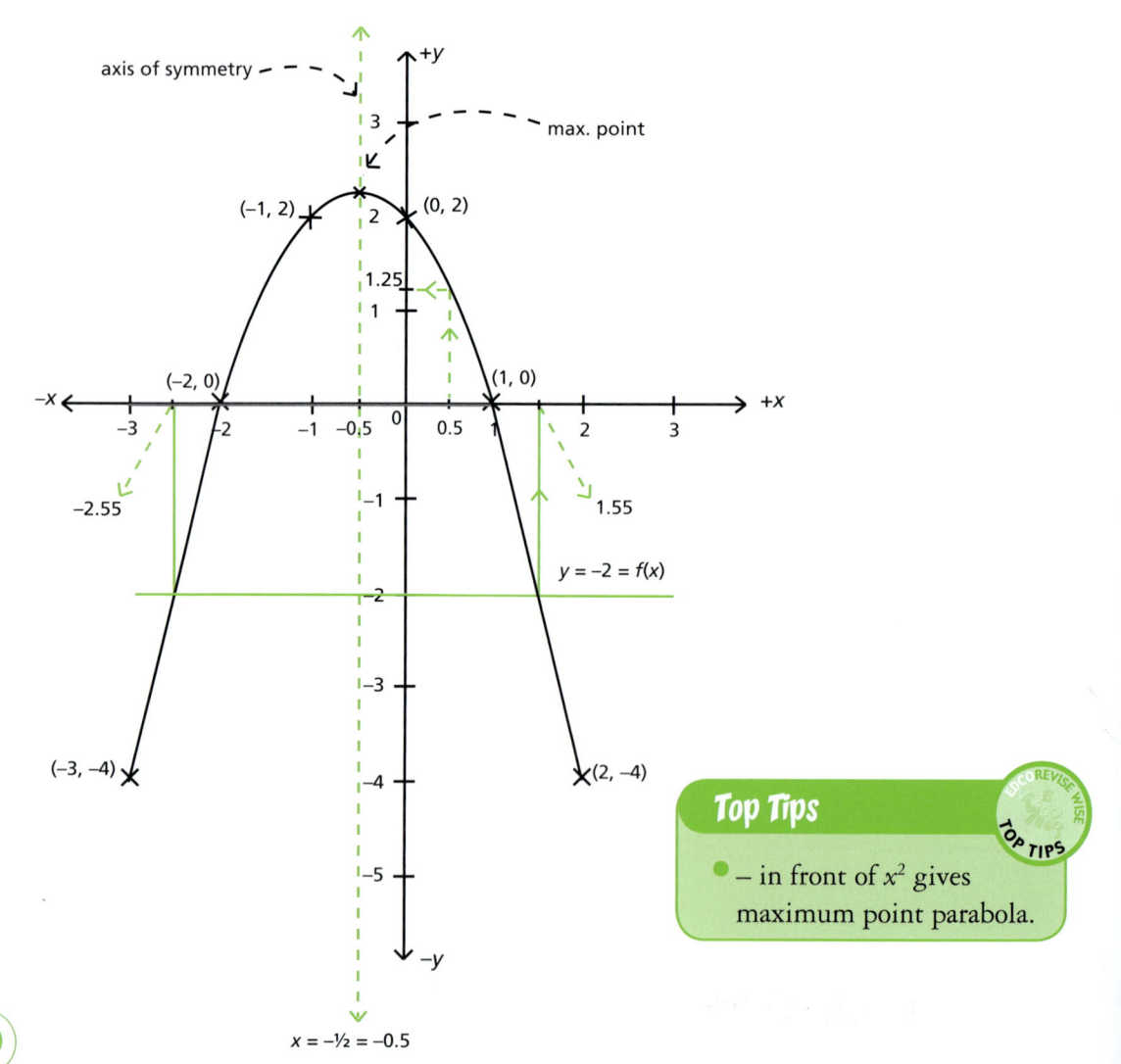

- $-$ in front of x^2 gives maximum point parabola.

Solution (a) $f(0.5) = 1.25$

(b) $f(x) = f(0) + f(2)$
$= 2 + (-4)$
$= 2 - 4$
$= -2$

then, from the graph
$x = -2.55, x = 1.55$

(c) Axis of symmetry
$x = -\frac{1}{2}$
or, $x = -0.5$

Help

- Locate $x = 0.5$ on the x-axis. Move up to the graph and read across to get $y = 1.25$ on the y-axis.

- Use the table to get $f(0)$ and $f(2)$. Using $f(x) = -2$, i.e. $y = -2$, draw a horizontal line through -2 on the y-axis. Where this line cuts the graph, read up to the x-axis to get $x = -2.55, x = 1.55$.

- We want the vertical line that divides the graph into two equal parts. Find the maximum point and through this point draw a vertical line perpendicular to the x-axis. This line passes through the x-axis at $x = \frac{1}{2} = -0.5$.

Self-test 1

1. $K = \{(1, 1), (4, 2), (9, 3)\}$. Write out the domain and range of K.

2. $f: x \to 5 - 4x$ has the domain $\{-1, 0, 1, 2\}$. Find the range of the function f.

3. $f(x) = 7x - 4$. Find (a) $f(-2)$ (b) $f(0)$ (c) $f(3)$.

4. If $g(x) = x - 3$, solve the following equations: (a) $g(x) = 0$ (b) $g(x) = 4$.

5. Draw the graph of the function $f: x \to x^2 + x - 2 = 0$ in the domain $-3 \leq x \leq 2$, $x \in R$. Use your graph to find (a) the value of $f(1.5)$ (b) the values of x for which $f(x) = 0$ (c) the minimum value of $f(x)$.

6. Draw the graph of the function $f(x) = 4x - x^2$ in the domain $-1 \leq x \leq 5, x \in R$. Use your graph to find (a) $f(2.5)$ (b) the values of x for which $f(x) = 3$, i.e. $y = 3$ (c) the maximum point and (d) draw the axis of symmetry of the graph $f(x)$.

Self-test answers

Self-test 1

1. $Do = \{1, 4, 9\}$; $Ra = \{1, 2, 3\}$
2. $Ra = \{9, 5, 1, -3\}$
3. (a) -18 (b) -4 (c) 17
4. (a) 3 (b) 7
5.

x	-3	-2	-1	0	1	2
$f(x)$	4	0	-2	-2	0	4

(a) 1.75 (b) $x = -2, x = 1$ (c) $-2\frac{1}{4}$

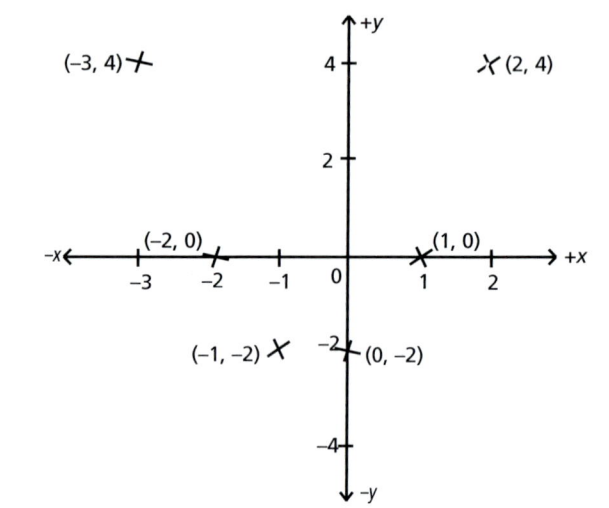

6.

x	-1	0	1	2	3	4	5
$f(x)$	-5	0	3	4	3	0	-5

(a) 3.75 (b) $x = 1, x = 3$ (c) $(2, 4)$ (d) $x = 2$

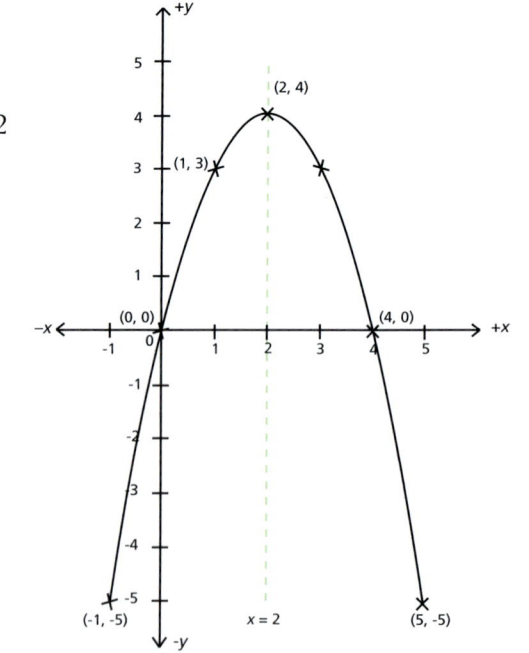

Key Points

- Every function (f) is a relation (R), but not every relation (R) is a function (f).

- The domain (Do) is the set of all first components.

- The range (Ra) is the set of all second components.

- A quadratic function with $+$ in front of x^2 gives a minimum point parabola, e.g. $\cup$.

- A quadratic function with $-$ in front of x^2 gives a maximum point parabola, e.g. $\cap$.

- Always join up the points of a parabola using 'free-hand' and not a ruler.

- An axis of symmetry divides a parabola into two equal parts and is perpendicular to the x-axis and passes through the minimum point or the maximum point.

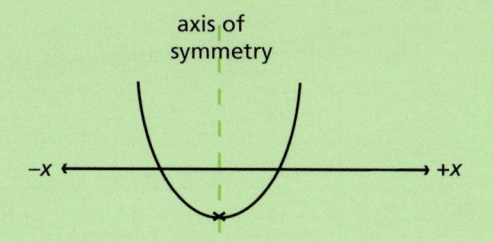

- The notation $f(x) = x^2 - 7x + 12$ is the same as $f: x \rightarrow x^2 - 7x + 12$ is the same as $y = x^2 - 7x + 12$.

Junior Certificate Examination 2004

Paper 1, Q6

6. (a) $P = \{(1, 5), (2, 5), (3, 6), (4, 6)\}$. Write out the domain and range of P.

    Solution Domain = $\{1, 2, 3, 4\}$

    Range = $\{5, 6\}$

    (b) Draw the graph of the function $f: x \to x^2 - 4x + 2$ in the domain $0 \le x \le 4$, where $x \in R$.

    Solution Use $y = x^2 - 4x + 2$ and $D_o = \{0, 1, 2, 3, 4\}$.

x	0	1	2	3	4
x^2	0	1	4	9	16
$-4x$	0	-4	-8	-12	-16
2	2	2	2	2	2
y	2	-1	-2	-1	2
Points	(0, 2)	(1, -1)	(2, -2)	(3, -1)	(4, 2)

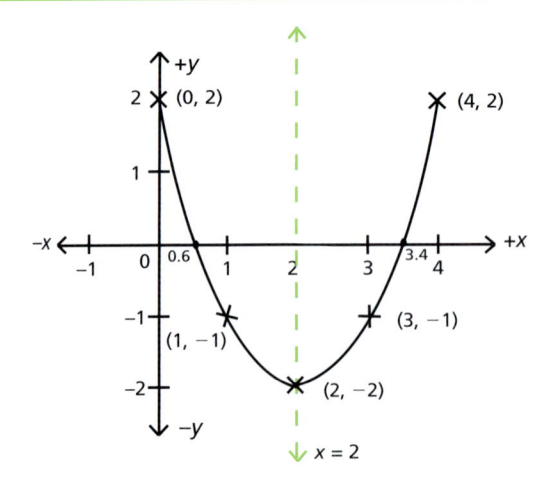

    (c) i. Draw the axis of symmetry of the graph drawn in (b) above. Work to be shown on the graph.

      Solution Axis of symmetry is $x = 2$

    ii. Use the graph to estimate the values of x for which $f(x) = 0$. Work to be shown on the graph and answers to be written here.

      (In other words, find the x values where the graph cuts the x-axis.)

      Solution $x = 0.6$, $x = 3.4$

Junior Certificate Examination 2005

Paper 1, Q6

6. (a) $f(x) = 5x - 6$. Find: (i) $f(3)$ (ii) $f(-2)$.

   Solution i. $f(3) = 5(3) - 6$
   $= 15 - 6 = 9$

   ii. $f(-2) = 5(-2) - 6$
   $= -10 - 6 = -16$

(b) Draw the graph of the function $f: x \to x^2 + x - 3$ in the domain $-3 \leq x \leq 2$, where $x \in R$.

   Use $y = x^2 + x - 3$ and $D_0 = \{-3, -2, -1, 0, 1, 2\}$.

   Solution

x	-3	-2	-1	0	1	2
x^2	9	4	1	0	1	4
x	-3	-2	-1	0	1	2
-3	-3	-3	-3	-3	-3	-3
y	3	-1	-3	-3	-1	3
Points	$(-3, 3)$	$(-2, -1)$	$(-1, -3)$	$(0, -3)$	$(1, -1)$	$(2, 3)$

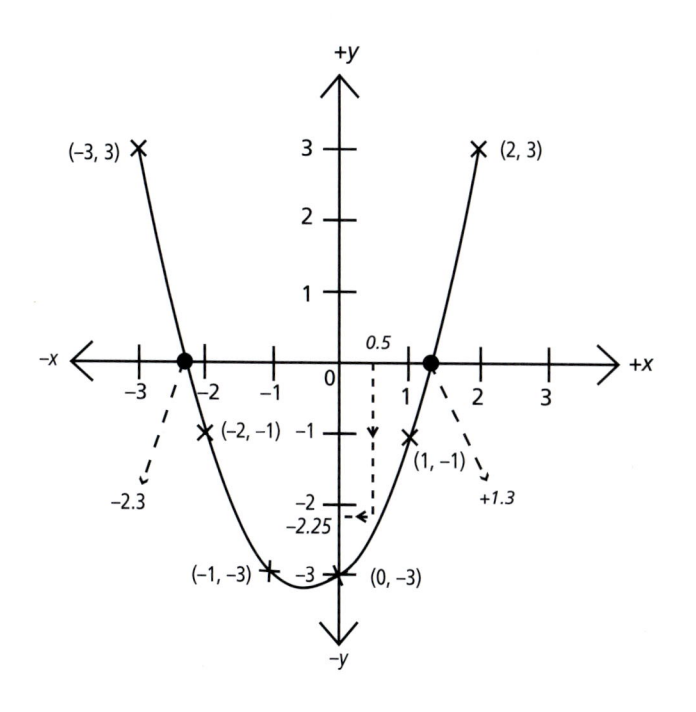

(c) Use the graph drawn in (b) to estimate:

  i. The values of x for which $f(x) = 0$.

   Work to be shown on the graph and answers to be written here.

   Solution $x = +1.3, \; x = -2.3$

  ii. The value of $f(x)$ when $x = 0.5$.

   Work to be shown on the graph and answers to be written here.

   Solution $f(x) = y = -2.25$

CHAPTER 7
Two-Dimensional and Three-Dimensional Figures

Learning Objectives

- Calculate the area and perimeter of rectangles and squares.
- Apply appropriate units to calculations involving area and perimeter.
- Calculate the area and perimeter of irregular shapes of a rectangular nature.
- Calculate the circumference and area of a circle given its radius length.
- Calculate the areas of regions enclosed by combinations of rectangles and circles.
- Calculate the surface area and volume of rectangular solids and cubes.
- Use correct units in surface area and volume problems.
- Understand the relationship between volume and capacity.
- Use a calculator in evaluating surface areas and volumes.
- Calculate the surface area and volume of cylinders, spheres and hemispheres.
- Handle questions involving changes of liquid levels in hollow rectangular solids and cylinders.
- Understand the use of the different values for π.

Length and area

Rectangular area = $l \times b$
Perimeter = $2l + 2b$

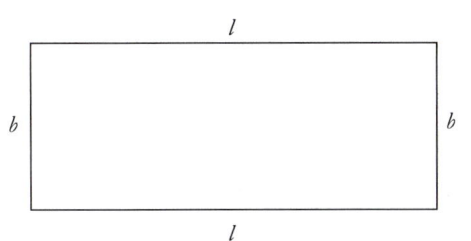

Square area = l^2
Perimeter = $4l$

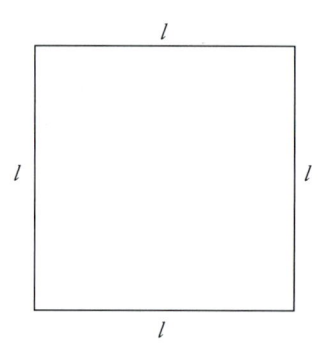

- The unit of length for short distances is the centimetre (cm).
- The unit of area is the square centimetre (cm²).

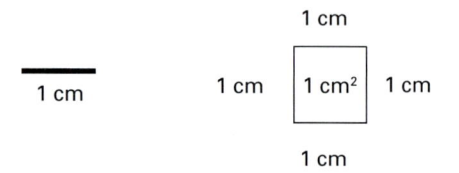

Top Tips

- 100 cm = 1 m.
- 10 000 cm² = 1 m².

- The unit of length for longer distances is the metre (m).
- The unit of area is the square metre (m²).

Example 1

A rectangle has dimensions length = 12 cm, breadth = 7 cm. Find its (*a*) area (*b*) perimeter.

Solution (*a*) Area = length × breadth
$$= 12 \times 7$$
$$= 84 \text{ cm}^2$$

(*b*) Perimeter = $2l + 2b$
$$= 2(12) + 2(7)$$
$$= 24 + 14$$
$$= 38 \text{ cm}$$

Example 2

The length of a rectangle is 13 cm. If its area is 91 cm², find its (*a*) breadth (*b*) perimeter.

Solution (*a*) $13 \times b = 91$
$$\text{So, } b = \frac{91}{13}$$
$$\Rightarrow b = 7 \text{ cm}$$

(*b*) Perimeter = $2l + 2b$
$$= 2(13) + 2(7)$$
$$= 26 + 14$$
$$= 40 \text{ cm}$$

Example 3

The breadth of a rectangle is 8 cm. If its perimeter is 44 cm, find its (a) length (b) area.

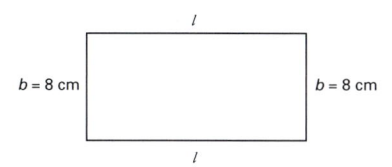

Solution (a) Perimeter $= 2l + 2b$

$2l + 16 = 44$

$2l = 28$

$l = 14$ cm

(b) Area $= l \times b$

$= 14 \times 8$

$= 112$ cm^2

Example 4

Find (a) the length of the side of a square whose area is 49 cm^2 (b) the perimeter of the square.

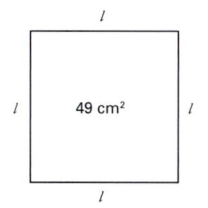

Solution (a) $l^2 = 49$

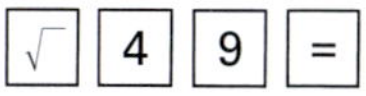

$\Rightarrow l = 7$ cm

CALCULATOR
√ 4 9 =

(b) Perimeter $= 4l = 4(7) = 28$ cm

Example 5

A rectangular garden consists of a lawn surrounded by a path. The dimensions of the garden are length = 21 m and breadth = 11 m. The width of the path is 1 m all round.

(a) **Find** the area of the entire garden.
(b) **Find** the area of the lawn.
(c) Hence **find** the area of the path.

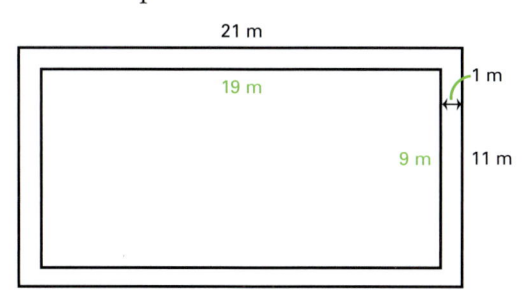

If the path is 1 m wide all round, then the dimensions of the lawn are length = 19 m, breadth = 9 m.

Solution (a) Area of garden $= 21 \times 11 = 231$ m^2

(b) Area of lawn $= 19 \times 9 = 171$ m^2

(c) Area of path $= 231 - 171 = 60$ m^2

Example 6

Find the area and perimeter of the following shapes.

(a)

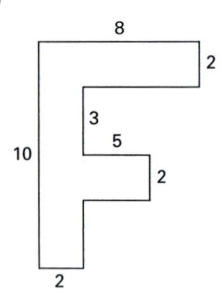

(b)

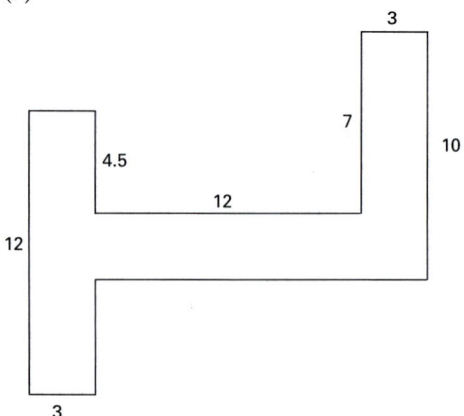

(c)

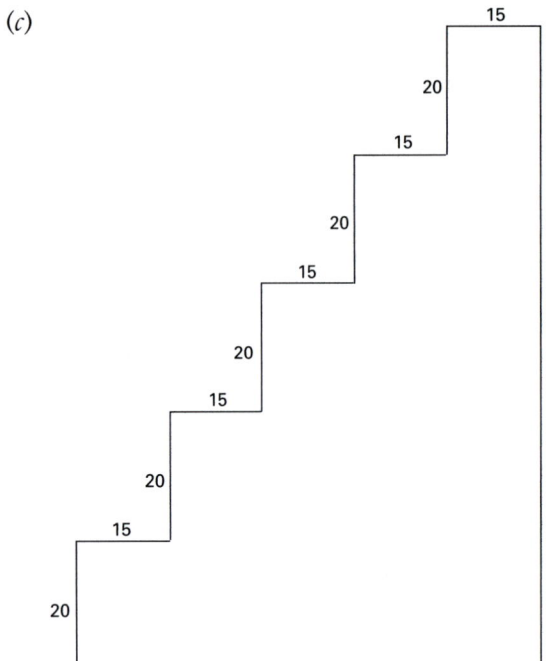

Solution (a) Area = (6 × 2) + (10 × 2) + (5 × 2)
 = 12 + 20 + 10
 = 42 cm²

Perimeter = 10 + 2 + 6 + 2 + 6 + 3 + 5 + 2 + 5 + 3 + 2
 = 46 cm

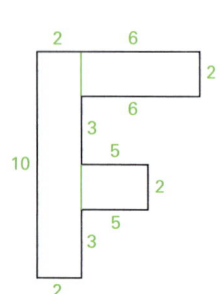

Solution

(b) Area = (12 × 3) + (12 × 3) + (10 × 3)
= 36 + 36 + 30
= 102 cm²

Perimeter = 12 + 3 + 4.5 + 12 + 7 + 3
+ 10 + 3 + 12 + 4.5 + 3
= 74 cm

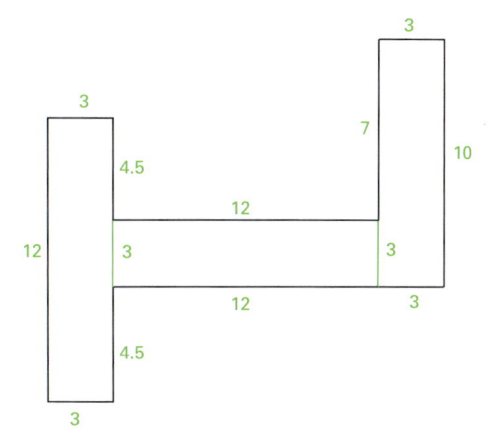

Solution

(c) Area = (15 × 100) + (15 × 80)
+ (15 × 60) + (15 × 40)
+ (15 × 20)
= 1500 + 1200 + 900
+ 600 + 300
= 4500 cm²

Perimeter = 100 + 75 + 20 + 15
+ 20 + 15 + 20 + 15
+ 20 + 15 + 20 + 15
= 175 + 175
= 350 cm

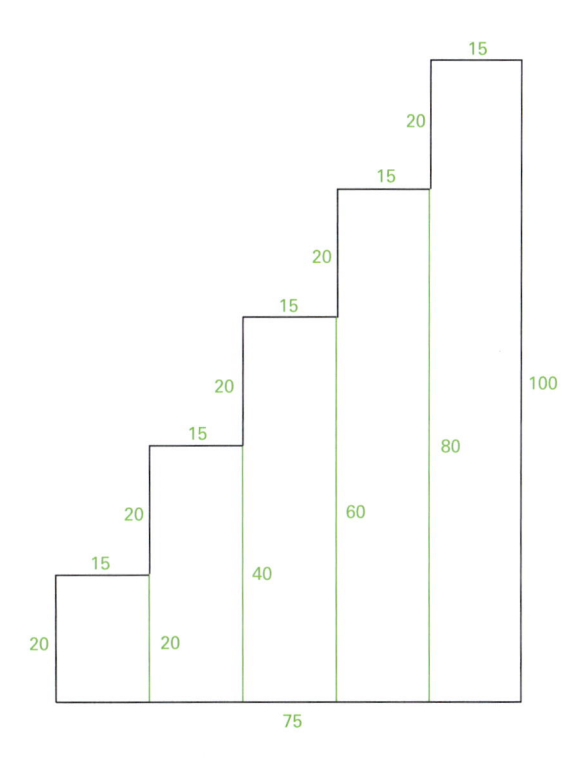

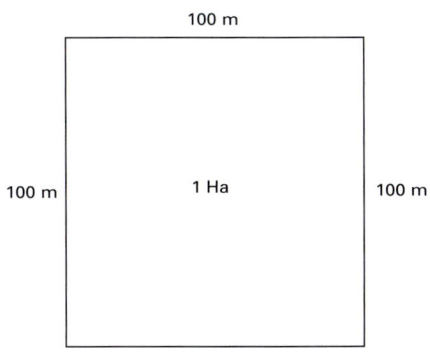

Top Tips

- The unit of area used for large enclosed spaces is the hectare (Ha). It is the area enclosed by a square of length 100 m.

- 1 hectare = 10 000 m².

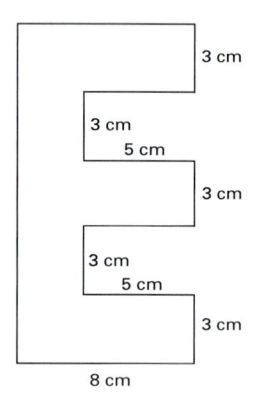

Example 7

If the area of a rectangular car park is 6 Ha and its breadth is 150 m, **calculate** its length.

Solution   Convert 6 Ha into 60 000 m².

$$l \times b = \text{area}$$
$$\Rightarrow l \times 150 = 60\,000$$
$$\Rightarrow 150\,l = 60\,000$$
$$\Rightarrow l = \frac{60\,000}{150}$$
$$= 400 \text{ m}$$

Self-test 1

1. The length of a rectangle is 10 cm. If its perimeter is 36 cm, **calculate** its (a) breadth (b) area.

2. **Find** (a) the length of the side of a square whose area is 64 cm² (b) the perimeter of the square.

3. **Find** the area and perimeter of the following shapes:

(a) H-shape: vertical bars 2 cm wide, total height 14 cm, horizontal connector 2 cm tall and 6 cm wide.

(b) E-shape: 8 cm tall on the left; arms of 5 cm with 3 cm heights; gaps of 3 cm.

4. The diagram shows a plan of a building with an indoor swimming pool. A tiled area surrounds the pool and is 5 m wide. **Calculate** the area of (*a*) the swimming pool (*b*) the building (*c*) the tiled area. (*d*) **How many** tiles measuring 0.2 m square are needed to tile the area surrounding the pool?

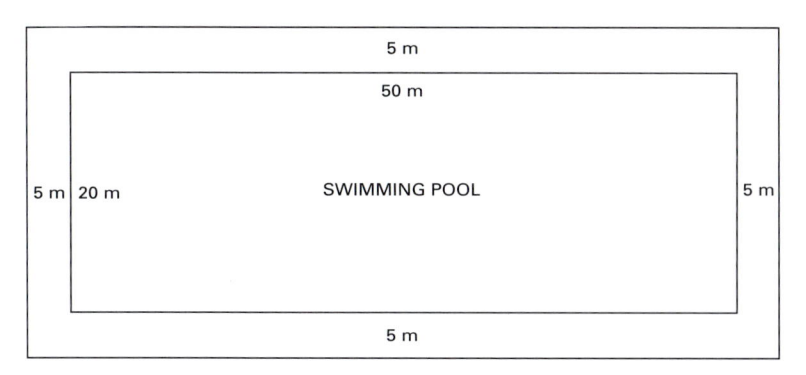

```
                    5 m
                    50 m
       ┌─────────────────────────────┐
 5 m │ 20 m    SWIMMING POOL    │ 5 m
       └─────────────────────────────┘
                    5 m
```

Circle

- Area = πr^2.

- Length of circumference = $2\pi r$.

- r = length of radius.

- $\pi = \frac{22}{7}$ or 3.14.

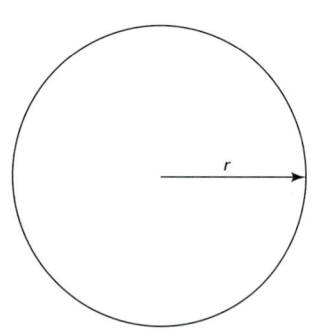

Top Tips

- When dealing with questions involving circles, you will be told to take $\pi = \frac{22}{7}$ or $\pi = 3.14$ or 3.1, depending on the degree of accuracy required in the answer.

Example 1

Find (*a*) the area and (*b*) the length of the circumference of a circle whose radius is 14 cm. Take $\pi = \frac{22}{7}$.

Solution (*a*) Area = πr^2

$$= \frac{22}{7} \times 14 \times 14$$

$$= 22 \times 28$$

$$= 616 \text{ cm}^2$$

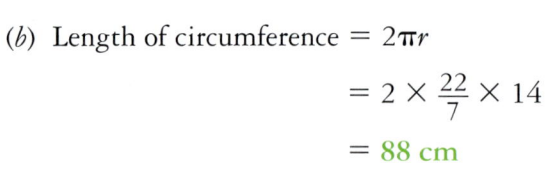

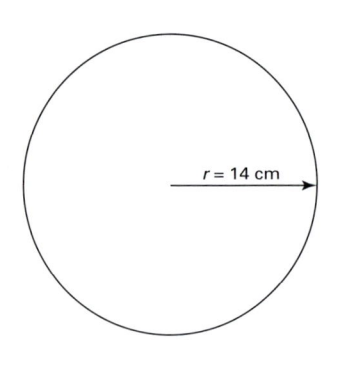

(*b*) Length of circumference = $2\pi r$

$$= 2 \times \frac{22}{7} \times 14$$

$$= 88 \text{ cm}$$

Example 2

Find (*a*) the area and (*b*) the length of the circumference of a circle whose radius is 8 cm. Take $\pi = 3.14$.

Solution (*a*) Area = πr^2

$$= 3.14 \times 64$$

$$= 200.96 \text{ cm}^2$$

(*b*) Length of circumference = $2\pi r$

$$= 2 \times 3.14 \times 8$$

$$= 6.28 \times 8$$

$$= 50.24 \text{ cm}$$

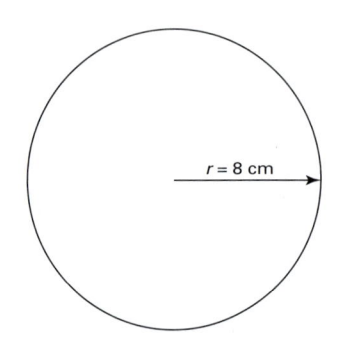

Example 3

If the area of a circle is 78.5 cm², find (a) the length of its radius (b) the length of its circumference. Take $\pi = 3.14$.

Solution (a)
$$\pi r^2 = A$$
$$\Rightarrow 3.14 r^2 = 78.5$$
$$\Rightarrow r^2 = \frac{78.5}{3.14}$$
$$\Rightarrow r^2 = 25$$
$$\Rightarrow r = 5 \text{ cm}$$

(b) Length of circumference $= 2\pi r$
$$= 2 \times 3.14 \times 5$$
$$= 31.4 \text{ cm}$$

Example 4

If the length of the circumference of a circle is 88 cm, find (a) the length of its radius (b) the area of the circle. Take $\pi = \frac{22}{7}$.

Solution (a)
$$2\pi r = C$$
$$2 \times \frac{22}{7} \times r = 88$$
$$\Rightarrow \frac{44}{7} \times r = 88$$
$$\Rightarrow 44r = 616$$
$$\Rightarrow r = \frac{616}{44}$$
$$\Rightarrow r = 14 \text{ cm}$$

(b) Area $= \pi r^2$
$$= \frac{22}{7} \times 14 \times 14$$
$$= 44 \times 14$$
$$= 616 \text{ cm}^2$$

Example 5

Find the area of the shaded region in each of the following diagrams. Take $\pi = \frac{22}{7}$. Give answers correct to one decimal place.

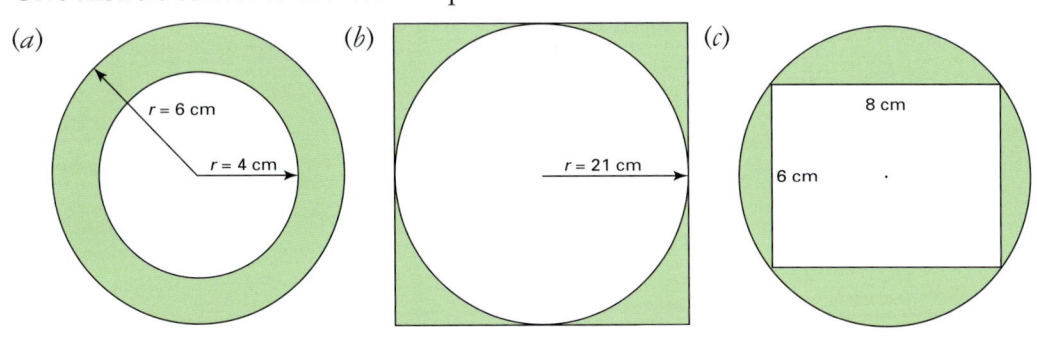

(a) r = 6 cm, r = 4 cm

(b) r = 21 cm

(c) 8 cm, 6 cm

Solution (a) Shaded area = area enclosed by large circle − area enclosed by small circle
$$= \frac{22}{7} \times 6 \times 6 - \frac{22}{7} \times 4 \times 4$$
$$= \frac{22}{7} \times 36 - \frac{22}{7} \times 16$$
$$= 113.14 - 50.29$$
$$= 62.85$$
$$\approx 62.9 \text{ cm}^2 \text{ correct to 1 decimal place}$$

Solution (*b*) Length of side of square = 42 cm

Shaded area = area of square − area enclosed by circle
$$= 42 \times 42 - \frac{22}{7} \times 21 \times 21$$
$$= 1764 - 1386$$
$$= 378.0 \text{ cm}^2$$

Solution (*c*) The diagonal of the rectangle passes through the centre of the circle and is therefore a diameter of the circle.

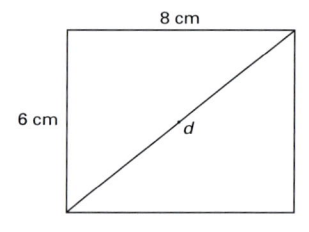

8 cm

6 cm

d

Use Pythagoras' Theorem: $d^2 = 6^2 + 8^2$

$\Rightarrow d^2 = 36 + 64$

$\Rightarrow d^2 = 100$

$\Rightarrow d = 10$ cm

$\Rightarrow$ radius = **5 cm**

Shaded area = area enclosed by circle − area of rectangle
$$= \frac{22}{7} \times 5 \times 5 - 8 \times 6$$
$$= 78.57 - 48$$
$$= 30.57 \text{ cm}^2$$
$$\approx 30.6 \text{ cm}^2$$

Example 6

Find the area and perimeter of the following shapes. Take $\pi = \frac{22}{7}$.

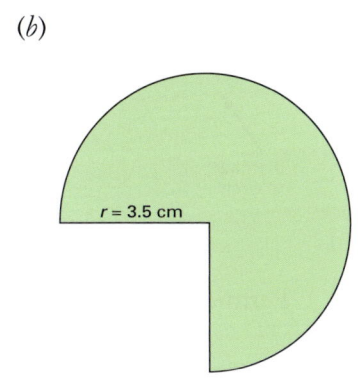

(a) 44 cm, 100 cm

(b) $r = 3.5$ cm

(c) 90 m, 70 m

Solution (a) Radius of both semi-circles $= (100 - 44) \div 2$
$$= 56 \div 2$$
$$= 28 \text{ cm}$$

Area of 2 semi-circles = area of one circle
$$= \frac{22}{7} \times 28 \times 28$$
$$= 2464 \text{ cm}^2$$

Shaded area = area of rectangle − area of circle
$$= 100 \times 56 - 2464$$
$$= 5600 - 2464$$
$$= 3136 \text{ cm}^2$$

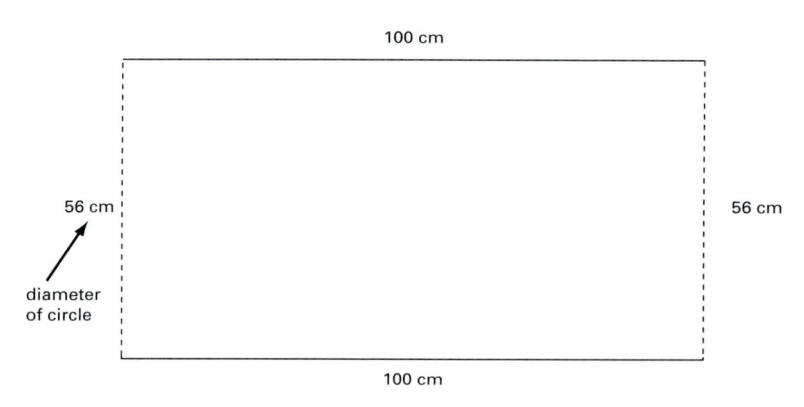

Perimeter of shape = length of circumference of circle + 2 straight edges

$$= (2 \times \tfrac{22}{7} \times 28) + 100 + 100$$

$$= 176 + 200$$

$$= 376 \text{ cm}$$

Solution (b) Area = $\tfrac{3}{4} \times$ area of a full circle

$$= \tfrac{3}{4} \times \tfrac{22}{7} \times 3.5 \times 3.5$$

$$= 28.875 \text{ cm}^2$$

Perimeter = $\tfrac{3}{4} \times$ length of circumference + 2 radii

$$= \left[\tfrac{3}{4} \times 2 \times \tfrac{22}{7} \times 3.5\right] + 3.5 + 3.5$$

$$= 16.5 + 7$$

$$= 23.5 \text{ cm}$$

Solution (c) Area of shaded region = area of 2 semi-circles + area of rectangle

$$= \text{area of 1 complete circle} + \text{area of rectangle}$$

$$= \left[\tfrac{22}{7} \times 35 \times 35\right] + (90 \times 70)$$

$$= 3850 \text{ m}^2 + 6300 \text{ m}^2$$

$$= 10150 \text{ m}^2$$

$$= 1.015 \text{ hectares}$$

Perimeter = length of circumference + length of 2 straight edges

$$= \left[2 \times \tfrac{22}{7} \times 35\right] + 90 + 90$$

$$= 220 + 180$$

$$= 400 \text{ m}$$

Self-test 2

1. Find (*a*) the area and (*b*) the length of the circumference of a circle whose radius is 14 cm. Take $\pi = \frac{22}{7}$.

2. The circumference of a circle is 132 cm. Find its (*a*) radius length and (*b*) its area. Take $\pi = \frac{22}{7}$.

3. Find the area of the shaded region in each of the figures. Take $\pi = \frac{22}{7}$. Give answers correct to two decimal places.

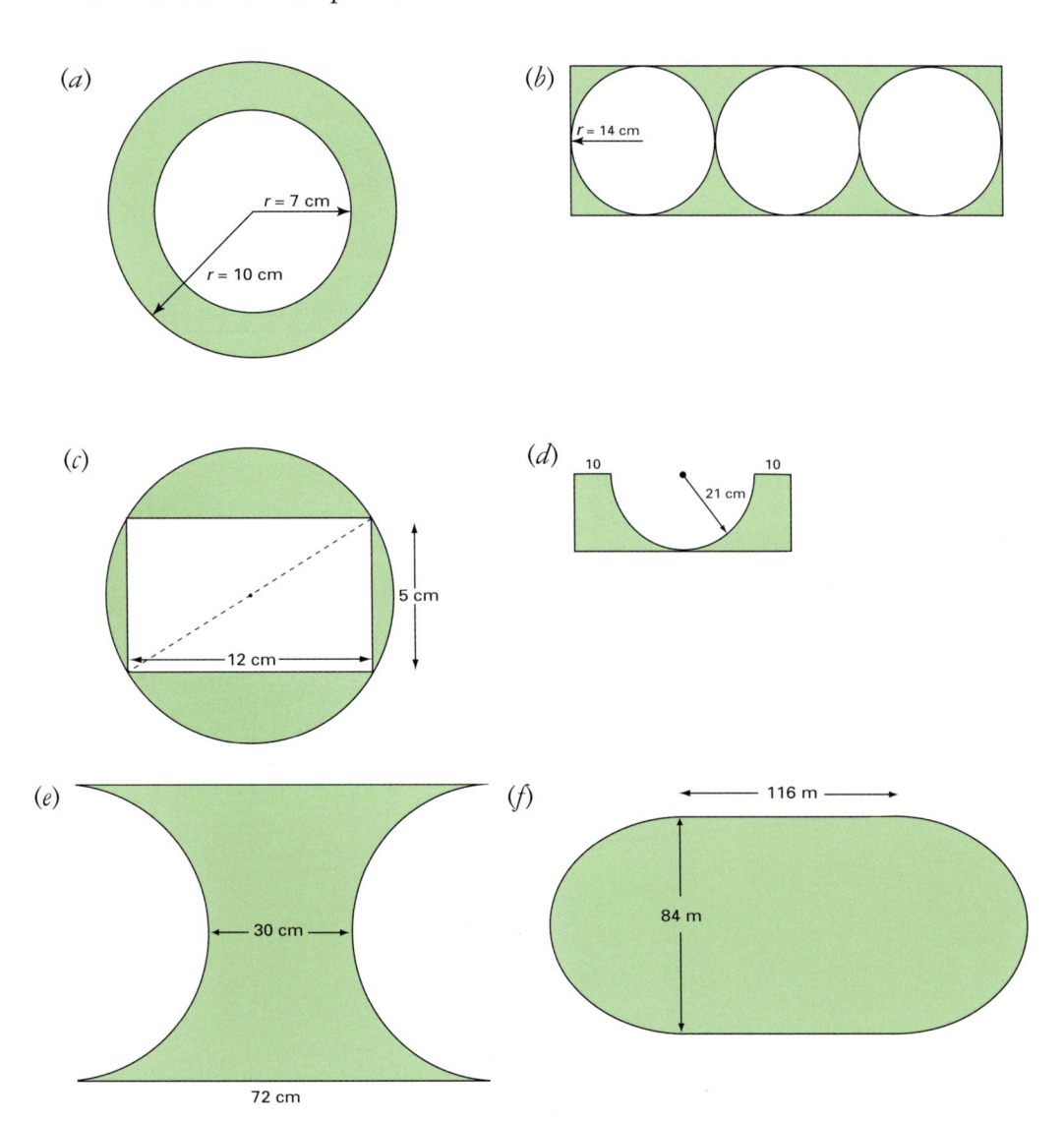

(*a*)

r = 7 cm
r = 10 cm

(*b*)

r = 14 cm

(*c*)

5 cm
12 cm

(*d*)

10   10
21 cm

(*e*)

30 cm
72 cm

(*f*)

116 m
84 m

4. Find the perimeter of the shapes in question 3 above, parts (*d*), (*e*) and (*f*).

Surface area and volume

- Unit of length is the centimetre (cm).
- Unit of area is the square centimetre (cm²).
- Unit of volume is the cubic centimetre (cm³).

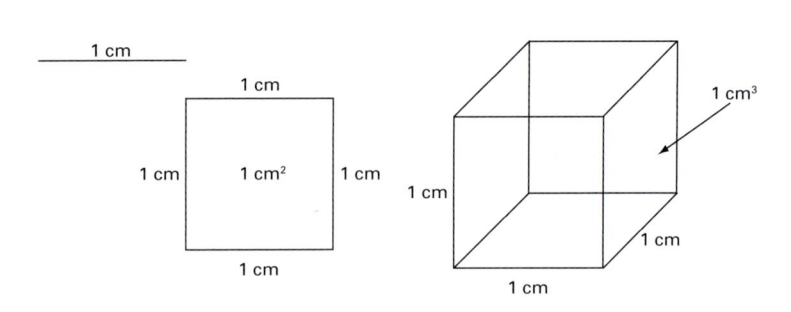

Rectangular solid

Volume = $l \times b \times h$

Surface area = $(2 \times l \times b) + (2 \times l \times h) + (2 \times b \times h)$

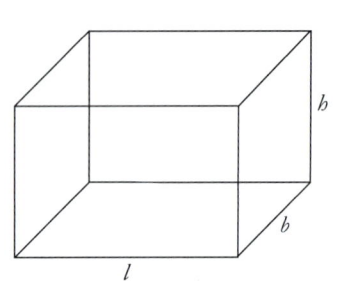

- Capacity is the amount of liquid that can be put into a certain volume.
- Liquid is measured in millilitres (ml).
- A volume of 1 cm³ can accommodate 1 ml of liquid.

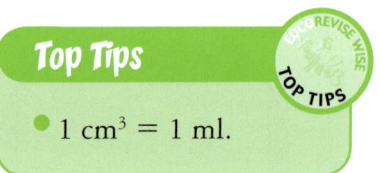

Hollow cube filled with liquid

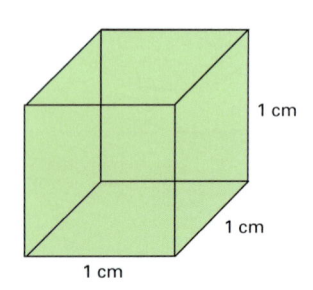

Top Tips

- 1 cm³ = 1 ml.

Cube

Volume = $l \times l \times l$
= l^3

Surface area = $6l^2$

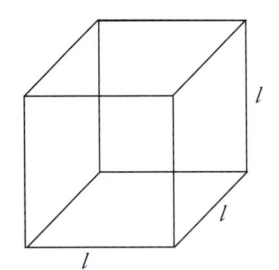

Example 1

A rectangular box has the following dimensions: length = 20 cm, breadth = 30 cm and height = 15 cm. **Find** its (*a*) surface area (*b*) volume and capacity.

Solution (*a*) Surface area = $(2 \times l \times b) + (2 \times l \times h) + (2 \times b \times h)$
= $(2 \times 20 \times 30) + (2 \times 20 \times 15) + (2 \times 30 \times 15)$
= $1200 + 600 + 900$
= **2700 cm²**

(*b*) Volume = $l \times b \times h$
= $20 \times 30 \times 15$
= **9000 cm³**

Capacity = 9000 ml because each 1 cm³ holds 1 ml of liquid.
Capacity = **9 litres** because 1000 ml = 1 litre.

> **Note**
>
> • Remember: 1000 cm³ = 1 litre.

Example 2

The capacity of a rectangular tank is 3.2 litres. If its length = 16 cm and its breadth = 10 cm, **calculate** its height.

Solution Capacity = 3.2 litres = 3200 ml

$$\Rightarrow \text{Volume} = 3200 \text{ cm}^3$$
$$\text{So, } 16 \times 10 \times h = 3200$$
$$\Rightarrow 160 \times h = 3200$$
$$\Rightarrow h = \frac{3200}{160}$$
$$\Rightarrow h = 20 \text{ cm}$$

Example 3

A cube has a volume of 125 cm³. Find
(a) the length of the side of the cube
(b) the surface area of the six faces.

Solution

(a) $l^3 = 125$
$\Rightarrow l = \sqrt[3]{125}$
$\Rightarrow l = 5$ cm

CALCULATOR: $\sqrt[3]{\ }$ 1 2 5 =

(b) Surface area $= 6l^2$
$= 6 \times 5^2$
$= 6 \times 25$
$= 150$ cm²

Top Tips

- The unit of length for larger distances is the metre (m).
- The unit of area for larger areas is the square metre (m²).
- The unit of volume for larger volumes is the cubic metre (m³).
- 1 m = 100 cm
- 1 m² = 10 000 m²
- 1 m³ = 1 000 000 cm³

- Another important relationship is that between litres and m³. A volume of 1 m³ can accommodate 1000 litres of liquid.

Top Tips

- 1 m³ = 1000 litres

Example 4

An empty rectangular tank has the following dimensions: length = 3 m, breadth = 2 m, height = 1.5 m. Water is being released into the tank at a rate of 3 litres per second. **How long** will it take to fill the tank?

Solution $V = l \times b \times h$

$= 3 \times 2 \times 1.5$

$= 9 \text{ m}^3$

Capacity = 9000 litres because 1 m^3 = 1000 litres.

$$\text{time taken to fill tank} = \frac{\text{total capacity}}{\text{rate of flow}}$$

$$\Rightarrow \text{time} = \frac{9000 \text{ litres}}{3 \text{ litres/sec}} = 3000 \text{ seconds}$$

$$\Rightarrow \text{time} = \frac{3000}{60} = 50 \text{ minutes}$$

Self-test 3

1. **Find** the volume and capacity (in litres) of the following hollow rectangular boxes.

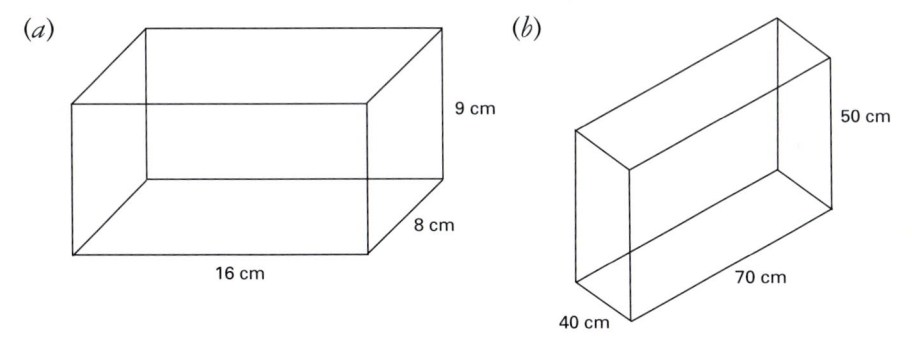

   (a) 16 cm, 8 cm, 9 cm

   (b) 40 cm, 70 cm, 50 cm

2. **Find** the surface area in cm^2 of the rectangular solids in question 1 above.

3. A rectangular solid has a breadth of 14 cm and a height of 10 cm.
   (a) **Find** its length if its capacity is 2.8 litres.
   (b) **Find** the total surface area of its six faces.

4. If the surface area of a cube is 96 cm^2, **find** (a) the length of its side and (b) its volume.

5. Fuel is leaking from a rectangular tank at a rate of 5 litres per second. The tank has the following dimensions: length = 4 m, breadth = 3 m, height = 2 m. If the tank was originally full, **how long** will it take for all the fuel to leak out?

Cylinder

- Volume = $\pi r^2 h$
- Total surface area = $2\pi rh$ (curved area) + $2\pi r^2$ (2 circular ends)

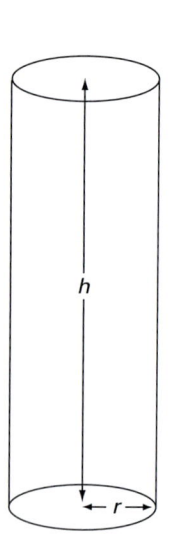

Sphere

- Volume = $\frac{4}{3}\pi r^3$
- Surface area = $4\pi r^2$

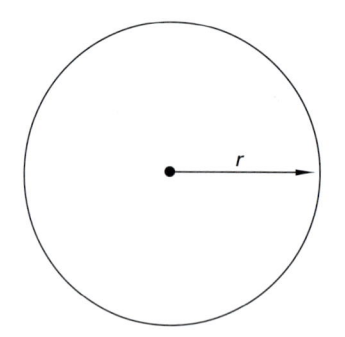

Hemisphere

- Volume = $\frac{2}{3}\pi r^3$
- Total surface area = $3\pi r^2$

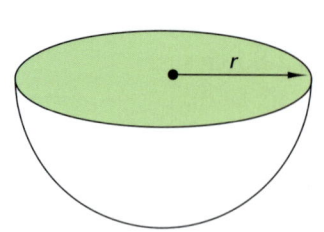

Example 1

Find (a) the volume of a cylindrical chimney whose internal diameter is 3 m and whose height is 21 m and (b) its curved surface area. Take $\pi = \frac{22}{7}$.

Solution   (a) Volume $= \pi r^2 h$

$$= \frac{22}{7}_1 \times 1.5 \times 1.5 \times \cancel{21}^3 \quad \text{...Radius} = 1.5\text{m}$$

$$= 148.5 \text{ m}^3$$

(b) Curved surface area $= 2\pi r h$

$$= 2 \times \frac{22}{7}_1 \times 1.5 \times \cancel{21}^3$$

$$= 198 \text{ m}^2$$

Example 2

(a) Find the surface area and volume of a sphere whose radius is 14 cm.

(b) How many litres of water would it accommodate? Take $\pi = \frac{22}{7}$.

Solution   (a) Surface area $= 4\pi r^2$

$$= 4 \times \frac{22}{7}_1 \times \cancel{14}^2 \times 14$$

$$= 88 \times 28$$

$$= 2464 \text{ cm}^2$$

Volume $= \frac{4}{3}\pi r^3$

$$= \frac{4}{3} \times \frac{22}{7}_1 \times \cancel{14}^2 \times 14 \times 14$$

$$= \frac{88}{3} \times 2 \times 196$$

$$= 11\,498.67 \text{ cm}^3$$

(b) It will accommodate 11.5 litres of water (correct to one decimal place).

Example 3

A solid hemisphere has a volume of 452.16 cm³. **Find** (*a*) the length of its radius (*b*) its total surface area. Take $\pi = 3.14$.

Solution (*a*) $\frac{2}{3}\pi r^3 = V$

$\frac{2}{3} \times 3.14 \times r^3 = 452.16$

$\Rightarrow 6.28 \times r^3 = 1356.48$ ← Multiplying both sides by 3

$\Rightarrow r^3 = \frac{1356.48}{6.28}$

$\Rightarrow r^3 = 216$

$\Rightarrow r = \sqrt[3]{216}$

$\Rightarrow r = 6$ cm

CALCULATOR

$\sqrt[3]{}$ | 2 | 1 | 6 | =

(*b*) Total surface area $= 3\pi r^2$

$= 3 \times 3.14 \times 6 \times 6$

$= 9.42 \times 36$

$= 339.12$ cm²

Example 4

(*a*) **Find** in terms of π the volume of a spherical ball with a radius of 6 cm.

(*b*) Three of these balls are placed in a cylindrical tube. **What** is the minimum volume of the tube?

(*c*) **Find** the volume of empty space in the tube.

(*d*) **Find** the percentage of unoccupied space.

Solution (*a*) $V = \frac{4}{3}\pi r^3$

$= \frac{4}{\cancel{3}_1} \times \pi \times \cancel{6}^2 \times 6 \times 6$

$= 288\pi$ cm³

Solution (*b*) Cylinder: radius = 6 cm, height = 36 cm (3 diameters)

$$\text{Volume of cylinder} = \pi r^2 h$$
$$= \pi \times 6 \times 6 \times 36$$
$$= 1296\pi \text{ cm}^3$$

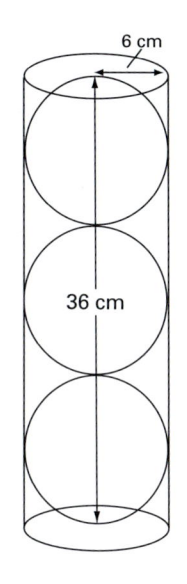

(*c*) Volume of 3 tennis balls = $288\pi \times 3$
$$= 864\pi \text{ cm}^3$$
Volume of empty space = $1296\pi - 864\pi$
$$= 432\pi \text{ cm}^3$$

(*d*) % of unoccupied space = $\dfrac{432\pi}{1296\pi} \times \dfrac{100}{1}$
$$= \dfrac{43\,200}{1296}$$
$$= 33\dfrac{1}{3}\%$$

Example 5

(*a*) **Find** the volume of a cylindrical stick of chalk whose diameter is 1 cm and whose length is 10.5 cm.

(*b*) Twelve sticks of chalk are placed into a rectangular cardboard box in two rows of six sticks. **Find** the volume of the smallest box which will contain the chalk.

(*c*) **Find** the volume of unoccupied space.

(*d*) **Find** the percentage of empty space to two decimal places. Take $\pi = \dfrac{22}{7}$.

Solution (*a*) $r = 0.5$ cm

$$V = \pi r^2 h$$
$$= \dfrac{22}{7}_1 (0.5)(0.5)(\cancel{10.5})^{1.5}$$
$$= 22 \times 0.25 \times 1.5$$
$$= 8.25 \text{ cm}^3$$

(b) Volume of rectangular box shown $= l \times b \times h$
$$= 6 \times 2 \times 10.5$$
$$= 6 \times 21$$
$$= 126 \text{ cm}^3$$

(c) 12 sticks of chalk have a volume of $12 \times 8.25 \text{ cm}^3 = 99 \text{ cm}^3$.

Volume of unoccupied space $= 126 - 99 = 27 \text{ cm}^3$.

(d) Percentage of empty space $= \dfrac{27}{126} \times \dfrac{100}{1} = \dfrac{2700}{126}$
$$= 21.43\%$$

Example 6

(a) A solid sphere made of candle wax has a radius of 9 cm. **Find** its volume in terms of π.

(b) The sphere is melted down and a cylindrical candle with a radius of 6 cm is made. **Calculate** the height of the candle.

Solution (a) Volume of sphere $= \dfrac{4}{3}\pi r^3$

$$V = \dfrac{4}{3} \times \pi \times 9 \times 9 \times 9$$
$$= 12 \times 81 \times \pi$$
$$= 972\pi \text{ cm}^3$$

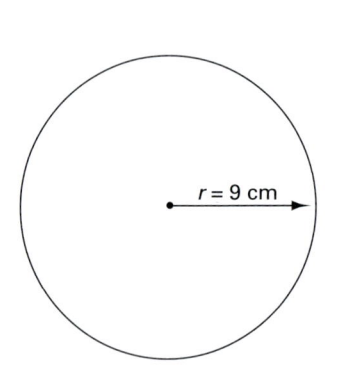

(b) The wax is now reshaped into a cylinder with no loss of wax.

So, let $\pi r^2 h = 972\pi$

$\Rightarrow 6 \times 6 \times h = 972$

$\Rightarrow 36 \times h = 972$

$\Rightarrow h = \dfrac{972}{36}$

$\Rightarrow h = 27 \text{ cm}$

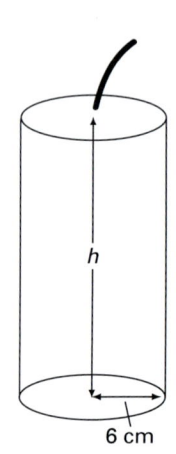

CHAPTER 7: TWO-DIMENSIONAL AND THREE-DIMENSIONAL FIGURES

Example 7

110 chocolate cubes of side 2 cm are melted and the liquid is collected in a cylindrical vessel of radius 4 cm. **To what height** does the liquid rise in the cylinder? Take $\pi = \frac{22}{7}$.

Solution Each cube has a volume of $2 \times 2 \times 2 = 8$ cm^3.

110 cubes have a volume of 880 cm^3.

No loss of chocolate occurs, so there is 880 cm^3 in the shape of a cylinder.

So, let $\pi r^2 h = 880$

$\Rightarrow \frac{22}{7} \times 4 \times 4 \times h = 880$

$\Rightarrow 22 \times 16 \times h = 6160 \leftarrow$ **Multiply by 7**

$\Rightarrow 352 \times h = 6160$

$\Rightarrow h = \frac{6160}{352}$

$\Rightarrow h = 17.5$ cm

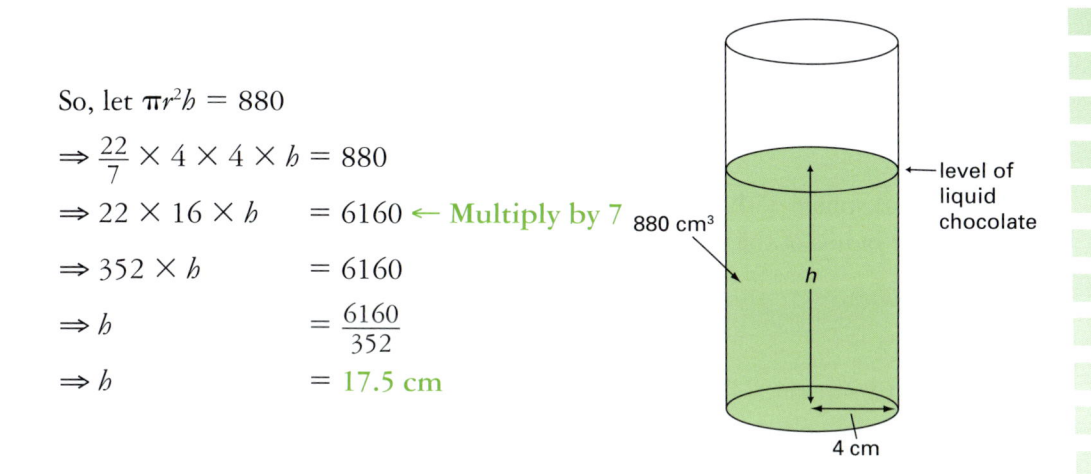

Example 8

A rectangular tank of length 44 cm and breadth 20 cm is full of water. A tap attached to the tank fills 10 cylindrical tumblers of radius 3.5 cm and height 20 cm. By **how much** does the level of the water drop in the tank? Take $\pi = \frac{22}{7}$.

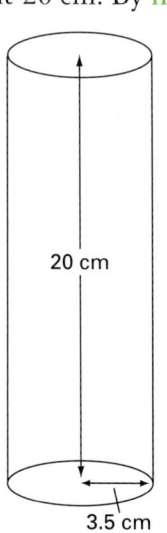

Solution Volume of each cylindrical tumbler

$= \pi r^2 h$

$= \frac{22}{7} \times 3.5 \times 3.5 \times 20$

$= \frac{22}{7} \times \overset{1}{\cancel{3.5}} \times 3.5 \times \overset{10}{\cancel{20}}$
    $\underset{1}{\cancel{2}}$

$= 22 \times 3.5 \times 10$

$= 770$ cm^3

10 cylindrical tumblers have a volume of 7700 cm³. When the 10 tumblers are filled, the volume of empty space at the top of the rectangular tank is 7700 cm³.

Solution   Let $l \times b \times h$ = 7700

$\Rightarrow 44 \times 20 \times h$ = 7700

$\Rightarrow 880 \times h$ = 7700

$\Rightarrow h = \dfrac{7700}{880}$

$\Rightarrow h$ = 8.75 cm

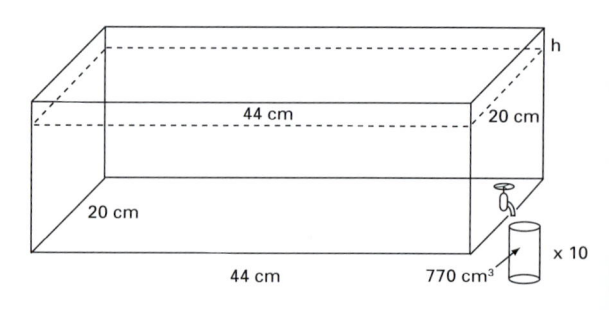

This is the amount by which the water level drops.

Example 9

A solid metal sphere with a radius of 3 cm is immersed in a cylinder partially filled with water. If the radius of the cylinder is 6 cm, **find** the height by which the water rises.

Top Tips

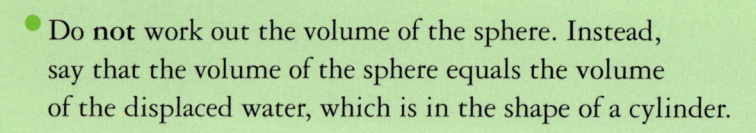

- **Do not** work out the volume of the sphere. Instead, say that the volume of the sphere equals the volume of the displaced water, which is in the shape of a cylinder.

Solution   Let $\pi r^2 h$ (volume of cylinder) = $\dfrac{4}{3}\pi r^3$ (volume of sphere)

$\Rightarrow \pi \times 6 \times 6 \times h = \dfrac{4}{3} \times \pi \times 3 \times 3 \times 3$

$\Rightarrow 36h = 36$ ← Dividing by π

$\Rightarrow h = 1$ cm

The water rises by 1 cm.

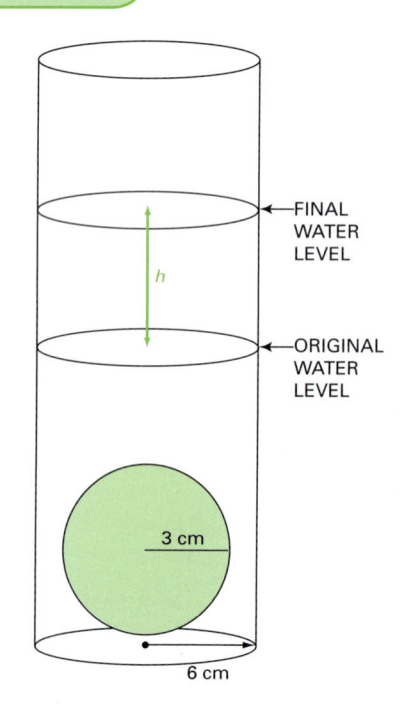

Self-test 4

1. **Find** (*a*) the volume and (*b*) surface area of a closed cylinder whose radius is 10 cm and whose height is 14 cm. Take $\pi = \frac{22}{7}$.

2. A cylinder whose volume is 2772 cm^3 has a radius of 10.5 cm.
   (*a*) **Calculate** its height.
   (*b*) **Calculate** its total surface area in cm^2. Take $\pi = \frac{22}{7}$.

3. (*a*) **Calculate** in terms of π (*a*) the volume of a sphere whose radius is 6 cm (*b*) its surface area.

4. (*a*) A sphere has a volume of 972π cm^3. **Find** its radius length.
   (*b*) Four of these spheres are placed in a cylindrical tube. **What is** the minimum volume of the tube?
   (*c*) **Find** the volume and percentage of empty space in the tube.

5. (*a*) A cylindrical cigar has a diameter of 2 cm and a length of 15 cm. **Find** its volume, taking $\pi = 3.14$.
   (*b*) Ten cigars are packed in two rows of five into a rectangular box. **Find** the dimensions of the smallest possible rectangular box into which the cigars are placed.
   (*c*) **Find** the percentage of empty space in the box correct to one decimal place.

6. (*a*) **Find**, in terms of π, the volume of a sphere with a radius of 2 cm.
   (*b*) Three of these spheres are totally immersed in water which is in a cylinder with a radius of 4 cm. **Find** the rise in the water level in the cylinder.

Self-test answers

Self-test 1

1. (a) 8 cm
   (b) 80 cm^2
2. (a) 8 cm
   (b) 32 cm
3. (a) area = 68 cm^2; perimeter = 72 cm
   (b) area = 90 cm^2; perimeter = 66 cm
4. (a) 1000 m^2
   (b) 1800 m^2
   (c) 800 m^2
   (d) 20 000 tiles are needed.

Self-test 2

1. (a) 616 cm^2
   (b) 88 cm
2. (a) 21 cm
   (b) 1386 cm^2
3. (a) 160.29 cm^2
   (b) 504 cm^2
   (c) 72.79 cm^2
   (d) 609 cm^2
   (e) 1638 cm^2
   (f) 15 288 m^2
4. (a) 256 cm
   (b) 276 cm
   (c) 496 m

Self-test 3

1. (a) volume = 1152 cm^3; capacity = 1.152 litres
   (b) volume = 140 000 cm^3; capacity = 140 litres
2. (a) 688 cm^2
   (b) 16 600 cm^2
3. (a) 20 cm
   (b) 1240 cm^2
4. (a) 4 cm
   (b) 64 cm^3
5. 80 minutes

Self-test 4

1. (a) 4400 cm^3
   (b) 1508.57 cm^2
2. (a) 8 cm
   (b) 1221 cm^2
3. (a) 288π cm^3
   (b) 144π
4. (a) 9 cm
   (b) 5832π cm^3
   (c) 1944π cm^3; 33$\frac{1}{3}$%
5. (a) 47.1 cm^3
   (b) dimensions: 10 × 4 × 15
   (c) 21.5%
6. (a) $\frac{32\pi}{3}$ cm^3
   (b) 2 cm

Key Points

- Area of rectangle = length × breadth.
- Perimeter of rectangle = $2l + 2b$.
- Area of square = l^2.
- Perimeter of square = $4l$.
- Area of circle = πr^2.
- Length of circumference of circle = $2\pi r$.
- $\pi \approx \frac{22}{7}$ or $\pi \approx 3.14$.
- Volume of rectangular box = $l \times b \times h$.
- Surface area of rectangular box = $(2 \times l \times b) + (2 \times l \times h) + (2 \times b \times h)$.
- Volume of cube = l^3.
- Surface area of cube = $6l^2$.
- Volume of cylinder = $\pi r^2 h$.
- Surface area of solid cylinder = $2\pi rh + 2\pi r^2$.
- Volume of sphere = $\frac{4}{3}\pi r^3$.
- Surface area of sphere = $4\pi r^2$.
- Volume of hemisphere = $\frac{2}{3}\pi r^3$.
- Surface area of solid hemisphere = $3\pi r^2$.
- 100 cm = 1 m.
- 10 000 cm² = 1 m²; 10 000 m² = 1 hectare.
- 1 000 000 cm³ = 1 m³.
- 1 cm³ = 1 ml.
- 1 m³ = 1000 litres.

Junior Certificate Examination 2004

Paper 2, Q1

1. (a) A swimming pool is 50 m in length. Mary swims 25 lengths of the pool. What distance, in kilometres, does Mary swim?

   Solution $50 \times 25 = 1250$ m

   $= 1.25$ km

   (b) A garden is made up of a rectangular lawn that is surrounded by a path. The garden is 16 m long and 10 m wide. The path is 2 m wide.

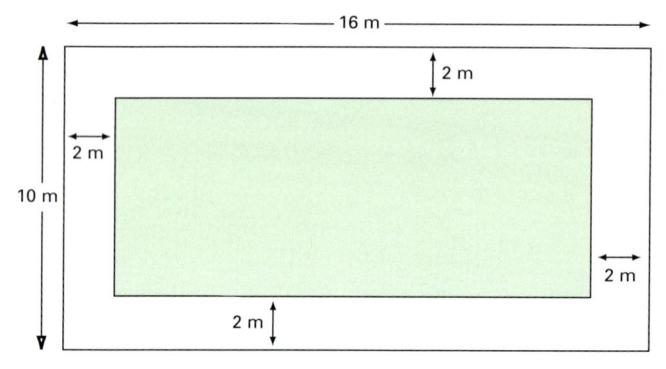

   i. Find, in m², the area of the garden.

   Solution $16 \times 10 = 160$ m²

   ii. Find, in m², the area of the lawn.

   Solution $12 \times 6 = 72$ m²

   iii. Find, in m², the area of the path.

   Solution $160 - 72 = 88$ m²

2. (a) A circle has a radius of 3.5 cm. Taking π as $\frac{22}{7}$, calculate the length of the circumference of the circle.

   Solution $C = 2\pi r$

   $C = 2 \times \frac{22}{7} \times 3.5$

   $C = 22$ cm

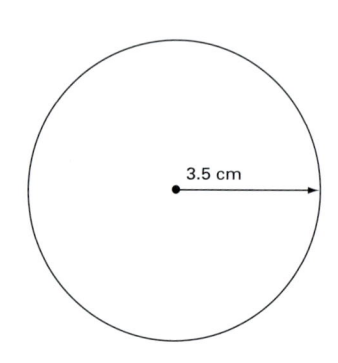

(b) A cube has side of length 2 cm.
 i. Find the volume of this cube in cm³.
    Solution $V = 2 \times 2 \times 2$
    $V = 8$ cm³

 ii. A rectangular block is built using 18 of these cubes. Find the volume of the rectangular block in cm³.
    Solution $V = 8 \times 18$
    $V = 144$ cm³

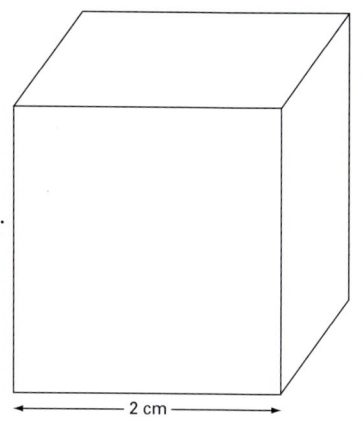

 iii. This rectangular block is 6 cm long, 6 cm wide and 4 cm high. Find its surface area in cm².
    Solution   Surface area $= (2 \times 6 \times 6) + (2 \times 6 \times 4) + (2 \times 6 \times 4)$
    $= 72 + 48 + 48$
    $= 168$ cm²

(c) A solid sphere made of lead has a radius of 6 cm.
 i. Find the volume of the sphere in terms of π.
    Solution $V = \frac{4}{3}\pi r^3$
    $V = \frac{4}{3} \times \pi \times 6 \times 6 \times 6$
    $V = 4 \times \pi \times 72$
    $V = 288\pi$ cm³

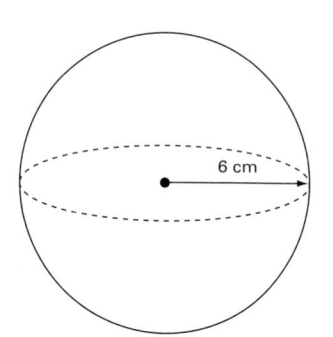

 ii. This sphere is melted down and all the lead is used to make a lead cylinder with a radius of 4 cm. Find the height of the cylinder.
    Solution   Let $\pi \times 4^2 \times h = 288\pi$
    $\Rightarrow 16h = 288$ ←Dividing by π
    $\Rightarrow h = \frac{288}{16}$
    $\Rightarrow h = 18$ cm

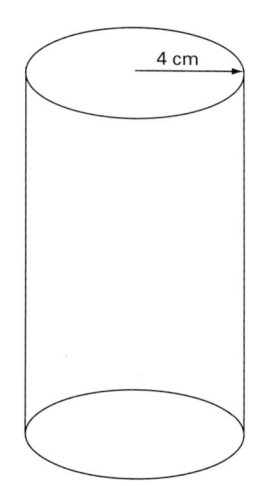

Junior Certificate Examination 2005

Paper 2, Q1 and Q2

1. (c) A field has shape and measurements as shown in the diagram.

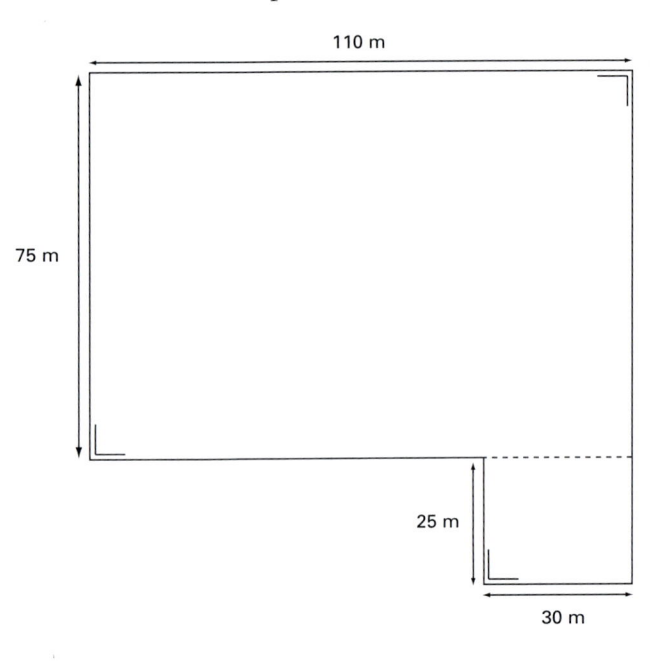

    i. Find, in metres, the length of the perimeter of the field.

    Solution $110 + 75 + 80 + 25 + 30 + 100$
    $= 420$ m

    ii. Find, in m², the area of the field.

    Solution   Area $= (110 \times 75) + (25 \times 30)$
    $= 8250 + 750$
    $= 9000$ m²

    iii. Mary bought the field at a cost of €20 000 per hectare. How much did Mary pay for the field?

    Solution   9000 m² $= 0.9$ Ha
    0.9 Ha @ €20 000 per Ha
    $=$ €18 000

2. (*a*) A rectangular box has measurements as shown. Find the volume of the box in cm³.

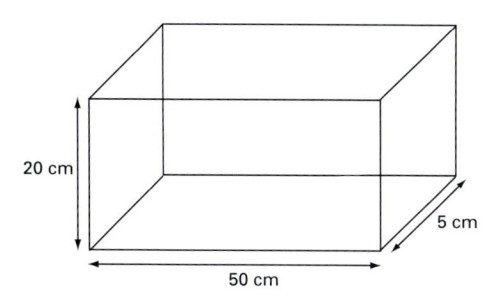

   20 cm, 5 cm, 50 cm

   Solution   Volume = 50 × 5 × 20
   $$= 5000 \text{ cm}^3$$

(*b*) The front wheel of a bicycle has a diameter of 56 cm.
   i.   Calculate, in cm, the length of the radius of the wheel.

   Solution   Radius = $\frac{1}{2}$ × 56 = 28 cm

   ii. Calculate, in cm, the length of the circumference of the wheel. Take π as $\frac{22}{7}$.

   Solution   C = 2π*r*
   $$= 2 \times \frac{22}{7} \times 28$$
   $$= 2 \times 22 \times 4$$
   $$= 176 \text{ cm}$$

   iii. How far does the bicycle travel when the wheel makes 250 complete turns? Give your answer in metres.

   Solution   176 × 250
   $$= 44\,000 \text{ cm}$$
   $$= 440 \text{ m}$$

(c) A solid cylinder has a radius of 4 cm and height of 14 cm.

  i. Find the volume of the cylinder in terms of π.

  Solution $V = \pi r^2 h$

  $V = \pi \times 4 \times 4 \times 14$

  $V = 224\pi$ cm^3

  ii. Find the curved surface area of the cylinder in terms of π.

  Solution $CSA = 2\pi r h$

  $= 2 \times \pi \times 4 \times 14$

  $= 112\pi$ cm^2

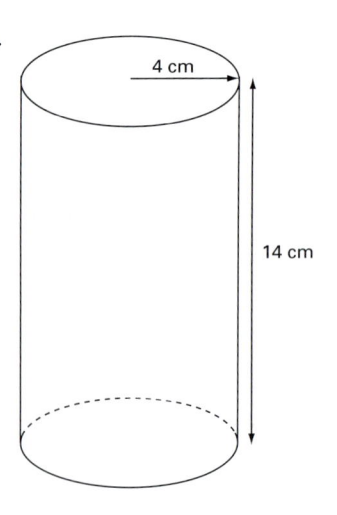

  iii. Find the total surface area of the cylinder in terms of π.

  Solution $TSA = 2\pi r h + 2\pi r^2$

  $= 112\pi + 2 \times \pi \times 4 \times 4$

  $= 112\pi + 32\pi$

  $= 144\pi$ cm^2

  iv. A sphere has the same surface area as the total surface area of the above cylinder. Find, in cm, the radius of this sphere.

  Solution Let $4\pi r^2 = 144\pi$

  $\Rightarrow r^2 = 36$

  CALCULATOR $\boxed{\sqrt{}}\ \boxed{3}\ \boxed{6}\ \boxed{=}$

  $\Rightarrow r = \sqrt{36}$

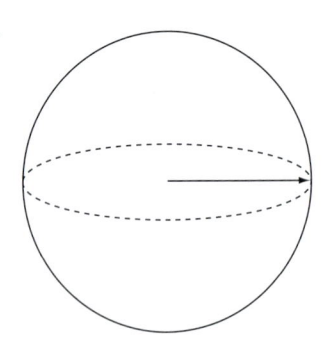

  $\Rightarrow r = 6$ cm

CHAPTER 8
Geometry

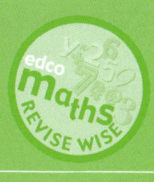

Learning Objectives

- Understand the notation and terminology used in geometry.
- Understand the statements of the theorems and how to apply the results in worked examples.
- Understand the meaning of congruence when applied to triangles.
- Prove that two triangles are congruent.
- Construct triangles and parallelograms.
- Bisect line segments and angles.
- Draw a circumcircle and incircle of a triangle.
- Trisect a line segment.
- Understand the concept of a transformation.
- Draw the images of figures and shapes by the three transformations axial symmetry, central symmetry and translation.

Revision of notation

1. Where a and b represent points on an infinite two-dimensional plane, ab is the line, infinite in both directions, passing through points a and b.

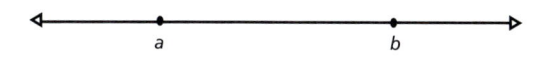

2. $[ab$ is the half line which terminates at a but goes to infinity beyond b.

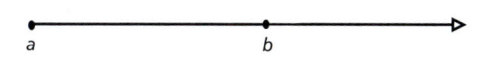

3. $[ab]$ is the line segment which terminates at both a and b. It is the set of points that lie between a and b.

4. |ab| means the distance between the points *a* and *b*. It also means the length of line segment [ab].

In this line segment [ab] we can see using a ruler that |ab| = 8 cm.

5. *ab* and *cd* are two lines that intersect at point o.

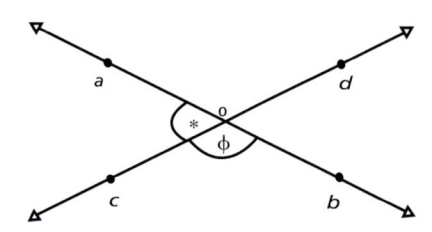

∠aoc describes the angle marked * in the diagram.
∠boc describes the angle marked φ in the diagram.

6. |∠aoc| means the measure of the angle ∠aoc.
By using a protractor we see that |∠aoc| = 45°.

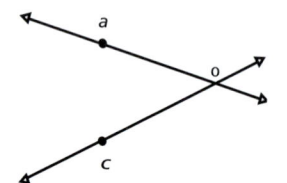

7. Sometimes single capital letters can be used to denote angles. Here, ∠aod is denoted by X. ∠bod is denoted by Y.

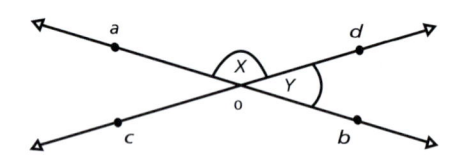

8. A total circle is divided into 360 parts, each of which is called 1 degree (1°). In the diagram, the 360 degrees are divided evenly into four equal parts of 90°. Each of these angles is said to be a **right angle**. So, |∠aoc| = |∠boc| = |∠aod| = |∠bod| = 90°. We say that *ab* is perpendicular to *cd* when the lines divide a circle into four equal parts.

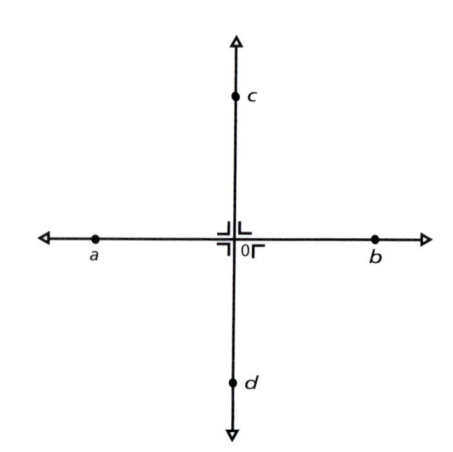

9. ∠*aoc* is an **acute angle** because |∠*aoc*| < 90°.
   ∠*aod* is an **obtuse angle** because |∠*aod*| > 90°
   and |∠*aod*| < 180°.

   The angle X shown in the second diagram is a
   reflex angle because X > 180°.

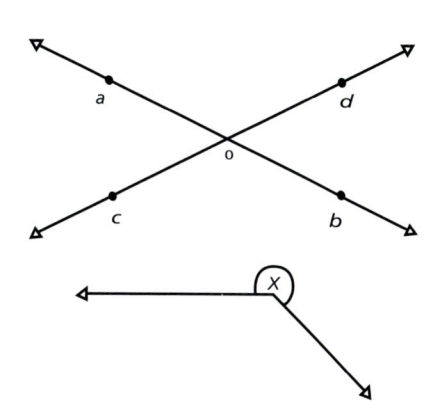

Theorems

Statements and examples

1. Vertically opposite angles are equal in measure.
   In the diagram, |∠A| = |∠B| and |∠C| = |∠D|.

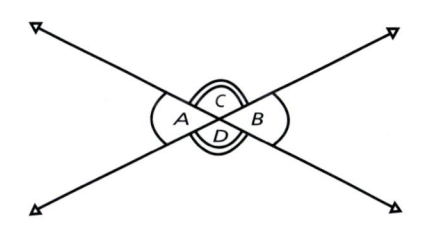

2. When a line cuts two parallel lines,
   corresponding angles are equal in measure.
   In the diagram, ∠A and ∠B are corresponding
   angles, therefore, |∠A| = |∠B|.

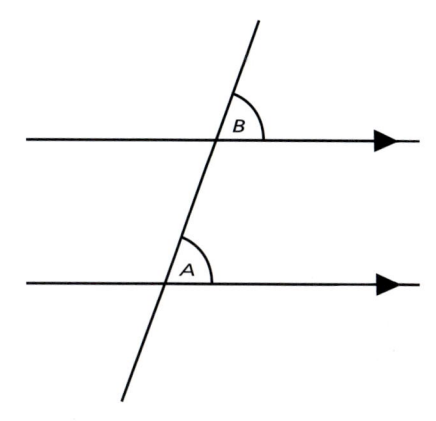

3. When a line cuts two parallel lines, **alternate angles** are equal in measure.

   In the diagram, $\angle C$ and $\angle D$ are alternate angles, therefore, $|\angle C| = |\angle D|$.

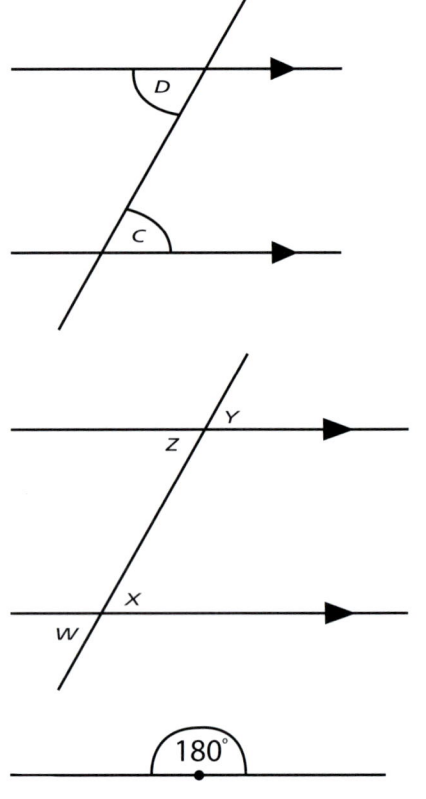

   Note also that a line cutting a series of parallel lines is referred to as a **transversal**. Corresponding angles are always on the same side of a transversal. Alternate angles are on opposite sides of a transversal.

   In the diagram:
   - $|\angle W| = |\angle X|$: Vertically opposite angles.
   - $|\angle X| = |\angle Y|$: Corresponding angles.
   - $|\angle X| = |\angle Z|$: Alternate angles.

4. A straight angle measures $180°$.

Example 1

Evaluate the unknown angles in these diagrams.

(a)

(b)

Solution

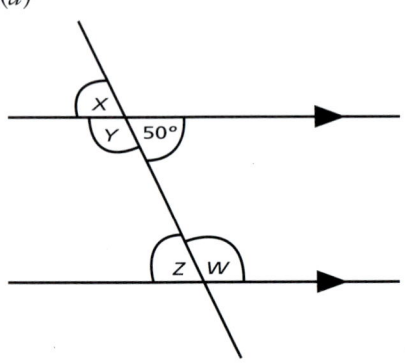

(a) $|\angle X| = 50°$: Vertically opposite.
$|\angle Y| = 130°$: $X + Y = 180°$ (straight angle).
$|\angle Z| = 50°$: Corresponding to $\angle X$.
$|\angle W| = 130°$: Alternate to $\angle Y$.

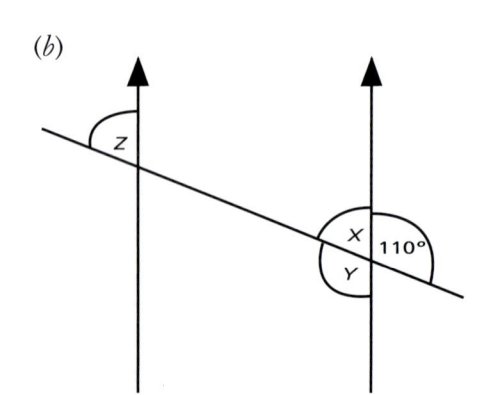

(b) $|\angle X| = 70°$: Straight angle. $(180°-110°)$
$|\angle Y| = 110°$: Vertically opposite.
$|\angle Z| = 70°$: Corresponding to $\angle X$.

5. The three angles in a triangle add up to 180°.

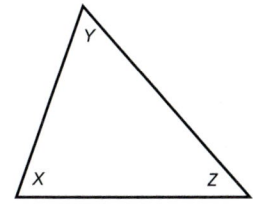

   $|\angle X| + |\angle Y| + |\angle Z| = 180°$

6. The exterior angle of a triangle equals the sum of the two interior opposite angles. In the diagram, $\angle X$ is the exterior angle of the $\triangle abc$. $\angle Y$ and $\angle Z$ are the interior opposite angles.

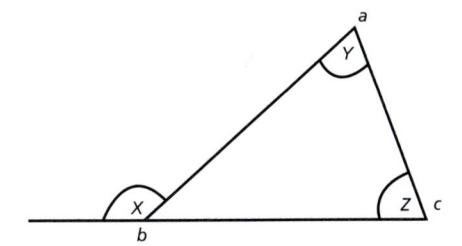

   $|\angle X| = |\angle Y| + |\angle Z|$

Top Tips

- An **isosceles triangle** is one in which two of the sides are equal in measure.

- In the diagram, $\triangle abc$ is isosceles because $|ab| = |ac|$. This is shown by putting notches on the line segments. $[bc]$ is called the base of the triangle.

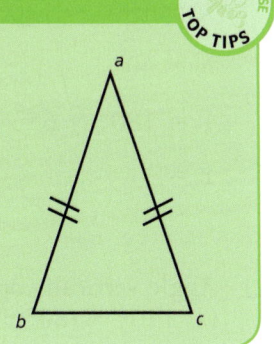

7. The angles at the base of an isosceles triangle are equal in measure. In the diagram, because $|ab| = |ac| \Rightarrow |\angle abc| = |\angle acb|$. (Angles marked * in the diagram are equal.)

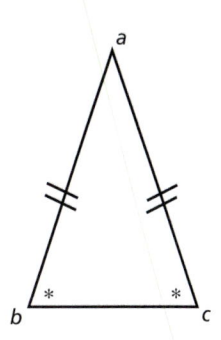

Example 2

Evaluate the unknown angles in these diagrams.

(a)

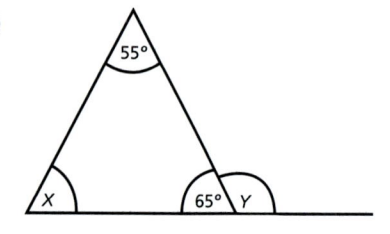

(b)

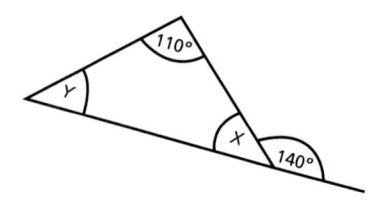

(c)

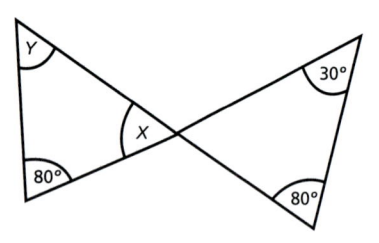

(d)

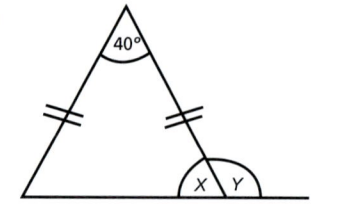

Solution

(a) $X = 180° - (55° + 65°)$

$X = 180° - 120°$

$X = 60°$

$Y = 180° - 65°$

$Y = 115°$

(b) $X = 180° - 140°$

$X = 40°$

$Y = 180° - (110° + 40°)$

$Y = 180° - 150°$

$Y = 30°$

(c) Angle vertically opposite X is 70°, i.e. $180° - (80° + 30°)$

$\Rightarrow X = 70°$

$Y = 180° - (80° + 70°)$

$Y = 180° - 150°$

$Y = 30°$

(d) $X = \frac{1}{2}$ of $140°$

$X = 70°$

$Y = 110°$

Example 3

Evaluate the letters *a* and *b* in the following diagrams.

(a)

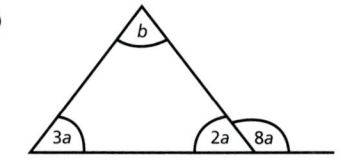

(b)

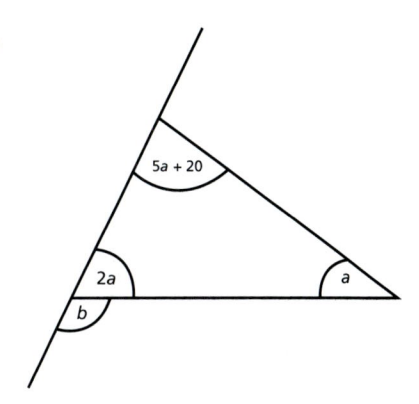

(c)

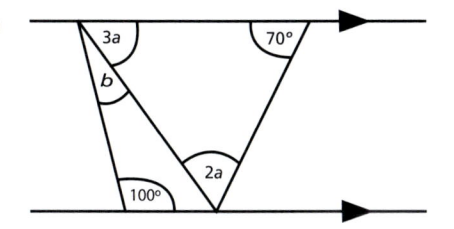

(d)

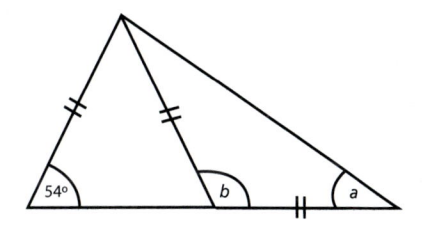

Solution

(a)
$$2a + 8a = 180°$$
$$\Rightarrow 10a = 180°$$
$$\Rightarrow a = 18°$$
Also, $3a + 2a + b = 180°$
$$\Rightarrow 5a + b = 180°$$
$$\Rightarrow 90° + b = 180°$$
$$\Rightarrow b = 90°$$

(b) $2a + a + 5a + 20° = 180°$
$$\Rightarrow 8a + 20° = 180°$$
$$\Rightarrow 8a = 160°$$
$$\Rightarrow a = 20°$$
Also, $2a + b = 180°$
$$\Rightarrow 40° + b = 180°$$
$$\Rightarrow b = 140°$$

(c) $\quad 3a + 2a + 70° = 180°$
$$\Rightarrow 5a + 70° = 180°$$
$$\Rightarrow 5a = 110°$$
$$\Rightarrow a = 22°$$
Also, $3a + b = 80°$
$$\Rightarrow 66° + b = 80°$$
$$\Rightarrow b = 14°$$

(d) $b + 54° = 180°$
$$\Rightarrow b = 180° - 54° \text{ (isosceles triangle)}$$
$$\Rightarrow b = 126°$$
Also, $a = \frac{1}{2}$ of $54°$ (isosceles triangle)
$$\Rightarrow a = 27°$$

JUNIOR CERTIFICATE MATHS – ORDINARY LEVEL

> **Top Tips**
> - Triangles drawn within circles, where one vertex of the triangle is the centre of the circle, are isosceles.

Example 4

Find the value of the angle marked X in each diagram.

(a)

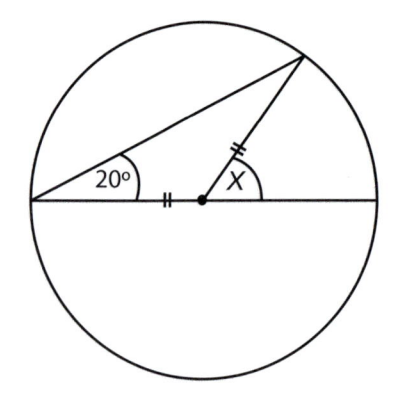

(b)

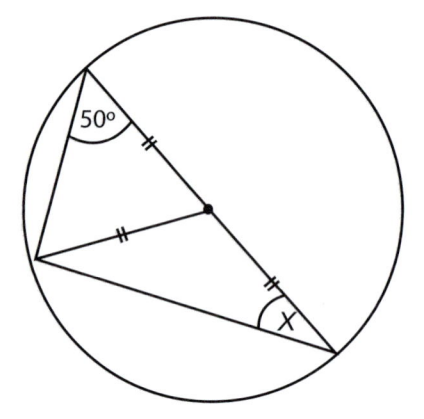

Solution

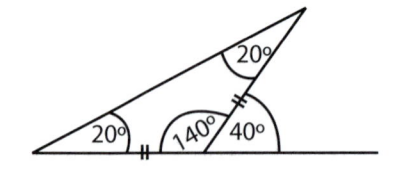

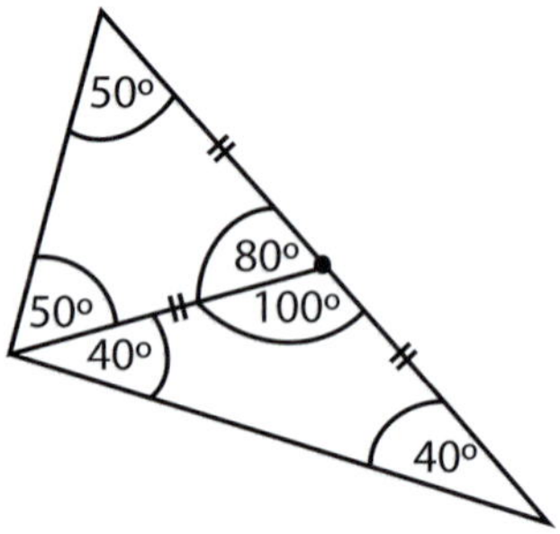

(a) X = 40°

(b) X = 40°

8. When a triangle is drawn on the diameter of a circle and the third vertex is on the circle, this angle is 90°.

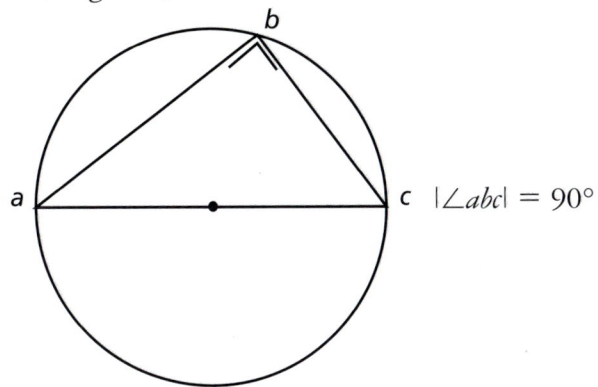

$|\angle abc| = 90°$

Example 5

Find the measures of the lettered angles in these diagrams.

(a)

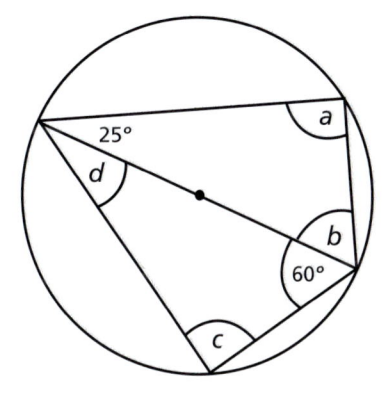

(b)

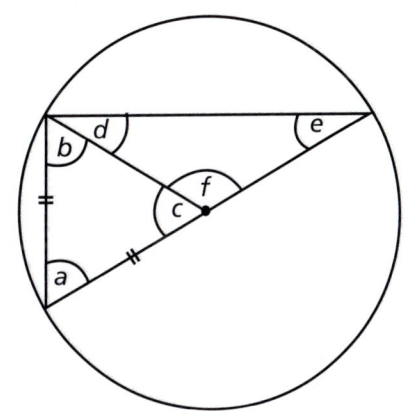

(c)

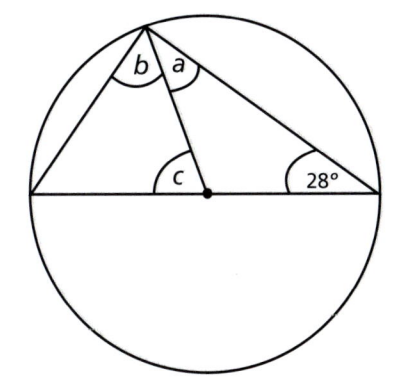

Solution

(a) $a = 90°$
  $b = 65°$ (i.e. $180° - 115°$)
  $c = 90°$
  $d = 30°$ (i.e. $180° - 150°$)

(b) $a = 60°$
  $b = 60°$
  $c = 60°$ (equilateral triangle)
  $d = 30°$ ($b + d = 90°$)
  $e = 30°$ (isosceles triangle)
  $f = 120°$ (i.e. $180° - 60°$)

(c) $a = 28°$ (isosceles triangle)
  $b = 62°$ (90° angle at circle)
  $c = 180° - 124°$
  $\Rightarrow c = 56°$

Self-test 1

1. **Evaluate** the lettered angles in the following diagrams.

    (a)

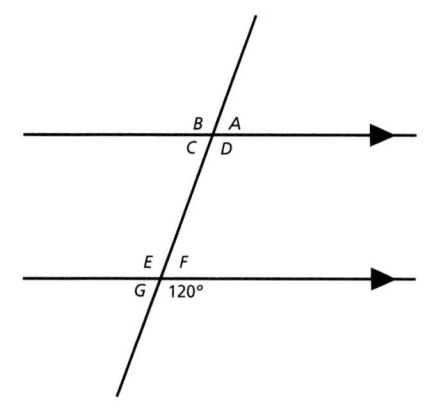

    (b)

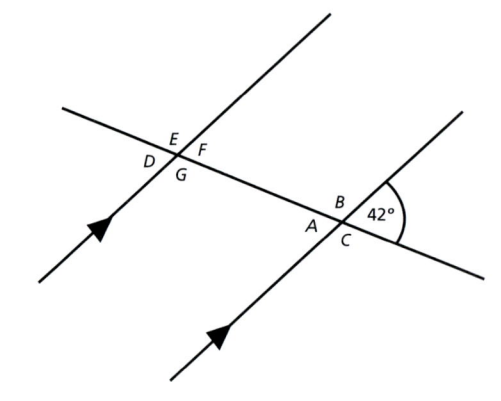

2. **Evaluate** the lettered angles in these diagrams.

    (a)

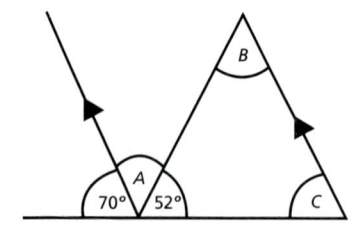

    (b)

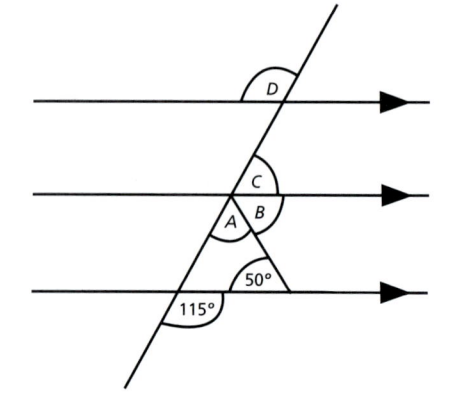

3. **Find** the lettered angles in these diagrams.

(a)

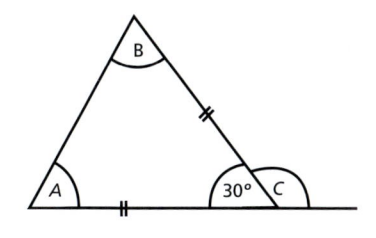

(b)

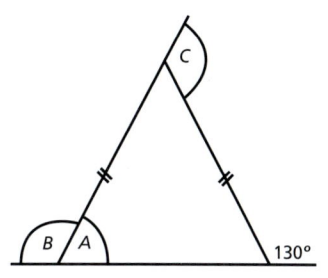

(c)

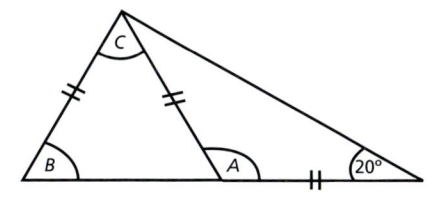

4. **Find** the measures of the lettered angles in these diagrams.

(a)

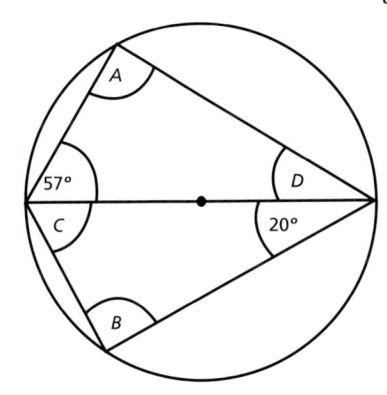

(b)

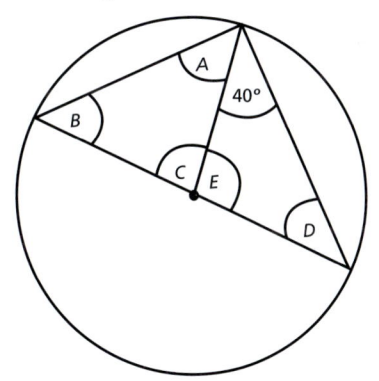

(c)

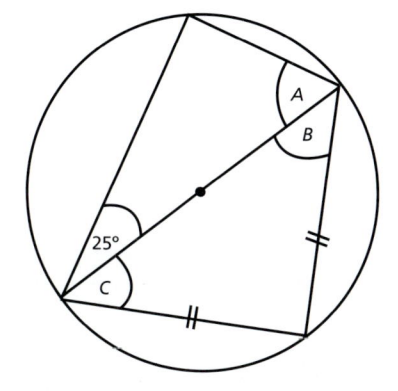

Definition

A **parallelogram** is a four-sided figure where the opposite sides are parallel to one another.

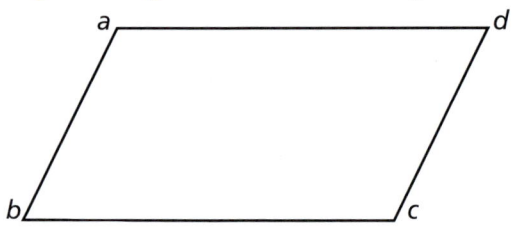

In this parallelogram $abcd$, we see that $ab//cd$ and $ad//bc$.

9. The opposite angles and opposite sides in a parallelogram are equal in measure.

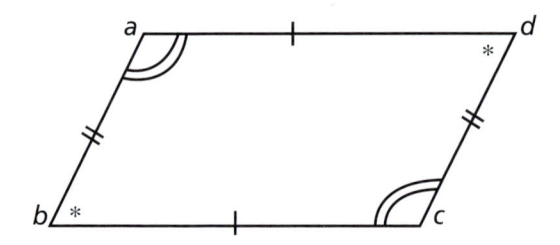

$|\angle bad| = |\angle bcd|$ and $|\angle abc| = |\angle adc|$
$|ab| = |cd|$ and $|ad| = |bc|$

10. The diagonals of a parallelogram bisect one another.

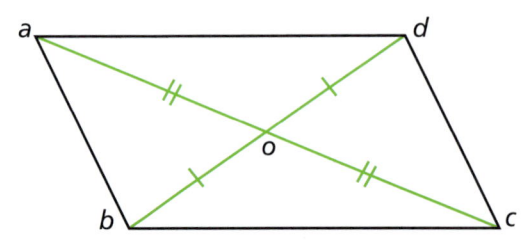

Draw the diagonals of the parallelogram $abcd$. They are $[ac]$ and $[bd]$.
Let $[ac] \cap [bd] = \{o\}$. Then, $|ao| = |oc|$ and $|bo| = |od|$.

Top Tips

- The four internal angles in a parallelogram add up to 360°. Therefore, we can determine all the internal angles provided we know one of them.

Example 6

Determine the values of X and Y in these diagrams.

(a)

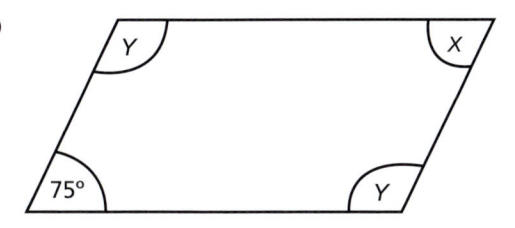

(b)

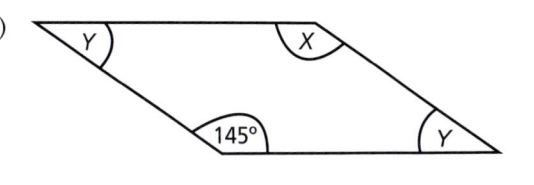

Solution

(a) $X = 75°$ [opposite angles equal]
$150° + 2Y = 360°$
$\Rightarrow 2Y = 210°$
$\Rightarrow Y = 105°$

(b) $X = 145°$ [opposite angles equal]
$290° + 2Y = 360°$
$\Rightarrow 2Y = 70°$
$\Rightarrow Y = 35°$

Example 7

Evaluate the missing angles in the following diagrams.

(a)

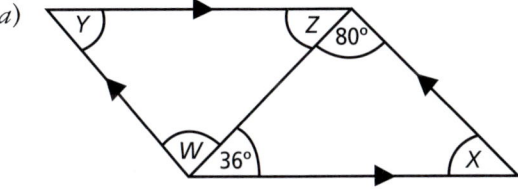

(b)

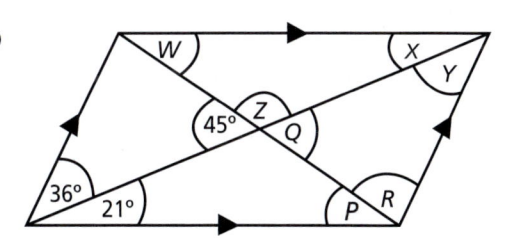

Solution

(a) $X = 180° - (80° + 36°)$
$X = 180° - 116°$
$X = 64°$
$Y = 64°$ [opposite to X]

$Z = 36°$ [alternate angles]
$W = 80°$ [alternate angles]

(b) $X = 21°$ [alternate angles]
$Y = 36°$ [alternate angles]
$Z = 135°$ [$Z + 45° = 180°$]
$W = 180° - [21° + 135°]$
$\Rightarrow W = 180° - 156°$
$\Rightarrow W = 24°$
$P = 24°$ [alternate to W]
$Q = 45°$ [vertically opposite]

131

Example 8

In the parallelogram *abcd* where *o* is the point of intersection of the diagonals [*ac*] and [*bd*], |*ao*| = 5 cm and |*od*| = 4 cm. **Write down** the lengths of the line segments: (*a*) [*oc*] (*b*) [*ac*] (*c*) [*bo*] (*d*) [*bd*].

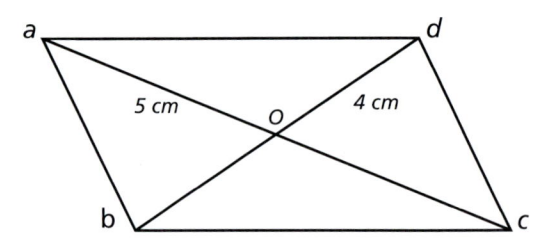

Solution
(*a*) |*oc*| = 5 cm

(*b*) |*ac*| = 10 cm

(*c*) |*bo*| = 4 cm

(*d*) |*bd*| = 8 cm

11. A **diagonal of a parallelogram** bisects its area.

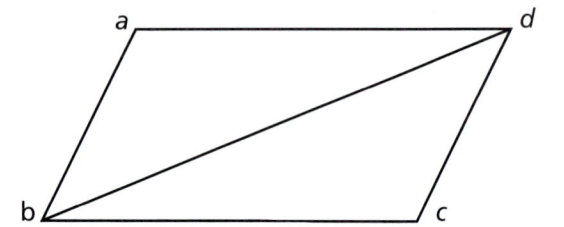

    In the ▱ *abcd*, area △*abd* = area △*bcd*.

12. The **area of a parallelogram** equals the length of the base multiplied by the perpendicular height.

    In the ▱ *abcd*, area = |*bc*| × *h*, where *h* is the perpendicular height.

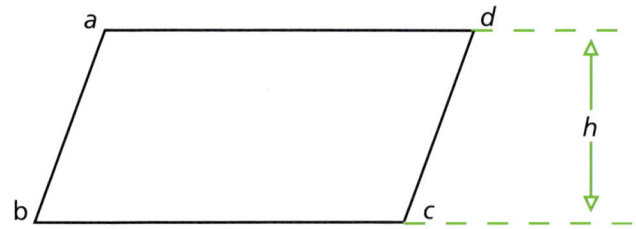

13. The area of a triangle equals half the length of the base multiplied by the perpendicular height.

    In the △*abc*, area = $\frac{1}{2}$ × |*bc*| × *h* where *h* is the perpendicular distance from point *a* to *bc*.

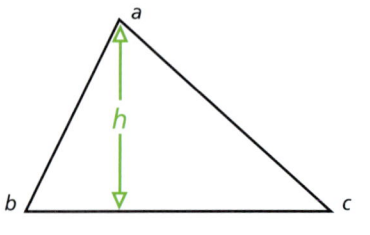

Example 9

Find the areas of the following figures.

(a) Rectangle abcd with width 8 cm and height 6 cm.

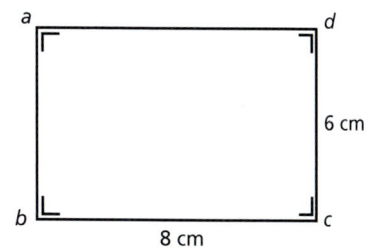

(b) Parallelogram abcd with base 10 cm and height 6 cm.

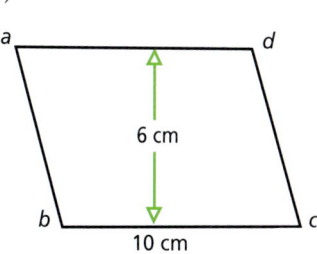

(c) Triangle abc with base 12 cm and height 14 cm.

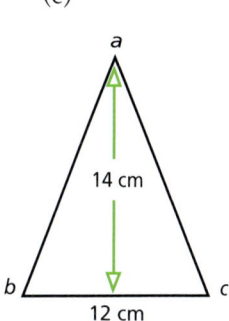

Solution

(a) Area of ▱abcd
 = 8 × 6
 = 48 cm²

(b) Area of ▱abcd
 = 10 × 6
 = 60 cm²

(c) Area of △abc
 = $\frac{1}{2}$ × 12 × 14
 = 6 × 14
 = 84 cm²

Note

• A rectangle is a parallelogram, as in the first diagram above.

Example 10

Find the length of the base in these figures.

(a) Rectangle abcd with Area = 120 cm² and height 10 cm.

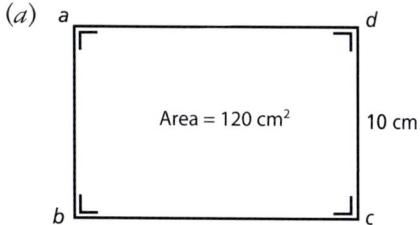

Solution

Area = base × height
120 = |bc| × 10
|bc| = $\frac{120}{10}$
|bc| = 12 cm

(b) Parallelogram with Area = 55 cm² and height 5 cm.

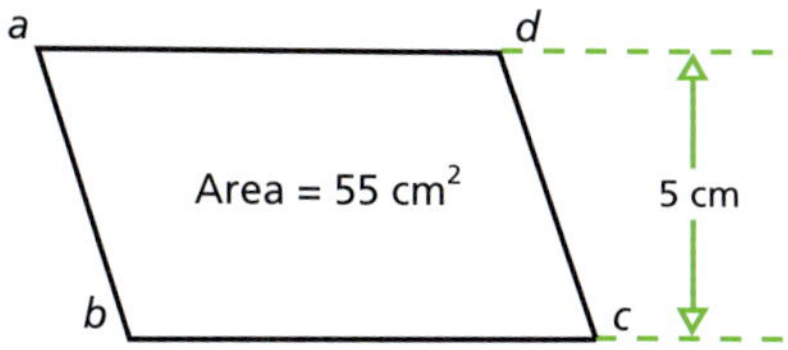

Solution

Area = base × height
55 = |bc| × 5
|bc| = $\frac{55}{5}$
|bc| = 11 cm

(c) Triangle with Area = 63 cm² and height 9 cm.

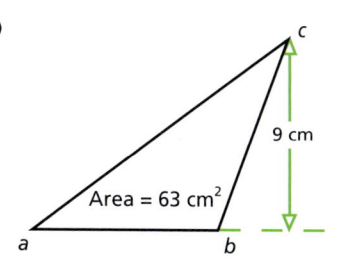

Solution

Area = $\frac{1}{2}$ × base × height
63 = $\frac{1}{2}$ × |ab| × 9
63 = 4.5|ab|
|ab| = $\frac{63}{4.5}$
|ab| = 14 cm

14. In a right-angled triangle, the square of the hypotenuse equals the sum of the squares of the other two sides.

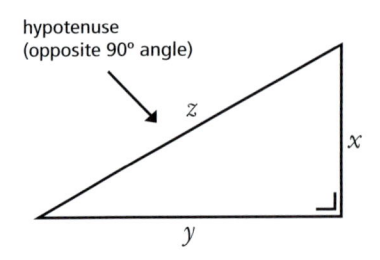

hypotenuse (opposite 90° angle)

$$z^2 = x^2 + y^2$$

Example 11

Find the length of the hypotenuse in this diagram.
Give your answer correct to two decimal places.

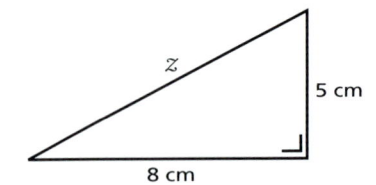

Solution

$z^2 = 8^2 + 5^2$ Square the short sides and add them.

$z^2 = 64 + 25$ Use your calculator to find $\sqrt{89}$.

$z^2 = 89$

$z = \sqrt{89}$

$z \approx 9.43$ cm

CALCULATOR

√ 8 9 =

Example 12

(a) **Find** the perpendicular height of this triangle correct to two decimal places.

(b) **Find** its area.

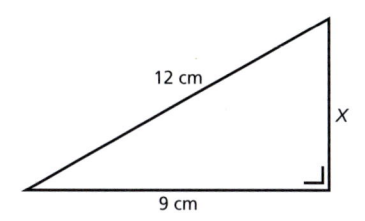

Solution (a)
$$12^2 = 9^2 + x^2$$
$$144 = 81 + x^2$$
$$144 - 81 = x^2$$
$$x^2 = 63$$
$$x = \sqrt{63}$$
$$x \approx 7.94 \text{ cm}$$

(b) Area = $\frac{1}{2} \times$ base $\times$ height

$\Rightarrow$ Area = $\frac{1}{2} \times 9 \times 7.94$

$\Rightarrow$ Area ≈ 35.73 cm^2

Self-test 2

1. **Determine** the values of the lettered angles in these diagrams.

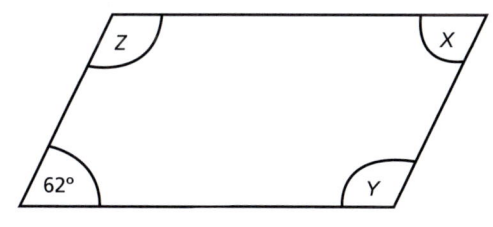

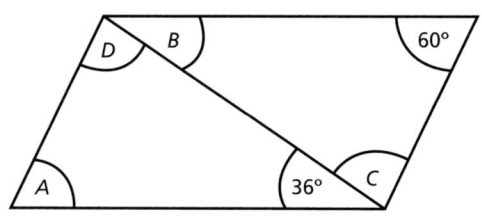

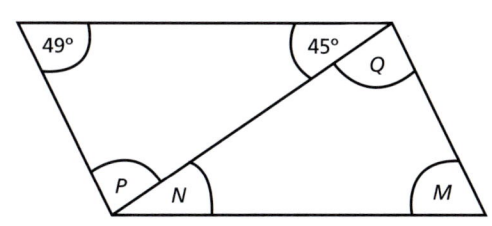

(a)

(b)

(c)

2. **Find** the area of the following shapes.

(*a*)

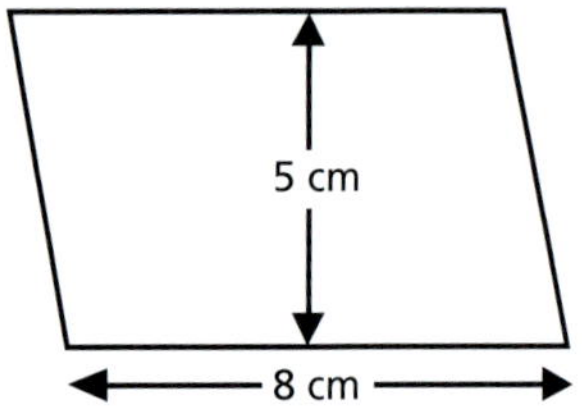
5 cm
8 cm

(*b*)

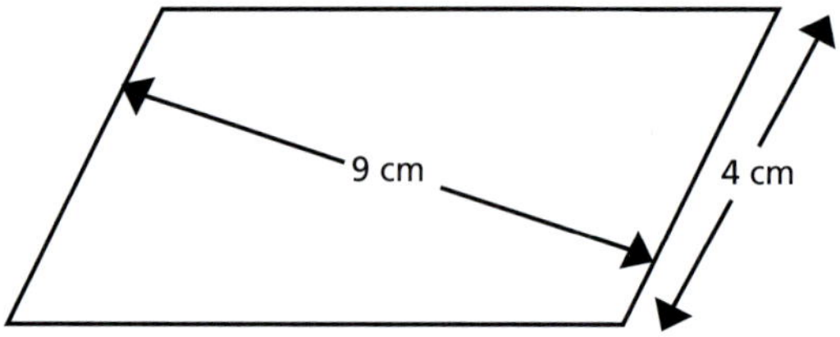
9 cm
4 cm

(*c*)

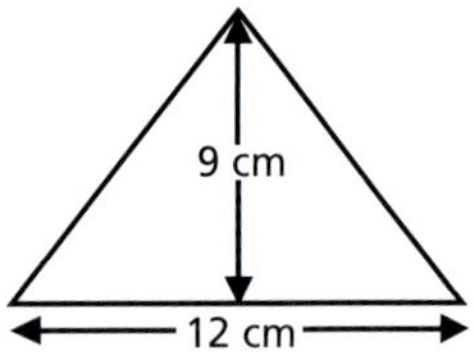
9 cm
12 cm

(*d*)

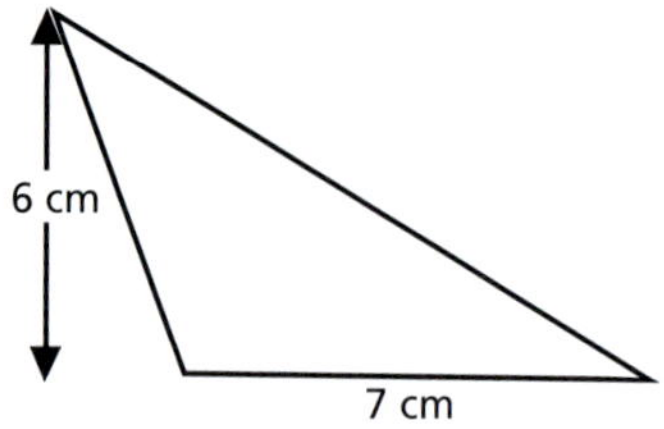
6 cm
7 cm

(*e*)

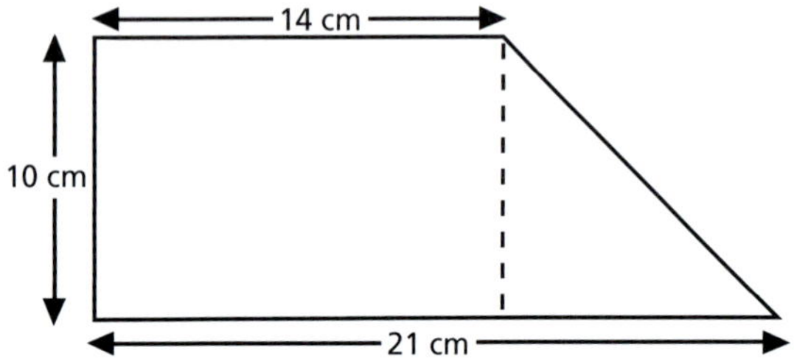
14 cm
10 cm
21 cm

3. **Find** the height *h* in the following shapes.

(*a*)

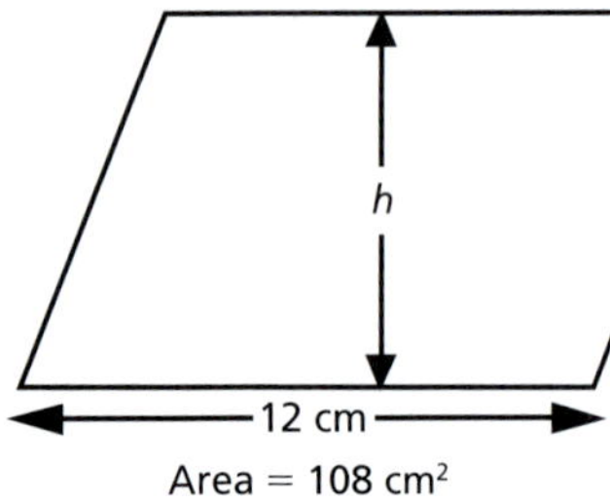
h
12 cm
Area = 108 cm²

(*b*)

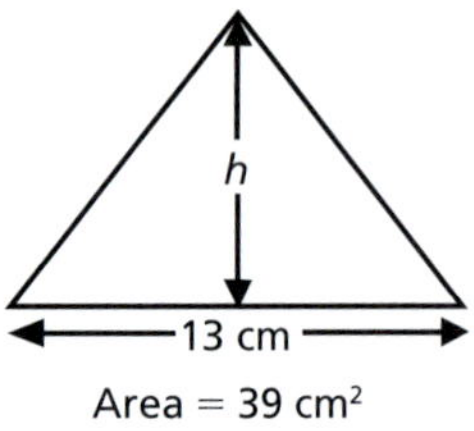
h
13 cm
Area = 39 cm²

(*c*)

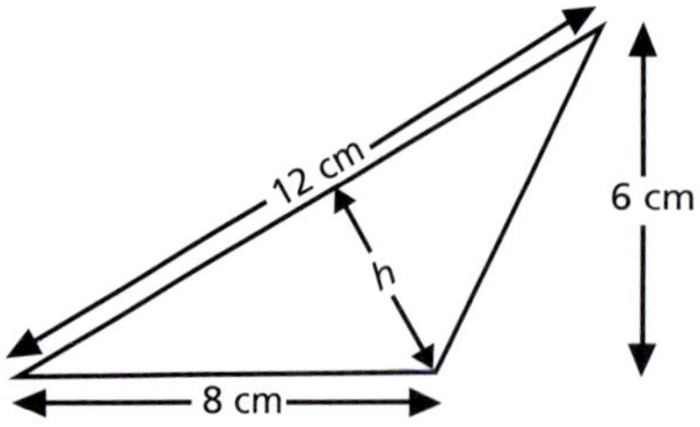
12 cm
h
6 cm
8 cm

4. **Find** the length of the side x in the following right-angled triangles.

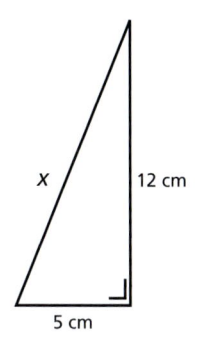

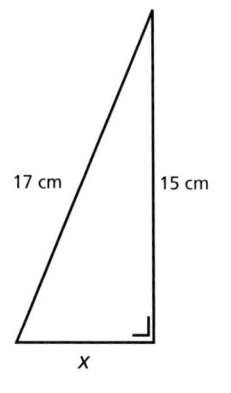

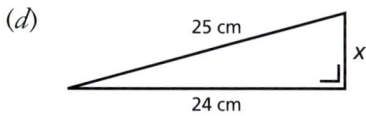

(a) 3 cm, 4 cm, x (hypotenuse)

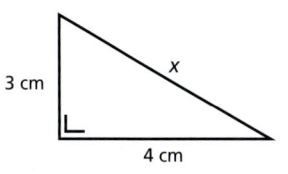

(b) 12 cm, 5 cm, x

(c) 17 cm, 15 cm, x

(d) 25 cm, 24 cm, x

(e) 6 cm, 4 cm, x (Leave this answer in Surd form, i.e. as a square root.)

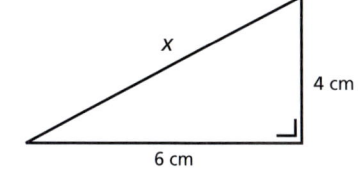

Congruence

If we are given two triangles where all three sides match and all three angles match, then they are congruent. They must be identical in every way.

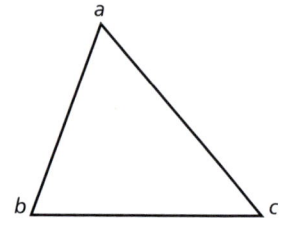

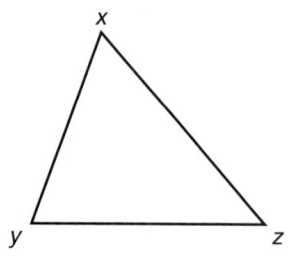

The triangles abc and xyz are congruent because by measurement we see that

$\left.\begin{array}{l}|ab| = |xy| \\ |ac| = |xz| \\ |bc| = |yz|\end{array}\right\}$ 3 sides identical

$\left.\begin{array}{l}|\angle bac| = |\angle yxz| \\ |\angle abc| = |\angle xyz| \\ |\angle acb| = |\angle xzy|\end{array}\right\}$ 3 angles identical

Top Tips

- In all cases where we are asked to prove that two triangles are congruent, it is sufficient to prove that three out of the six pieces of information match. If we can do this, the other three pieces of information are automatically equal.

1. In these triangles, the three sides match one another, as shown. These triangles are congruent because the corresponding angles are also equal.

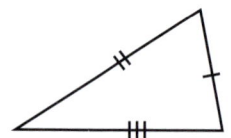

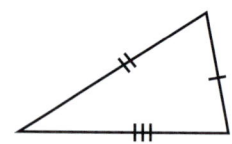

    This situation is often referred to as S.S.S. because congruence results from matching the three sides.

2. In these triangles, two of the sides are equal in length and the angles between the sides are equal in measure as shown. These triangles are congruent because in addition the two horizontal sides are equal in length and the corresponding angles are equal.

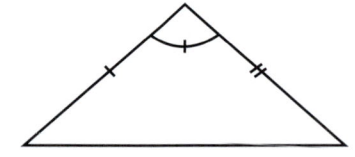

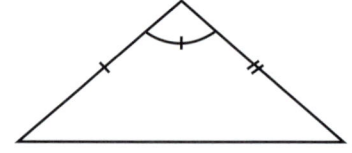

    This situation is referred to as S.A.S. because congruence results from matching side, angle, side.

3. In these triangles, two of the angles are equal in measure and the sides between the angles are equal in length, as shown. These triangles are congruent because in addition, the third angle in each of the triangles matches and the corresponding sides are equal.

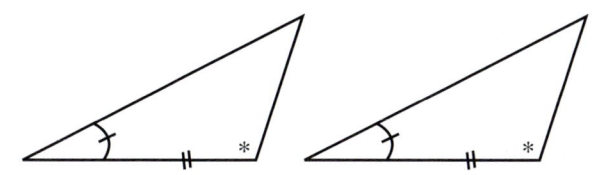

This situation is referred to as A.S.A. because congruence results from matching **a**ngle, **s**ide, **a**ngle.

4. In these triangles, the 90° angles match, the sides opposite the right angles match and one other side matches, as shown. These triangles are congruent because in addition, the third horizontal sides match, as do the corresponding angles.

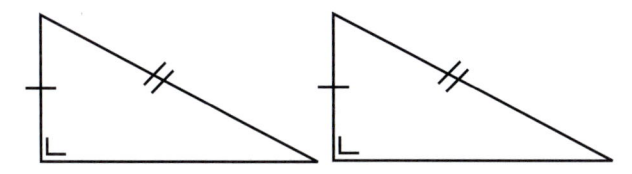

This situation is referred to as R.H.S. because congruence results from matching a **r**ight angle, a **h**ypotenuse and a **s**ide.

Example 1

In the parallelogram *abcd*, [*bd*] is a diagonal. **Prove** that △*abd* is congruent to △*bcd*.

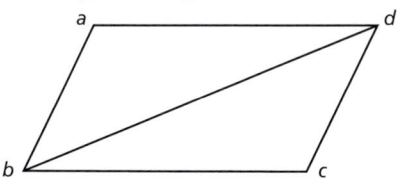

Solution   Match three measurements in △*abd* with three measurements in △*bcd*. We must match them based on sound reasoning.

(a) |*ab*| = |*cd*| [opposite sides in a parallelogram are equal in length.]
(b) |*ad*| = |*bc*| [opposite sides in a parallelogram are equal in length.]
(c) |∠*bad*| = |∠*bcd*| [opposite angles in a parallelogram are equal.]
⇒ △*abd* is congruent to △*bcd*   (S.A.S).

Example 2

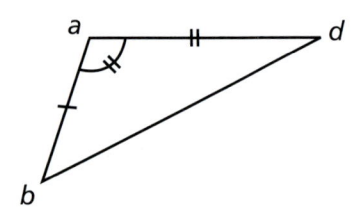

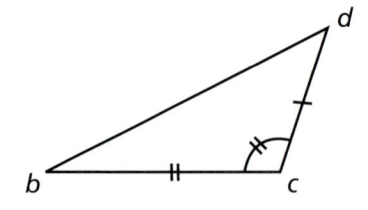

In the parallelogram *abcd*, [*ac*] and [*bd*] are diagonals intersecting at point *o*. **Prove** that the triangles *aob* and *cod* are congruent.

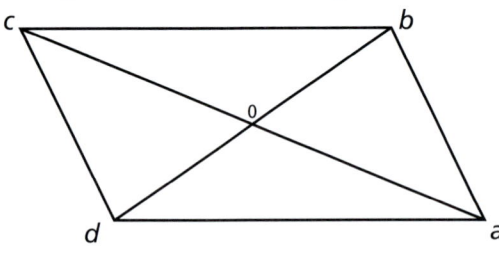

Solution
(a) |*ab*| = |*cd*| [opposite sides in a ▱ are equal in length.]
(b) |*ob*| = |*od*| [diagonals of a ▱ bisect one another.]
(c) |*oa*| = |*oc*| [diagonals of a ▱ bisect one another.]
⇒ △*aob* is congruent to △*cod* (S.S.S.).

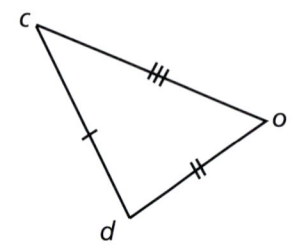

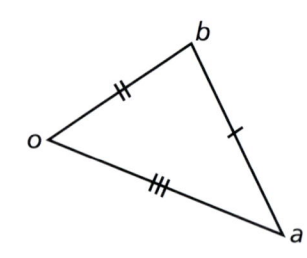

Constructions

In this section, we will deal with (*a*) constructing triangles (*b*) constructing parallelograms (*c*) bisecting line segments (*d*) bisecting angles (*e*) drawing circumcircles of triangles (*f*) drawing incircles of triangles (*g*) trisecting a line segment.

You will need a ruler, protractor, compass, set square and pencil.

Constructing triangles

We must always be given three pieces of information — three lengths *or* two lengths and one angle *or* one length and two angles.

Method is to firstly do a rough sketch of what you expect the diagram will look like. Then do an accurate construction.

Example 1

Construct a triangle *abc* in which $|ab| = 8$ cm, $|ac| = 3$ cm and $|bc| = 7$ cm.

Solution Start with a sketch. Use $[ab]$ as the base.

Sketch

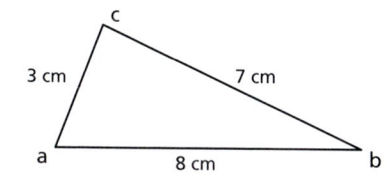

Construction
- Draw $|ab| = 8$ cm as a base.
- Open out compass 3 cm. Place point of compass on *a* and draw an arc **upwards** and to the **right** of *a*.
- Open out compass 7 cm. Place point of compass on *b* and draw an arc **upwards** and to the **left** of *b*.
- The point where the arcs intersect is *c*.
- Join *c* to *a*; join *c* to *b*.
- Finally, put all relevant information in on the diagram.

Final diagram

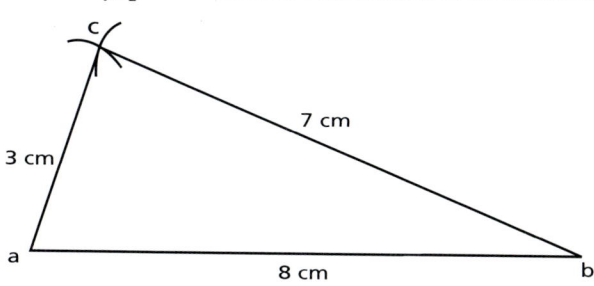

Example 2

Construct a triangle xyz where $|xy| = 6$ cm, $|xz| = 5$ cm and $|\angle yxz| = 70°$.

Solution

Sketch $[xy]$ is the base.

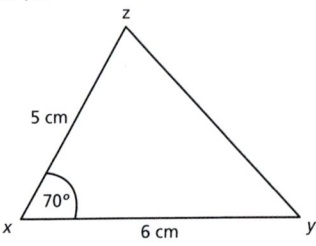

Construction
- Draw $|xy| = 6$ cm as a base.
- Open out compass 5 cm. Place point of compass on x and draw an arc upwards and to the right of x.
- Place the protractor centralised on point x and place an indicator point at 70°. Draw a line from x through the indicator point. The point where this line intersects the arc is point z.
- Put all the relevant information in on the diagram.

Final diagram

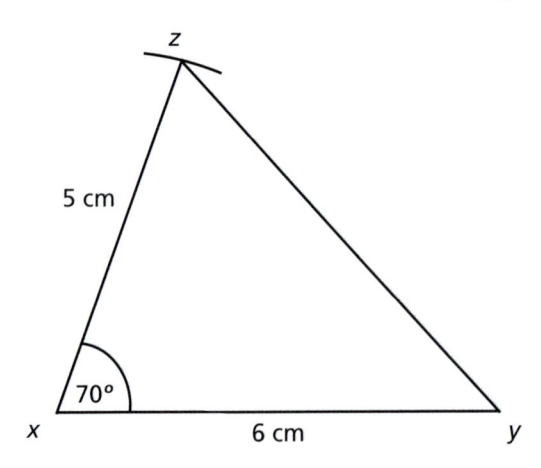

Constructing parallelograms

We must be given three pieces of information to construct a parallelogram.

Example 1

Construct a parallelogram *abcd* where $|ab| = 10$ cm, $|ad| = 6$ cm and $|\angle dab| = 60°$.

Solution Use $[ab]$ as the base in the sketch. Note that we are taking the letters *a, b, c, d* in order anticlockwise.

Sketch

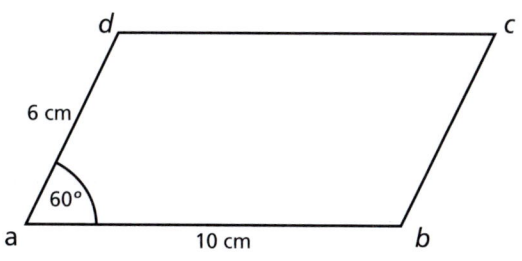

Construction
- Draw base line $[ab]$ with $|ab| = 10$ cm.

- Open out compass 6 cm. Place point on *a* and draw an arc upwards and to the right of *a*.

- Place the protractor on *a* and place an indicator point at 60°.

- Draw a line from *a* through the indicator point. The point where this line intersects the arc is *d*.

- Finally, we must locate *c*. Open out compass 6 cm. Place the compass on *b* and draw an arc upwards and to the right of *b*.

- Open out compass 10 cm. Place the compass on *d* and draw an arc to the right of *d*. The point where these arcs intersect is *c*.

- Join *b* to *c* and *d* to *c*.

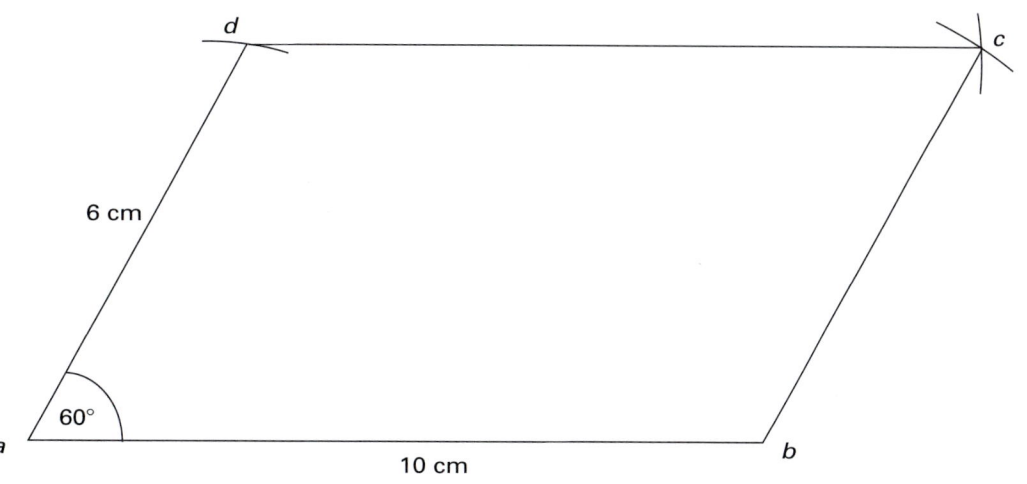

Bisecting a line segment perpendicularly

Method
- Start with line segment $[ab]$.
- Open out compass slightly more than half the distance from a to b. In our diagram $|ab| = 8$ cm, so open out the compass 5 cm.
- Place the point of the compass on a and draw an arc, as shown.
- Place the point of the compass on b and draw an arc, as shown. The arcs will intersect in two places.
- Draw a line through these points of intersection. This will be the perpendicular bisector of $[ab]$. Note also that every point on the bisector is the same distance from a and b.

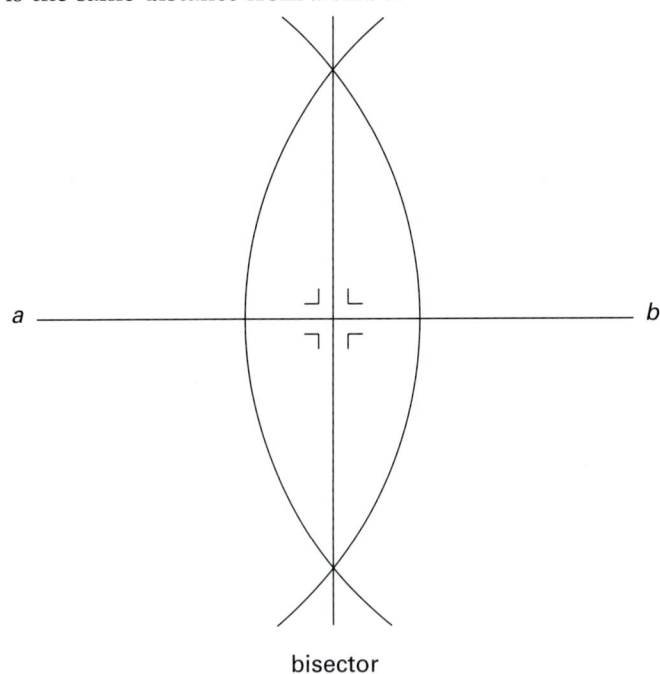

Circumcircle of a triangle

> **Top Tips**
>
> - When we are given a triangle *abc*, it is possible to find a point which is the same distance from *a* and *b* and *c*. By placing a compass on this point, a circle can be drawn through *a* and *b* and *c*. This circle is called the **circumcircle**.

Method

- Start with triangle *abc*.

- Draw the perpendicular bisector of [*ab*] as detailed in the previous section.

- Draw the perpendicular bisector of [*ac*] as before.

- The point where the bisectors meet is the same distance from *a* and *b* and *c*. This is called the circumcentre of the circumcircle. We call it *o*.

- Place the point of the compass on this point and draw the circle through *a* and *b* and *c*.

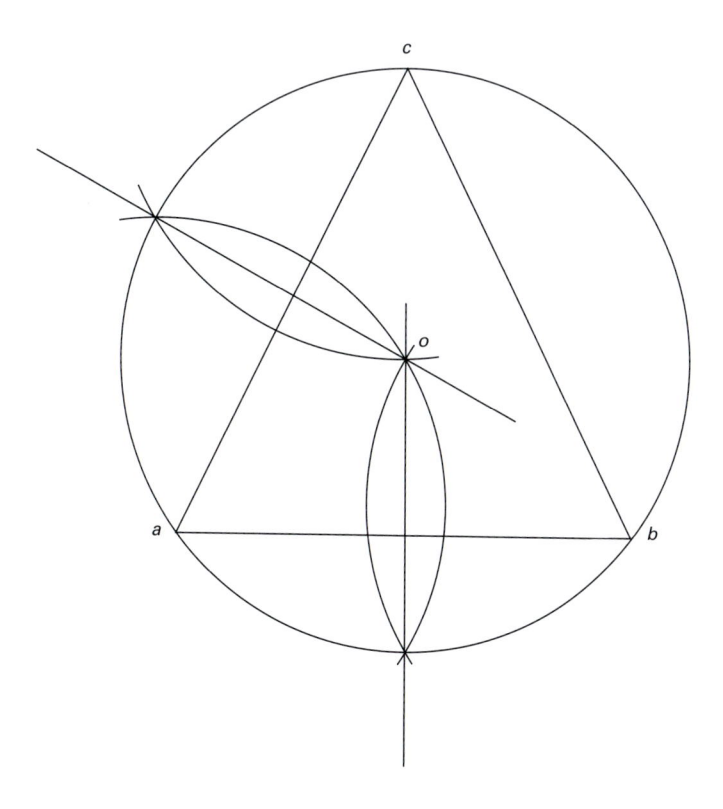

Bisecting an angle

Method

- Start with $\angle aob$.

- Place the point of the compass on *o* and draw an arc, as shown. Call the points of intersection of the arc with *oa* and the arc with *ob* *x* and *y*, respectively.

- Now place the point of the compass on *x* and draw an arc within the space included in the angle.

- Now place the point of the compass on *y* and draw a similar arc. The arcs will intersect.

- Finally, draw a line through *o* and the point of intersection of the arcs. This is the angle bisector.

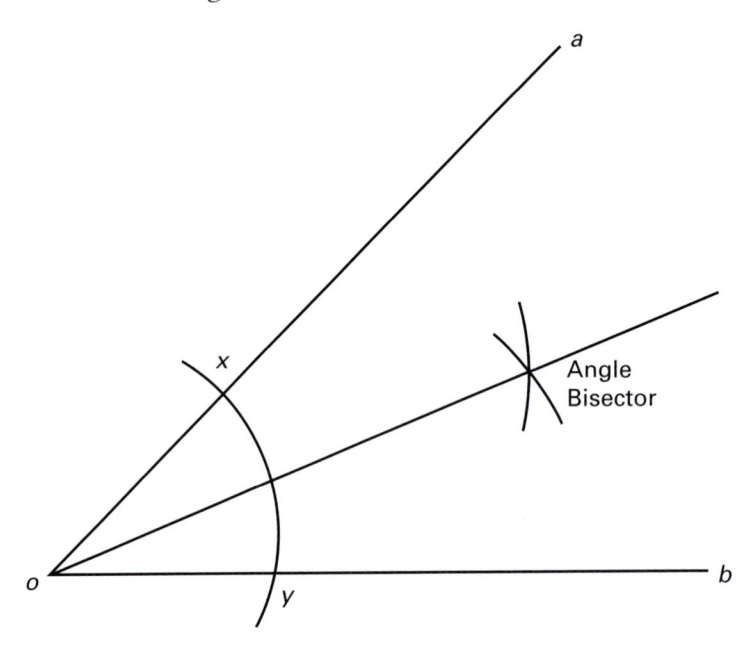

CHAPTER 8: GEOMETRY

Incircle of a triangle

> **Top Tips**
>
> - When we are given a triangle *abc*, it is possible to find a point within the triangle which is the same distance, measured perpendicularly, from each of the three sides. By placing a compass on this point, a circle can be drawn which touches each of the line segments [*ab*], [*ac*] and [*bc*]. This circle is called the **incircle**.

Method
- Start with triangle *abc*.
- Draw the bisector of ∠*bac* as outlined in the section above.
- Draw the bisector of ∠*abc* as outlined in the section above.
- The point where these angle bisectors meet is the incentre. Call it point *o*. This is the incentre of the triangle *abc*.
- Place the point of the compass on this point and open it out until it touches one of the sides. Now draw the incircle. The circle will touch all three sides provided enough care has been taken.

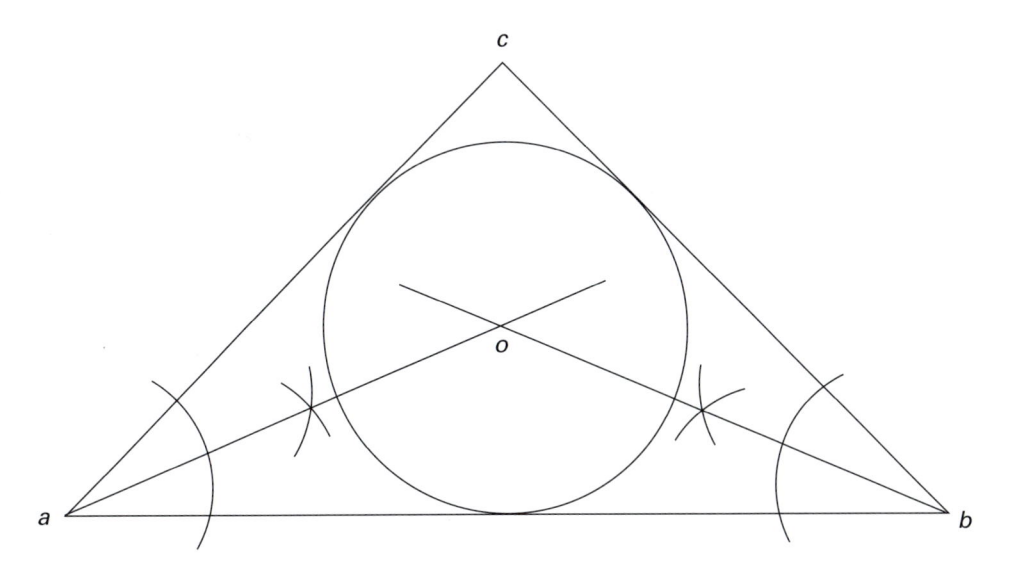

Trisecting a line segment

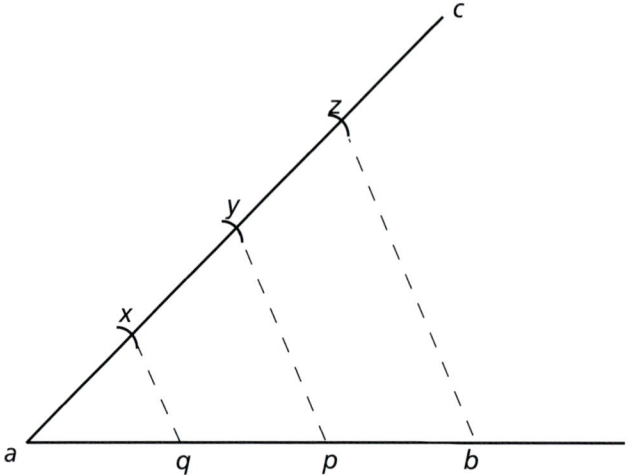

Method
- Start with a horizontal line segment $[ab]$, which we want to divide into three equal parts.
- Draw a line ac making an angle of about 60° to ab.
- Mark off three equal lengths along ac using a compass. Use a distance of about 2 cm. Put in points x, y, z so that the distances are all 2 cm.
- Now join z to b.
- Draw a line parallel to zb through y so that it intersects $[ab]$ at point p.
- Draw a line parallel to zb through x so that it intersects $[ab]$ at point q.

Result $|aq| = |qp| = |pb|$ and the line segment $[ab]$ is trisected.

Self-test 3

1. **Construct** a triangle abc where $|ab| = 7$ cm, $|ac| = 5$ cm and $|\angle abc| = 60°$. **Construct** the perpendicular bisectors of $[ab]$ and $[bc]$. Hence **draw** the circumcircle of $\triangle abc$.

2. **Construct** a triangle pqr where $|pq| = 9$ cm, $|pr| = 7$ cm and $|qr| = 6$ cm. **Construct** the bisectors of $\angle rpq$ and $\angle rqp$. Hence **draw** the incircle of $\triangle pqr$.

Transformation geometry

Axial symmetry

Finding the image of a shape by reflection in a line is referred to as **axial symmetry** in the line. Normally we call the line L, and S_L denotes reflection or axial symmetry in L.

Example 1

In the diagram we are given a capital letter M and asked to **find** the image of the letter by axial symmetry in line L.

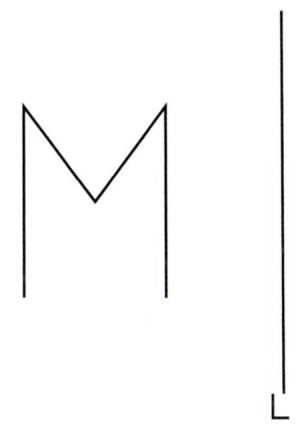

Solution   This is achieved by joining each of the five vertices on the letter perpendicularly to L and continuing out the same distance on the other side of L, as shown. Now connect the points on the image as they are connected on the original.

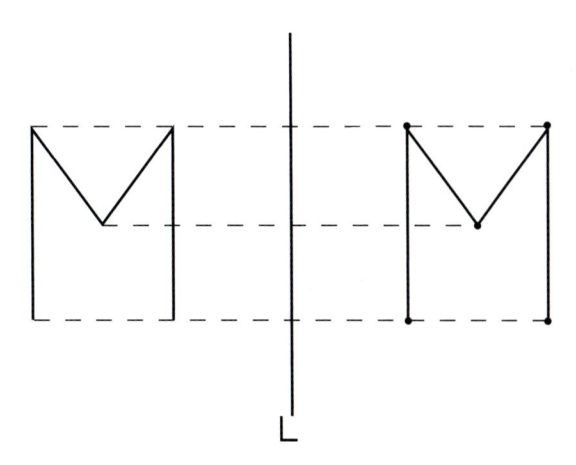

Example 2

Find the image of the parallelogram *abcd* with diagonals [*ac*] and [*bd*] under axial symmetry in the line *L*.

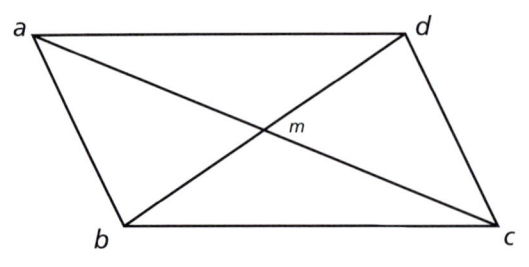

Solution   Call the images of *a, b, c, d* and *m* by their dashed equivalents, i.e. a', b', c', d', m'. Then join the vertices on the image as they are joined on the original figure.

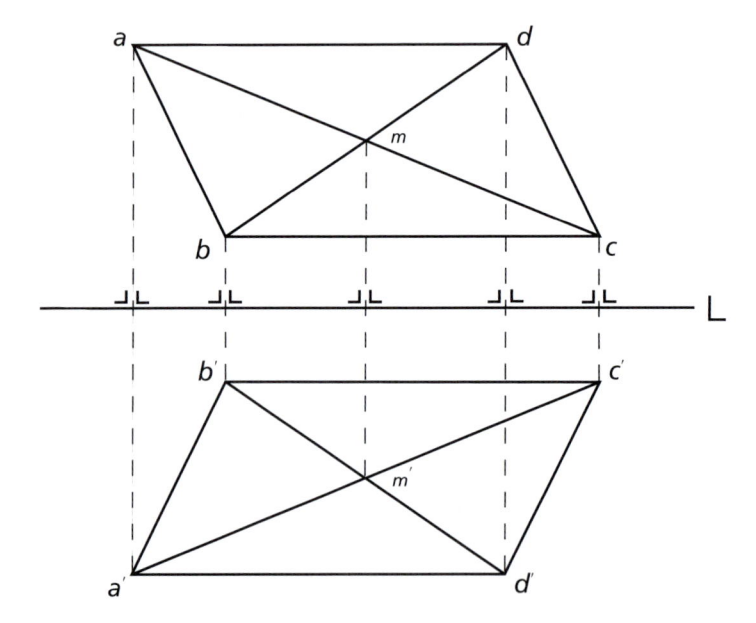

Top Tips

- Ensure that points are always joined to *L* at a 90° angle, as shown in previous diagram.

- $S_L(a)$ is often called a' or a_1. $S_L(b)$ is called b' or b_1, etc.

CHAPTER 8: GEOMETRY

> **Note**
>
> • Sometimes lines can be drawn through a shape so that when an axial symmetry is performed, the shape is its own image. Such a line is called an **axis of symmetry**.

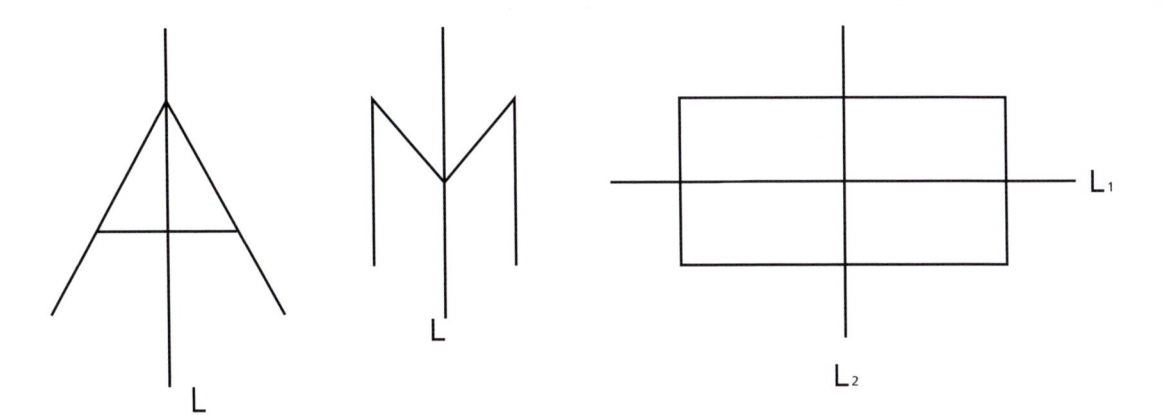

Example 3

Find the image of each of the following by S_L.

(a) a (f) [ad]

(b) e (g) [ao]

(c) g (h) [bd]

(d) c (i) △abd

(e) o (j) △efp

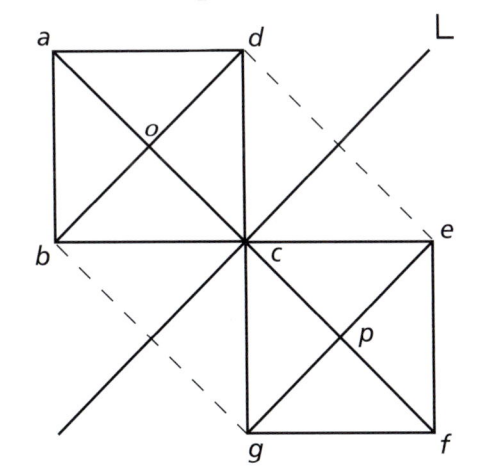

Solution
(a) $S_L(a) = f$ (e) $S_L(o) = p$ (i) $S_L(\triangle abd) = \triangle fge$

(b) $S_L(e) = d$ (f) $S_L[ad] = [fg]$ (j) $S_L(\triangle efp) = \triangle dao$

(c) $S_L(g) = b$ (g) $S_L[ao] = [fp]$

(d) $S_L(c) = c$ (h) $S_L[bd] = [ge]$

Self-test 4

1. **Draw** the images of the following shapes by axial symmetry in line *L*.

    (a)

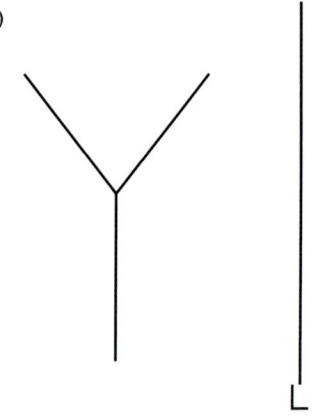

    (b)

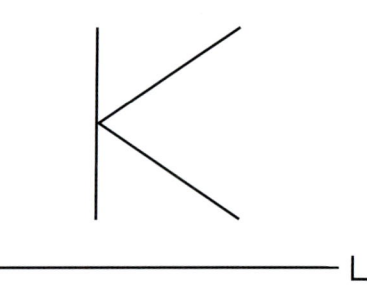

    (c)

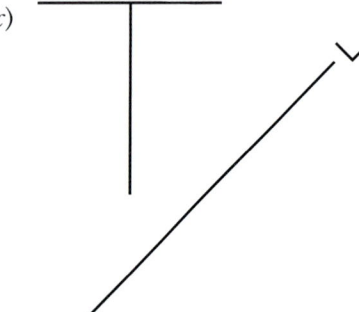

2. **Draw** in the axes of symmetry of the following shapes. (Note that some shapes may have more than one.)

    (a)   (b) 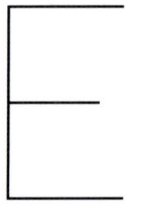   (c)

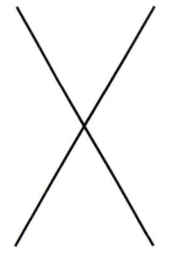

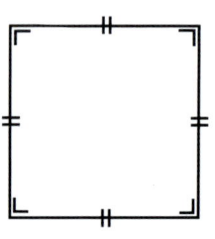

    (d) 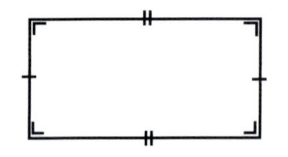   (e) 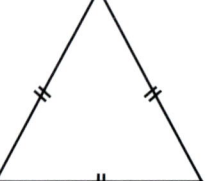   (f)

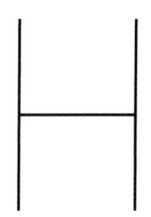

3. *abcd* is a square. The midpoints of the sides are *e, f, g, h*, as shown. Point *o* is the intersection of the diagonals. **Find** the image of △*aoe* by (*a*) axial symmetry in *ac* (*b*) axial symmetry in *bd* (*c*) axial symmetry in *ge* (*d*) axial symmetry in *hf*.

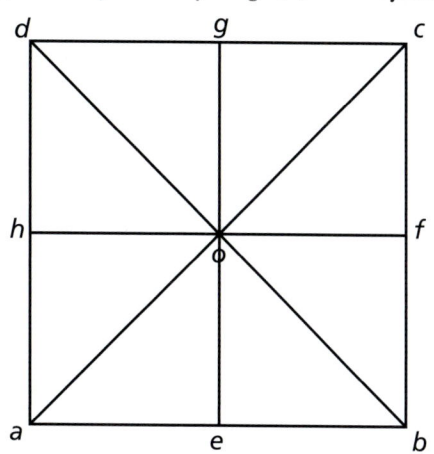

Central symmetry

Finding the image of a shape by reflection in a point is referred to as **central symmetry** in the point. If the point is *o*, then S_o denotes central symmetry in *o*.

Example 1

Find the image of capital letter *T* by central symmetry in point *o*.

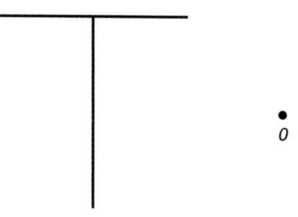

Solution Join each of the key points on the figure to *o* and continue the same distance beyond *o*. Connect the points on the image as they are connected on the original diagram.

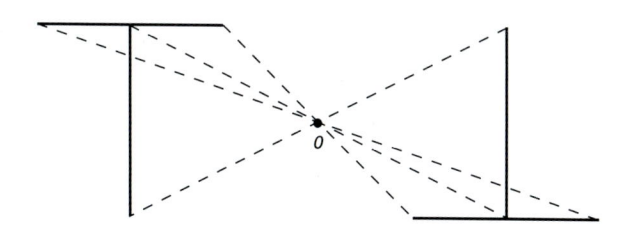

Example 2

Construct the image of the figure by central symmetry in the point x.

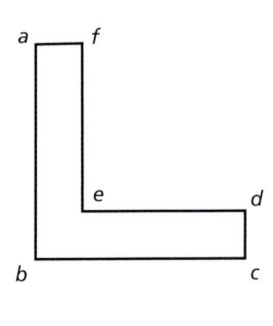

Solution Label the key points a, b, c, d, e, f. Join a to x and continue on the same distance to a_1.

Similarly, $S_x(b) = b_1$, $S_x(c) = c_1$, $S_x(d) = d_1$, $S_x(e) = e_1$, $S_x(f) = f_1$.

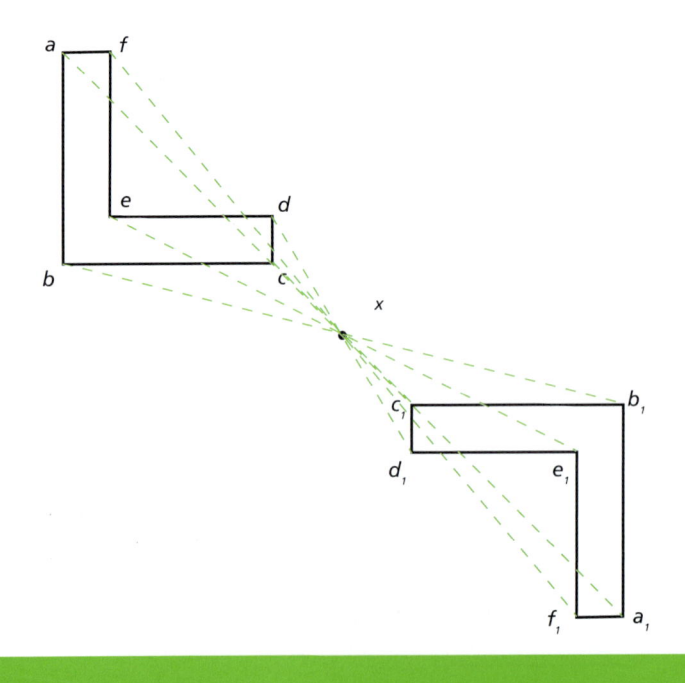

Top Tips

- Label the vertices on the shape if this has not already been done.
- Join each point to the 'mirror' point and continue on the same distance.
- When this process has been completed for all vertices, join up the image points in the same pattern as in the original shape.

Example 3

(a) Find $S_m(a)$, $S_m(b)$, $S_m([md])$.
(b) Find $S_c(\triangle bmc)$, $S_c(\triangle adc)$, $S_c(\square efgc)$.
(c) Find $S_n([ce])$, $S_n(\triangle gnf)$, $S_n(\triangle gnc)$, $S_n(\square efgc)$.

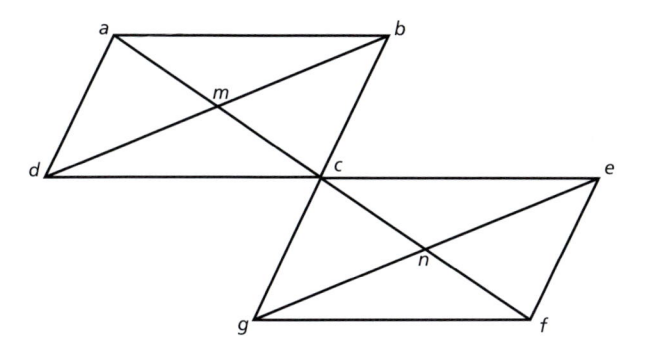

Solution

(a) $S_m(a) = c$; $S_m(b) = d$; $S_m([md]) = [mb]$
(b) $S_c(\triangle bmc) = \triangle gnc$; $S_c(\triangle adc) = \triangle fec$; $S_c(\square efgc) = \square dabc$.
(c) $S_n([ce]) = [fg]$; $S_n(\triangle gnf) = \triangle enc$; $S_n(\triangle gnc) = \triangle enf$; $S_n(\square efgc) = \square gcef$.

Self-test 5

1. Find the image of the following shapes by central symmetry in the point x.

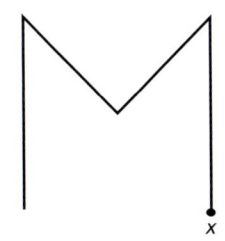

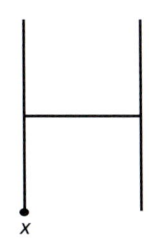

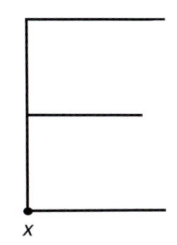

2. The rectangle $pqrs$ has diagonals $[pr]$ and $[qs]$ which intersect at point o.

   (a) Find $S_o(p)$, $S_o(q)$, $S_o(r)$.
   (b) Find $S_o([ps])$, $S_o([qs])$, $S_o([or])$.
   (c) Find $S_o(\triangle pos)$, $S_o(\triangle ors)$, $S_o(\triangle prs)$.

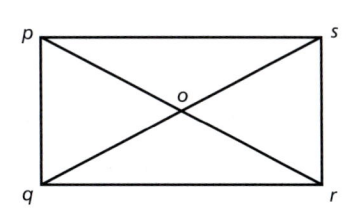

3. $abcd$ is a square. The midpoints of the sides are e, f, g, h. Point o is the intersection of the diagonals. Find the image of the following by central symmetry in o: (a) d (b) f (c) h (d) $[hc]$ (e) $[fb]$ (f) $[ac]$ (g) $\triangle doh$ (h) $\triangle aod$ (i) $\triangle cog$ (j) rectangle $hogd$.

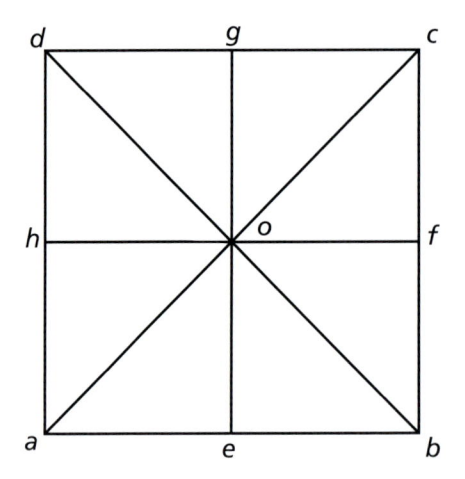

Translation

Finding the image of a shape by a translation involves moving the entire shape a given distance in a given direction.

Example 1

Find the image of the shape by the translation $\vec{xy}$.

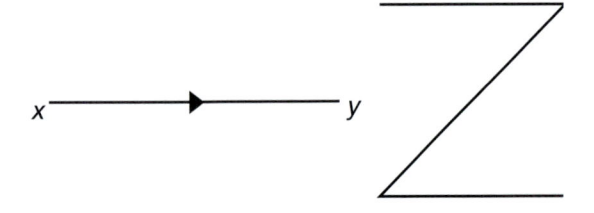

Solution

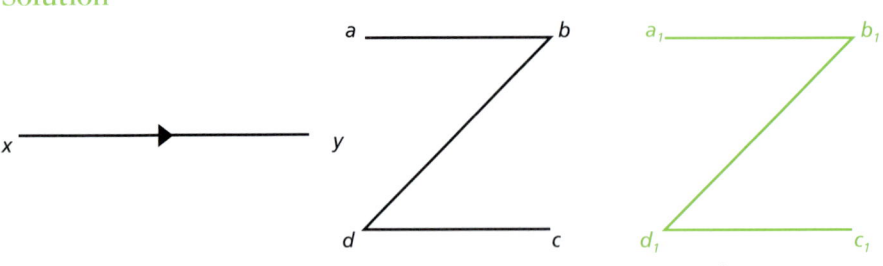

Label the key points on the shape a, b, c, d. The translation $\vec{xy}$ is 4 cm long from left to right. The image of each of the points a, b, c, d by the translation $\vec{xy}$ is a_1, b_1, c_1, d_1. Each of these points is 4 cm to the right of the original points. Finally, join the points in the image shape as they are joined in the original shape.

Example 2

Find the image of the shape by the translation $\vec{ab}$.

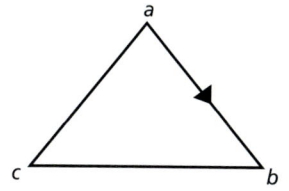

Solution

This time the translation is part of the shape to be translated. The method is the same as before. Move the shape in the direction of $\vec{ab}$ and the length of $\vec{ab}$.

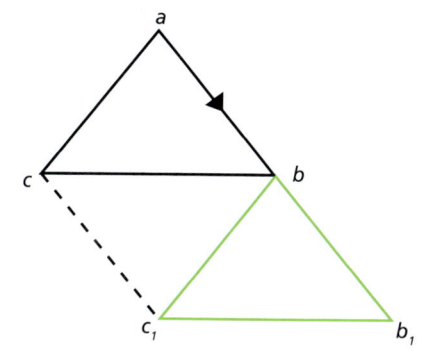

So $a \to b$, $b \to b_1$, $c \to c_1$.
Finally, join up points b, b_1, c_1.

Top Tips

- Label the vertices on the shape.
- Note the direction of the arrow on the translation and its length.
- Find the image of each of the vertices by the translation.
- Join up the image points in the same pattern as in the original shape.

Example 3

(a) What is the image of the following under translation $\vec{do}$: [dh], [he], [eo], △dho, △deo?

(b) What is the image of the following under translation $\vec{fo}$: △aef, △eof, △fgb, △fog?

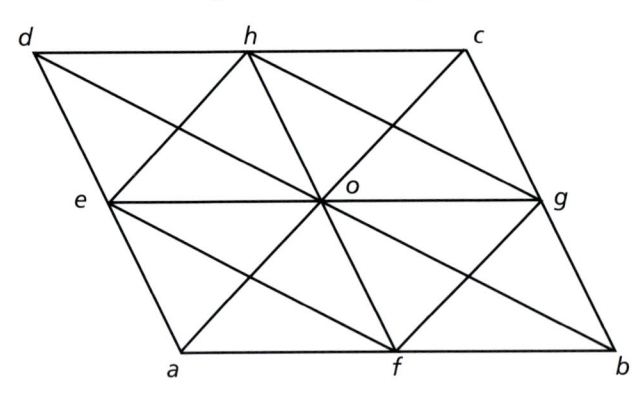

Solution

(a) By $\vec{do}$

[dh] → [og]

[he] → [gf]

[eo] → [fb]

△dho → △ogb

△deo → △ofb

(b) By $\vec{fo}$

△aef → △edo

△eof → △dho

△fgb → △ocg

△fog → △ohc

Self-test 6

1. **Draw** the image of the following shapes under the translation shown.

   (a)   (b) 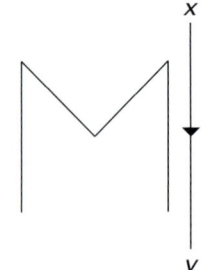   (c)

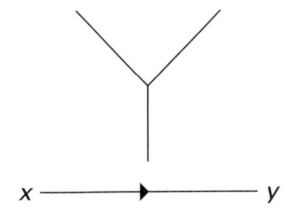

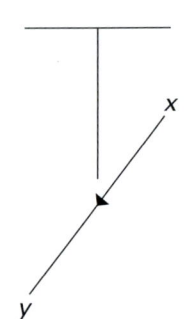

2. On separate diagrams, **find** the image of the parallelogram *xyzw* under (*a*) $\vec{xw}$ (*b*) $\vec{wz}$
   (*c*) $\vec{wy}$ (*d*) $\vec{xz}$.

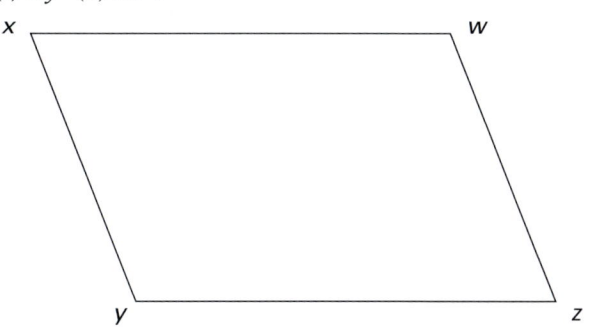

3. *abcd* is a square. *e, f, g, h* are the midpoints of the sides [*ad*], [*ab*], [*bc*] and [*cd*], respectively.

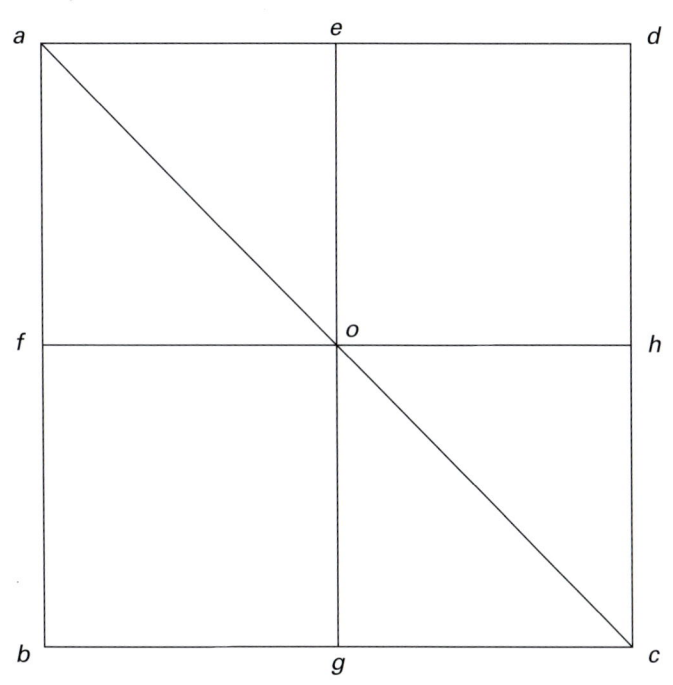

Find (*a*) the image of *f* by $\vec{ao}$ (*b*) the image of [*ae*] by $\vec{oc}$ (*c*) the image of △*afo* by $\vec{ao}$
(*d*) the image of △*och* by $\vec{co}$ (*e*) the image of rectangle *adhf* by $\vec{eo}$ (*f*) the image of △*ogc* by $\vec{fa}$.

Self-test answers

Self-test 1

1. (a) A = 60°
B = 120°
C = 60°
D = 120°
E = 120°
F = 60°
G = 60°
(b) A = 42°
B = 138°
C = 138°
D = 42°
E = 138°
F = 42°
G = 138°

2. (a) A = 58°
B = 58°
C = 70°
(b) A = 65°
B = 50°
C = 65°
D = 115°

3. (a) A = 75°
B = 75°
C = 150°
(b) A = 50°
B = 130°
C = 100°
(c) A = 140°
B = 40°
C = 100°

4. (a) A = 90°
B = 90°
C = 70°
D = 33°
(b) A = 50°
B = 50°
C = 80°
D = 40°
E = 100°
(c) A = 65°
B = 45°
C = 45°

Self-test 2

1. (a) X = 62°
Y = 118°
Z = 118°
(b) A = 60°
B = 36°
C = 84°
D = 84°
(c) M = 49°
N = 45°
P = 86°
Q = 86°

2. (a) 40 cm^2
(b) 36 cm^2
(c) 54 cm^3
(d) 21 cm^2
(e) 175 cm^2

3. (a) 9 cm
(b) 6 cm
(c) 4 cm

4. (a) 5 cm
(b) 13 cm
(c) 8 cm
(d) 7 cm
(e) $\sqrt{52}$

Self-test 3

No numerical answer to question 1 or question 2.

Self-test 4

3. (a) △aoh
   (b) △cof
   (c) △boe
   (d) △dog

Self-test 5

2. (a) r, s, p
   (b) [rq], [sq], [op]
   (c) △roq, △opq, △rpq
3. (a) b
   (b) h
   (c) f
   (d) [fa]
   (e) [hd]
   (f) [ca]
   (g) △bof
   (h) △cob
   (i) △aoe
   (j) foeb

Self-test 6

3. (a) g
   (b) [oh]
   (c) △ogc
   (d) △aoe
   (e) fhcb
   (f) △eoh

Key Points

- ab is a line, infinite in both directions, passing through a and b.
- $[ab$ is the half-line, terminating at a but going to infinity beyond b.
- $[ab]$ is the line segment terminating at a and b. It is the set of points lying between a and b.
- $|ab|$ is the distance between points a and b.
- Angles which measure less than 90° are acute angles.
- Angles which measure greater than 90° but less than 180° are obtuse angles.
- Angles which measure greater than 180° but less than 360° are reflex angles.
- Vertically opposite angles are equal in measure.
- Corresponding angles are equal in measure.
- Alternate angles are equal in measure.
- A straight angle measures 180°.
- The three angles in a triangle add up to 180°.
- The exterior angle of a triangle equals the sum of the two interior opposite angles.
- The angles at the base of an isosceles triangle are equal in measure.
- An angle at the circle standing on the diameter measures 90°.
- The opposite angles and opposite sides of a parallelogram are equal in measure.
- The diagonals of a parallelogram bisect one another.
- A diagonal of a parallelogram bisects its area.
- The area of a parallelogram = base × perpendicular height.
- The area of a triangle = $\frac{1}{2}$ × base × perpendicular height.
- In a right-angled triangle, the square on the hypotenuse equals the sum of the squares on the other two sides.
- Two triangles are congruent when all three sides and all three angles match in each triangle.
- The four ways for showing congruence are (a) S.S.S. (b) S.A.S. (c) A.S.A. (d) R.H.S.
- When constructing triangles and parallelograms, all construction lines must be clearly shown.
- All vertices must be labelled and all the given information must be transferred to the diagram.
- A rough sketch should be drawn before the construction is attempted.
- When finding the axial symmetry of a shape in a line, ensure that all points on the shape are joined perpendicularly to the line and continued the same distance beyond the line.
- An axis of symmetry of a shape is a line drawn through the middle of the shape which makes the shape its own image by an axial symmetry.
- When finding the central symmetry of a shape in a point, ensure that all points on the shape are joined to the 'mirror point' and continued the same distance beyond.
- Translations move shapes a given distance in a given direction.

Junior Certificate Examination 2004

Paper 2, Q4

4. (a) Calculate the value of x and the value of y in the diagram.

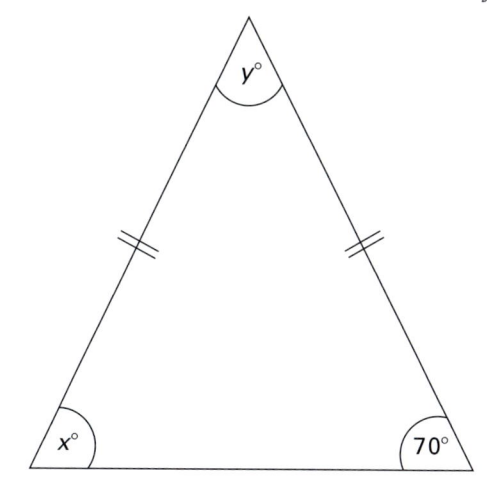

    Solution $x = 70°$: Isosceles triangle.

    $y = 40°$: Three angles add up to $180°$.

(b) $abcd$ is a parallelogram. The diagonals $[ac]$ and $[bd]$ intersect at m.

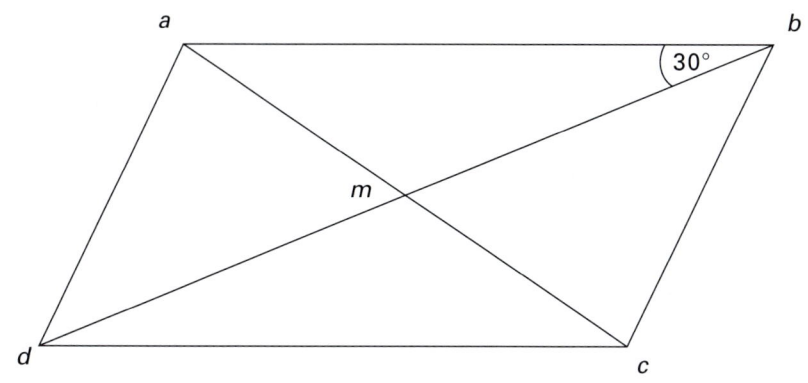

   i. The parallelogram $abcd$ has an area of 36 cm². Write down the area of $\triangle adc$ and give a reason for your answer.

   Solution   Area of $\triangle adc = 18$ cm²

   Reason: The diagonal $[ac]$ bisects the area of the parallelogram.

ii. Given that $|\angle abd| = 30°$, find $|\angle bdc|$ and give a reason for your answer.

   Solution $|\angle bdc| = 30°$

   Reason: **Alternate angles are equal in measure.**

iii. Given that $|am| = 2.25$ cm, find $|ac|$ and give a reason for your answer.

   Solution $|ac| = 4.5$ cm

   Reason: *m is the midpoint of [ac].*

iv. Show that $\triangle amb$ and $\triangle dmc$ are congruent.

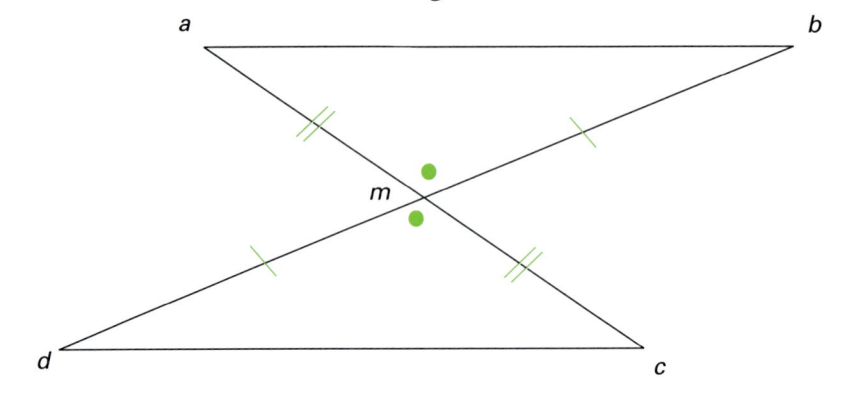

   Solution Reasons: $|am| = |mc|$

   $|bm| = |md|$

   $|\angle amb| = |\angle dmc|$

   $\Rightarrow \triangle amb$ is congruent to $\triangle dmc$ (S.A.S.)

(c) $[ab]$ is a diameter of a circle with centre c. d is a point on the circle. $dc \perp ab$.

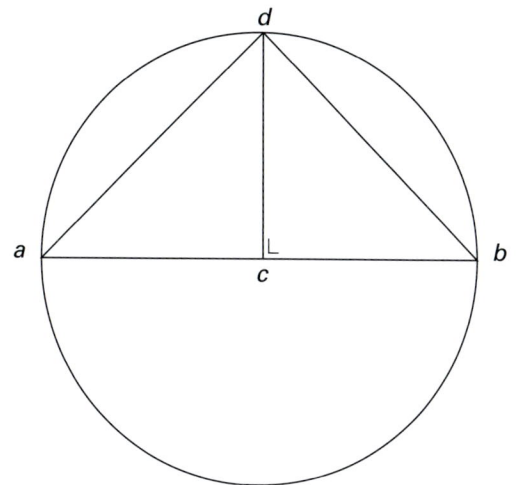

i. Name the image of $\triangle dcb$ under S_{dc}, the axial symmetry in line dc.

Solution $\triangle dcb \rightarrow \triangle dca$

ii. Given that $|\angle dac| = 45°$, write down two other angles equal in measure to $\angle dac$.

Solution $|\angle dac| = |\angle adc| = 45°$

$|\angle dac| = |\angle dbc| = 45°$

iii. Write down $|\angle adb|$ and give a reason for your answer.

Solution $|\angle adb| = 90°$

Reason: $|\angle adc| + |\angle bdc| = 45° + 45° = 90°$

iv. Given that $|ad| = |db| = 2$, show that $|ab| = \sqrt{8}$.

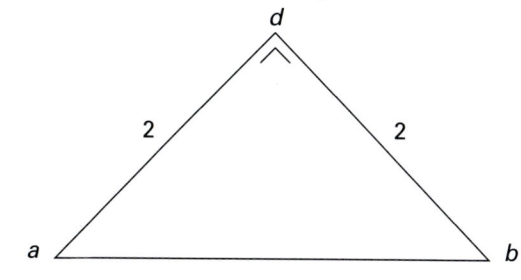

Solution $|ab|^2 = |ad|^2 + |db|^2$: Pythagoras' Theorem.

$\Rightarrow |ab|^2 = 2^2 + 2^2$

$\Rightarrow |ab|^2 = 4 + 4$

$\Rightarrow |ab|^2 = 8$

$\Rightarrow |ab| = \sqrt{8}$

Junior Certificate Examination 2005

Paper 2, Q4

4. (a) Construct a triangle pqr with $|pq| = 8$ cm, $|qr| = 10$ cm and $|\angle pqr| = 30°$. Label your diagram clearly.

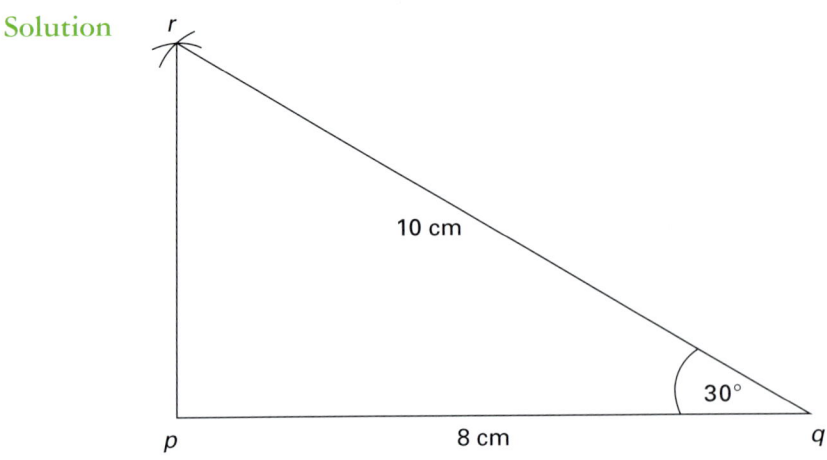

   Solution

   (b) abc is an isosceles triangle with $|ca| = |cb|$. The side $[ab]$ is extended to d and $ce \perp ab$.

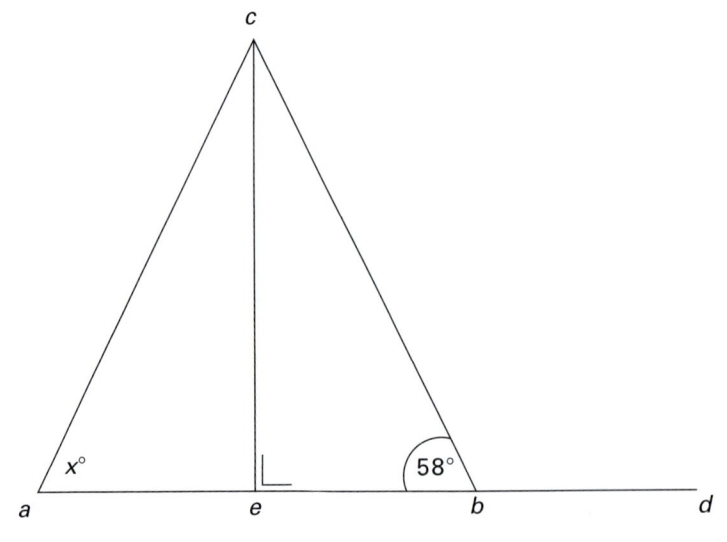

   i. Name an angle equal in measure to $\angle abc$. Give a reason for your answer.

   Solution   Name of angle: $\angle cab$

   Reason: $\triangle abc$ is isosceles.

ii. Given that $|\angle abc| = 58°$, find $|\angle cbd|$ and give a reason for your answer.

   Solution $|\angle cbd| = 122°$

   Reason: **Because $122° + 58° = 180°$: Straight angle.**

iii. Given that $|ab| = 10$ cm and $|ce| = 8$ cm, find the area of $\triangle abc$.

   Solution Area $= \frac{1}{2} \times$ base $\times$ perpendicular height

   $= \frac{1}{2} \times 10 \times 8$

   $= 40 \text{ cm}^2$

iv. ce is the bisector of $\angle acb$. Show that $\triangle ace$ and $\triangle bce$ are congruent.

   Solution Reasons: $|ac| = |bc|$: given.

   $|\angle ace| = |\angle bce|$: given.

   $|ce| = |ce|$: common side.

   $\Rightarrow \triangle ace$ is congruent to $\triangle bce$. [S.A.S]

(c) $[ac]$ and $[bd]$ are diameters of a circle with centre o. L is a line touching the circle at the point b only.

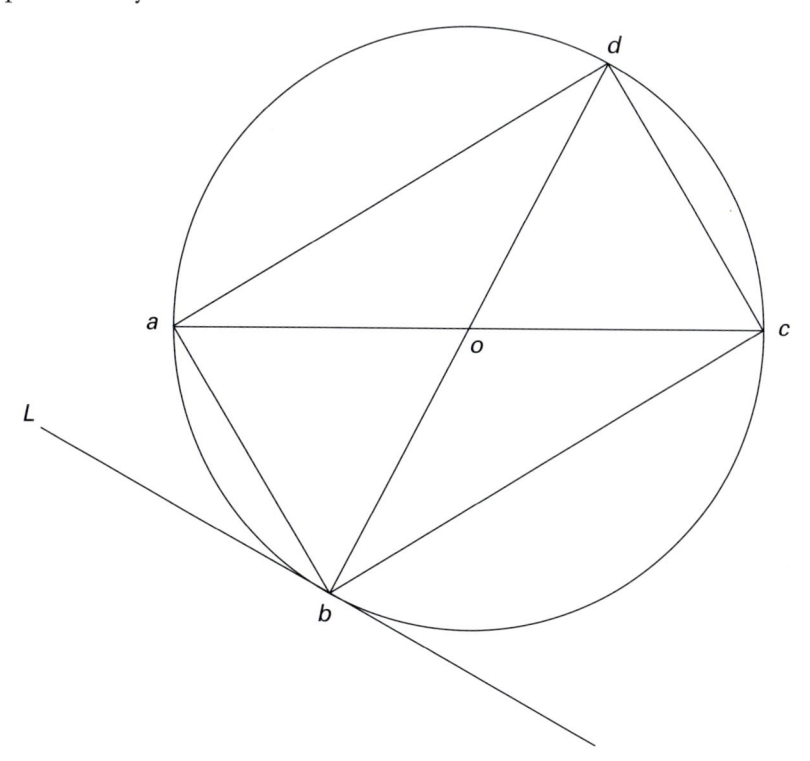

i. Name the image of the △*aod* under S_o, the central symmetry in the point *o*.

Solution △*aod* → △*cob* under S_o.

ii. What is the name given to a line, such as the line *L*, that touches the circle at one point only?

Solution Tangent.

iii. Write down |∠*abc*| and give a reason for your answer.

Solution |∠*abc*| = 90°

Reason: [*ac*] is a diameter and *b* is on the circle.

iv. Given that |*ad*| = 4 and |*dc*| = 3, use the Theorem of Pythagoras to find |*ac*|.

Solution
$|ac|^2 = 4^2 + 3^2$
$\Rightarrow |ac|^2 = 16 + 9$
$\Rightarrow |ac|^2 = 25$
$\Rightarrow |ac| = \sqrt{25}$
$\Rightarrow |ac| = 5$

CHAPTER 9
Co-ordinate Geometry

Learning Objectives

- How to apply the distance formula, midpoint formula, slope formula and equation of a line formula.
- How to draw vertical and horizontal lines.
- How to draw diagonal lines using the x and y intercepts.
- How to find the equation of a line parallel to a given line.
- How to test if a point is on a line.
- How to find images of points by axial symmetry, central symmetry and translation.

Applying formulae

Let $a = (x_1, y_1)$; let $b = (x_2, y_2)$.

- Length of the line segment $[ab] = \sqrt{(x_2 - x_1)^2 + (y_2 - y_1)^2}$.
- Midpoint of the line segment $[ab] = \left(\dfrac{x_1 + x_2}{2}, \dfrac{y_1 + y_2}{2}\right)$.
- Slope of the line passing through a and b: $m = \dfrac{y_2 - y_1}{x_2 - x_1}$.
- Equation of the line through a and b: $y - y_1 = m(x - x_1)$.

The formulae required for the Junior Cert question will be given on the test paper for you to apply.

Top Tips

- $|ab|$ means length of line segment $[ab]$.
- The letter m is used to denote the slope. So $m = \dfrac{y_2 - y_1}{x_2 - x_1}$.
- In order to find the equation of a line, we must first find its slope m.

Example 1

Find the length of the line segment $[ab]$ when $a = (3, 1)$ and $b = (-1, 4)$.

Solution

Let $(x_1, y_1) = (3, 1)$
$(x_2, y_2) = (-1, 4)$

Formula: $|ab| = \sqrt{(x_2 - x_1)^2 + (y_2 - y_1)^2}$
$\Rightarrow |ab| = \sqrt{(-1 - 3)^2 + (4 - 1)^2}$
$\Rightarrow |ab| = \sqrt{(-4)^2 + 3^2}$
$\Rightarrow |ab| = \sqrt{16 + 9}$
$\Rightarrow |ab| = \sqrt{25}$
$\Rightarrow |ab| = 5$

We can see that when the points are plotted, $|ab|$ is found from Pythagoras' Theorem by drawing the right-angled triangle as shown.

Example 2

Find the midpoint of the line segment joining $a = (-4, 3)$ and $b = (-6, -5)$.

Solution Let $(x_1, y_1) = (-4, 3)$

Let $(x_2, y_2) = (-6, -5)$

Formula: Midpoint of $[ab] = \left(\dfrac{x_1 + x_2}{2}, \dfrac{y_1 + y_2}{2} \right)$

$$\Rightarrow \text{Midpoint} = \left(\dfrac{-4 + (-6)}{2}, \dfrac{3 + (-5)}{2} \right)$$

$$= \left(\dfrac{-4 - 6}{2}, \dfrac{3 - 5}{2} \right)$$

$$= \left(\dfrac{-10}{2}, \dfrac{-2}{2} \right)$$

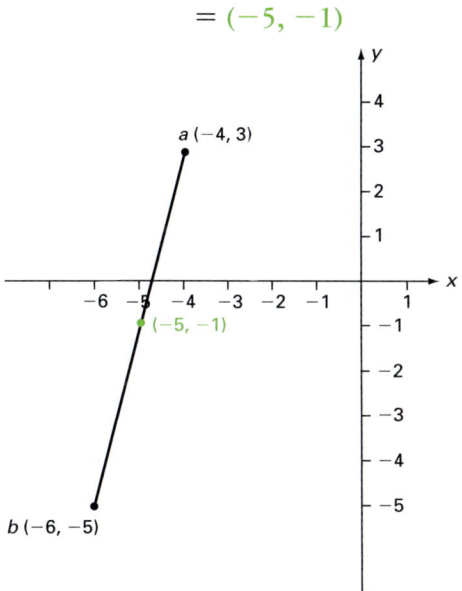

$$= (-5, -1)$$

Example 3

Find the slope of the line passing through the points $p = (-2, 1)$ and $q = (-4, 5)$.

Solution Formula: Slope $m = \dfrac{y_2 - y_1}{x_2 - x_1}$

Let $(x_1, y_1) = (-2, 1)$

Let $(x_2, y_2) = (-4, 5)$

$\Rightarrow m = \dfrac{5 - 1}{-4 - (-2)}$

$\Rightarrow m = \dfrac{5 - 1}{-4 + 2}$

$\Rightarrow m = \dfrac{4}{-2}$

$\Rightarrow m = -2$

We see that when the two points are plotted and the right-angled triangle is drawn as shown that the slope is obtained by **dividing the vertical distance by the horizontal distance.**

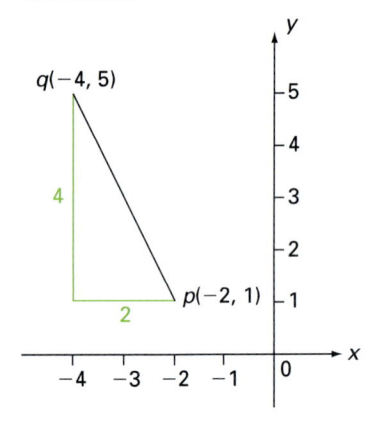

Because the line slopes downwards from left to right, the slope m is negative (minus).

So, $m = -\dfrac{4}{2} \Rightarrow m = -2$

Example 4

Find the equation of the line joining $p(-2, 1)$ and $q(-4, 5)$.

Solution Formula: $y - y_1 = m(x - x_1)$

Let $(x_1, y_1) = (-2, 1)$

$m = -2$ [from previous example]

So, $y - 1 = -2(x - [-2])$

$\Rightarrow y - 1 = -2(x + 2)$

$\Rightarrow y - 1 = -2x - 4$

$\Rightarrow 2x + y + 3 = 0$

Top Tips

- When using this formula, it is important to remember that x and y are variables and therefore no values are assigned to them.

- m is the slope of the line.

Example 5

Find the equation of the line passing through $r(-2, 1)$ and $s(4, 3)$.

Solution Step 1: Find slope $m = \dfrac{y_2 - y_1}{x_2 - x_1}$

Let $(x_1, y_1) = (-2, 1)$

Let $(x_2, y_2) = (4, 3)$

$\Rightarrow m = \dfrac{3 - 1}{4 - (-2)}$

$\Rightarrow m = \dfrac{2}{4 + 2}$

$\Rightarrow m = \dfrac{2}{6}$

$\Rightarrow m = \dfrac{1}{3}$

Step 2: Find equation

Let $(x_1, y_1) = (-2, 1)$

Let $m = \dfrac{1}{3}$

$y - y_1 = m(x - x_1)$
$\Rightarrow y - 1 = \tfrac{1}{3}(x - [-2])$
$\Rightarrow y - 1 = \tfrac{1}{3}(x + 2)$
$\Rightarrow 3y - 3 = 1(x + 2)$ ← Multiply both sides by 3
$\Rightarrow 3y - 3 = x + 2$
$\Rightarrow -x + 3y - 5 = 0$
$\Rightarrow x - 3y + 5 = 0$

Self-test 1

1. $a = (5, -2)$, $b = (-1, -4)$
   - (a) Find |ab| correct to two decimal places.
   - (b) Find the midpoint of [ab].
   - (c) Find the slope of the line ab.
   - (d) Find the equation of the line ab.

2. $p = (-3, 4)$, $q = (7, -1)$
   - (a) Find |pq| in Surd form.
   - (b) Find the midpoint of [pq].
   - (c) Find the slope of the line pq.
   - (d) Find the equation of the line pq.

Drawing lines on the Cartesian plane

- All horizontal lines have the form y = constant.
- All vertical lines have the form x = constant.

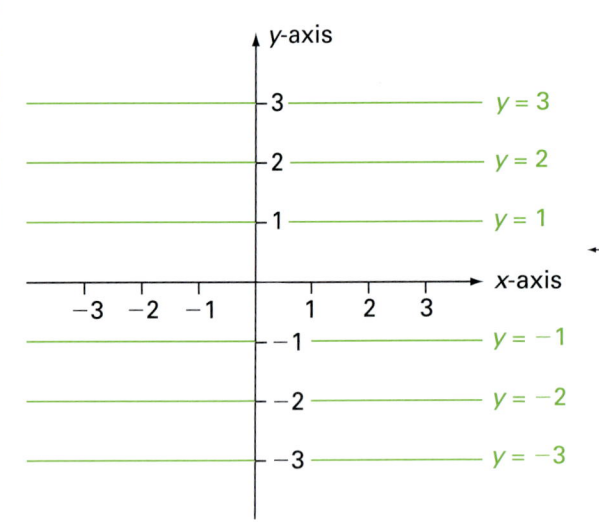

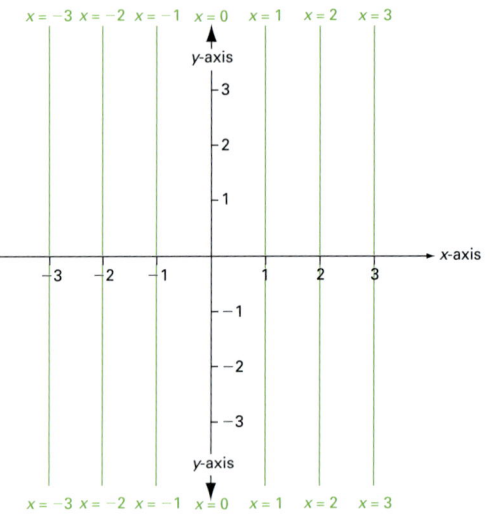

Top Tips

- The x-axis has equation $y = 0$.
- The y-axis has equation $x = 0$.
- Drawing diagonal lines can be achieved by finding where the line cuts both the x-axis and the y-axis. These are called the x intercept and the y intercept.

Example 1

Graph the line L: $3x + 2y = 6$.

Solution Find the x intercept

Let $y = 0 \Rightarrow 3x + 2(0) = 6$
$\Rightarrow 3x = 6$
$\Rightarrow x = 2$

So, $(2, 0)$ is the x intercept.

Find the y intercept

Let $x = 0 \Rightarrow 3(0) + 2y = 6$
$\Rightarrow 2y = 6$
$\Rightarrow y = 3$

So, $(0, 3)$ is the y intercept.

Now, plot the points and join them. The line continues infinitely in both directions.

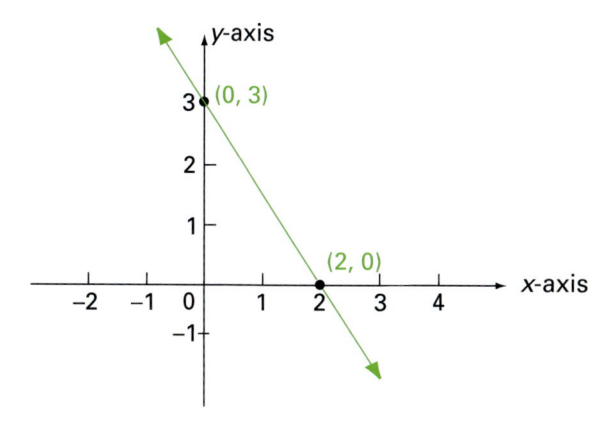

Example 2

Graph the $L: 4x - 3y = 12$ and hence find its slope.

Solution **Find the x intercept**

Let $y = 0 \Rightarrow 4x - 3(0) = 12$

$\Rightarrow 4x = 12$

$\Rightarrow x = 3$

So, $(3, 0)$ is the x intercept.

Find the y intercept

Let $x = 0 \Rightarrow 4(0) - 3y = 12$

$\Rightarrow -3y = 12$

$\Rightarrow y = -4$

So, $(0, -4)$ is the y intercept.

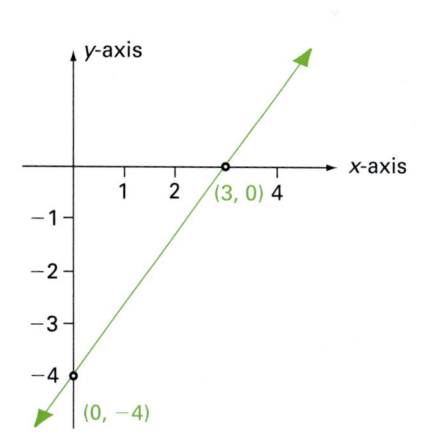

Find slope: $m = \dfrac{y_2 - y_1}{x_2 - x_1}$

Let $(x_1, y_1) = (3, 0)$

Let $(x_2, y_2) = (0, -4)$

slope $m = \dfrac{y_2 - y_1}{x_2 - x_1}$

$\Rightarrow m = \dfrac{-4 - 0}{0 - 3}$

$\Rightarrow m = \dfrac{-4}{-3}$

$\Rightarrow m = \dfrac{4}{3}$

Example 3

(a) **Graph** the line $L: 2x + y = 5$.

(b) Hence, **find** the slope of the line.

(c) **Find** the equation of the line K through the point $(3, 2)$, which is parallel to L.

Top Tips

- Parallel lines have equal slopes.

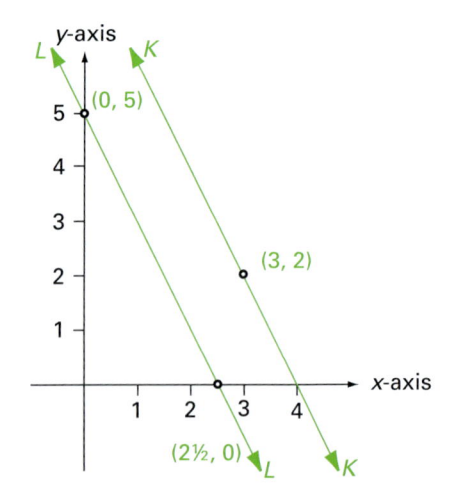

Solution (a) $L: 2x + y = 5$

x **intercept**: Let $y = 0$

$\Rightarrow 2x + 0 = 5$

$\Rightarrow 2x = 5$

$\Rightarrow x = 2\tfrac{1}{2}$

So, $(2\tfrac{1}{2}, 0)$ is on L.

y **intercept**: Let $x = 0$

$\Rightarrow 2(0) + y = 5$

$\Rightarrow y = 5$

So, $(0, 5)$ is on L.
See graph on right.

(b) Let $(x_1, y_1) = (2\tfrac{1}{2}, 0)$

Let $(x_2, y_2) = (0, 5)$

$m = \dfrac{y_2 - y_1}{x_2 - x_1}$

$\Rightarrow m = \dfrac{5 - 0}{0 - 2\tfrac{1}{2}}$

$\Rightarrow m = \dfrac{5}{-2\tfrac{1}{2}}$

$\Rightarrow m = -2$

(c) K is parallel to L, so K has a slope of -2.

Let $m = -2$

Let $(x_1, y_1) = (3, 2)$

Equation

$y - y_1 = m(x - x_1)$

$\Rightarrow y - 2 = -2(x - 3)$

$\Rightarrow y - 2 = -2x + 6$

$\Rightarrow 2x + y = 8$

How to test if a point is on a line

- The point under test is substituted into the equation of the line. If the value for the left-hand side equals the value for the right-hand side, then the point is on the line.

Example 1

Investigate if the point $(2, -1)$ is on the line $3x - 4y = 10$.

Solution   Substitute $x = 2$ and $y = -1$.
Left-hand side $= 3(2) - 4(-1)$ Right-hand side $= 10$
$\qquad\qquad\quad\; = 6 + 4$ So, $(2, -1)$ is on the line $3x - 4y = 10$.
$\qquad\qquad\quad\; = 10$

Example 2

L is the line $5x + 2y = -1$.
Investigate if $(1, -3)$ and $(-2, -4)$ are on L.

Solution   Test $(1, -3)$
Left-hand side $= 5(1) + 2(-3)$ Right-hand side $= -1$
$\qquad\qquad\quad\; = 5 - 6$ So, $(1, 3)$ is on L.
$\qquad\qquad\quad\; = -1$

Test $(-2, -4)$
Left-hand side $= 5(-2) + 2(-4)$ Right-hand side $= -1$
$\qquad\qquad\quad\; = -10 - 8$ So, $(-2, -4)$ is *not* on L.
$\qquad\qquad\quad\; = -18$

Example 3

The point $(2, k)$ is on the line $L: 2x - 7y = -17$. Find the value of k.

Solution   Left-hand side $= 2(2) - 7(k)$ Right-hand side $= -17$
$\qquad\qquad\qquad\quad = 4 - 7k$

$\qquad\qquad\qquad$ Let $LHS = RHS$
$\qquad\qquad\qquad \Rightarrow 4 - 7k = -17$
$\qquad\qquad\qquad \Rightarrow \quad -7k = -17 - 4$
$\qquad\qquad\qquad \Rightarrow \quad -7k = -21$
$\qquad\qquad\qquad \Rightarrow \quad\;\; k = 3$

Self-test 2

1. Draw the lines $L: x = 2$ and $K: y = -1$. What is the point of intersection of L and K?
2. Sketch the line $L: 5x - 2y = 10$. Hence find the slope of the line.
3. Sketch the line $L: 3x + 5y = 15$. Hence find the slope of the line. Find the equation of the line K through the point $(2, -1)$, which is parallel to L. Finally, sketch K.
4. L is the line $4x - 3y = 15$. Investigate if the points $(3, -1)$, $(-2, 1)$ and $(6, 3)$ are on L.

Axial symmetry, central symmetry and translation

Notation

- $S_X(a, b)$ means the image of the point (a, b) by axial symmetry in the x-axis.
- $S_Y(a, b)$ means the image of the point (a, b) by axial symmetry in the y-axis.
- $S_0(a, b)$ means the image of the point (a, b) by central symmetry in the point $(0, 0)$.

Top Tips

- $S_X(a, b) = (a, -b)$
- $S_Y(a, b) = (-a, b)$
- $S_0(a, b) = (-a, -b)$

Example 1

Find the image of the point $(-1, 2)$ by S_X. Draw a diagram to illustrate the answer.

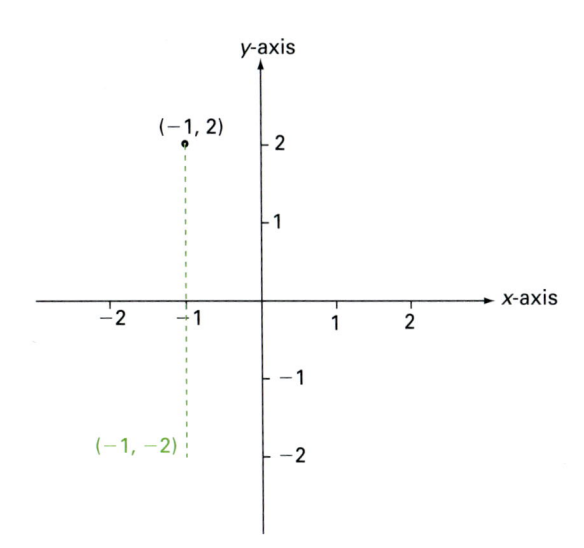

Solution $S_X(-1, 2) = (-1, -2)$

Example 2

Find the image of the point $(3, 2)$ by S_Y. Illustrate the answer on a diagram.

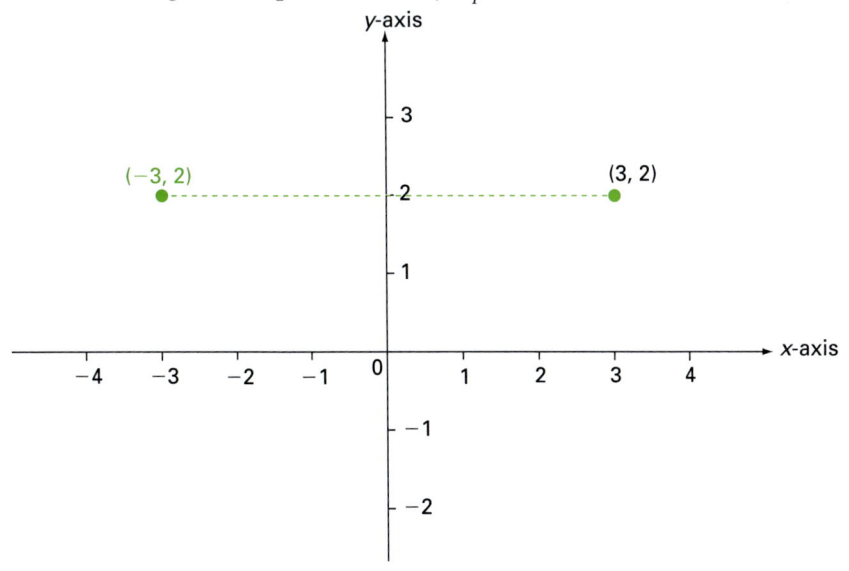

Solution $S_Y(3, 2) = (-3, 2)$

Example 3

Find the image of the point $(3, -1)$ by S_0. **Draw** a diagram to illustrate the answer.

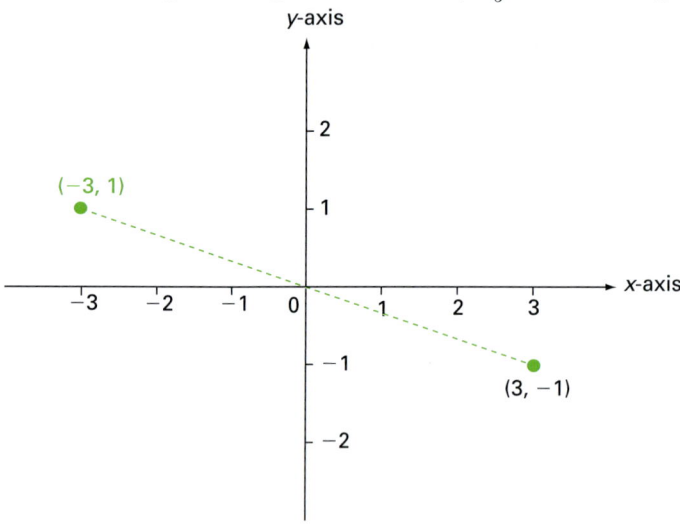

Solution $S_0(3, -1) = (-3, 1)$

- Finding the image of a point by a translation involves determining the horizontal and vertical movement associated with the translation. Then this movement is applied to the point.

- If a translation originates at point a and ends at point b, it is written as $\vec{ab}$.

Example 4

If $a = (-1, 2)$ and $b = (1, 3)$, **find** the horizontal and vertical movement of translation $\vec{ab}$. Hence, **find** the image of the point $c(2, 1)$ under the translation $\vec{ab}$.

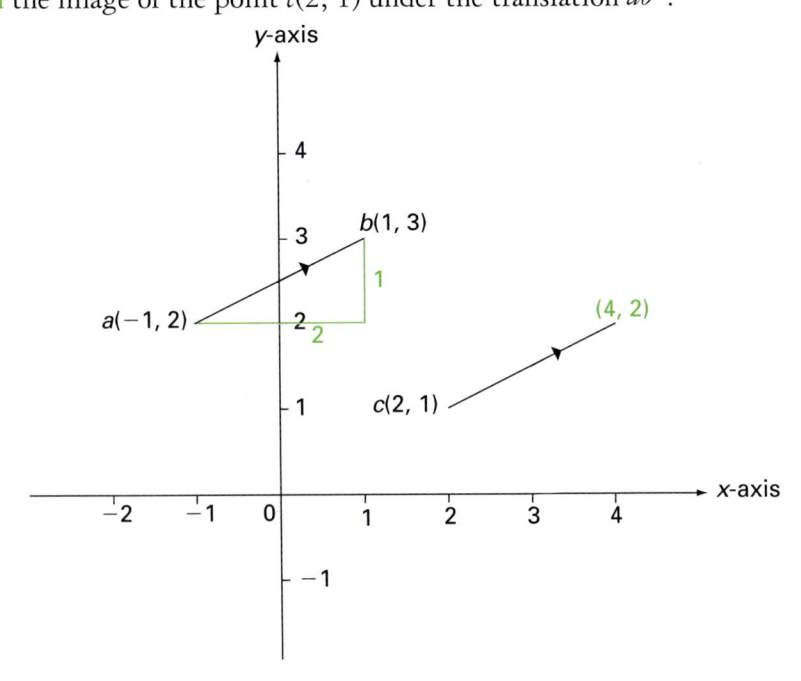

Solution   Mark in the translation on the diagram. Draw an arrow in the direction from a to b.

The horizontal movement is $+2$ units. The vertical movement is $+1$ unit.

Now apply this movement to the point $(2, 1)$.
$\Rightarrow (2, 1) \rightarrow (4, 2)$

So, image of $c(2, 1)$ under translation $\vec{ab}$ is $(4, 2)$.

Self-test 3

1. Find the image of each of the following points by axial symmetry in the x-axis, S_X: (a) (4, 2) (b) (−3, 2) (c) (2, −11) (d) (−5, −3).

2. Find the image of each of the following points by axial symmetry in the y-axis, S_Y: (a) (3, 1) (b) (−4, 3) (c) (−1, −2) (d) (2, −5).

3. Find the image of each of the following points by central symmetry in the point (0, 0), S_0: (a) (−5, −4) (b) (2, 3) (c) (−4, 1) (d) (2, −5).

4. Find the image of each of the following points under the translation (1, −2) → (3, 1): (a) (−1, 3) (b) (−3, −2) (c) (4, 2) (d) (0, −2).

5. Find the image of each of the following points under the translation (2, 4) → (−1, 0): (a) (5, 6) (b) (3, 2) (c) (−1, −2) (d) (−2, 2).

Self-test answers

Self-test 1
1. (a) 6.32
   (b) (2, −3)
   (c) $m = \frac{1}{3}$
   (d) $x - 3y = 11$
2. (a) $\sqrt{125}$
   (b) $(2, 1\frac{1}{2})$
   (c) $m = -\frac{1}{2}$
   (d) $x + 2y = 5$

Self-test 2
1. L ∩ K = (2, −1)
2. $m = \frac{5}{2}$
3. $m = -\frac{3}{5}$; $3x + 5y = 1$
4. (3, −1) ∈ L
   (−2, 1) ∉ L
   (6, 3) ∈ L

Self-test 3
1. (a) (4, −2)
   (b) (−3, −2)
   (c) (2, 11)
   (d) (−5, 3)
2. (a) (−3, 1)
   (b) (4, 3)
   (c) (1, −2)
   (d) (−2, −5)
3. (a) (5, 4)
   (b) (−2, −3)
   (c) (4, −1)
   (d) (−2, 5)
4. (a) (1, 6)
   (b) (−1, 1)
   (c) (6, 5)
   (d) (2, 1)
5. (a) (2, 2)
   (b) (0, −2)
   (c) (−4, −6)
   (d) (−5, −2)

Key Points

- Length of a line segment = $\sqrt{(x_2 - x_1)^2 + (y_2 - y_1)^2}$.

- Midpoint of a line segment = $\left(\dfrac{x_1 + x_2}{2}, \dfrac{y_1 + y_2}{2}\right)$.

- Slope of a line passing through (x_1, y_1) and (x_2, y_2) is given by the formula $m = \dfrac{y_2 - y_1}{x_2 - x_1}$.

- Equation of a line passing through (x_1, y_1) and (x_2, y_2) is $y - y_1 = m(x - x_1)$.

- All horizontal lines are given by equations of the form $y = $ constant.

- All vertical lines are given by equations of the form $x = $ constant.

- The x-axis has the equation $y = 0$.

- The y-axis has the equation $x = 0$.

- To graph a line, let $x = 0$ and get the y value. So, $(0, *)$ is the y intercept.
  Then let $y = 0$ and get the x value. So, $(*, 0)$ is the x intercept.

- To test if a point is on a line, substitute the point into the line. If the left-hand side equals the right-hand side, then the point is on the line.

- $S_X(a, b) = (a, -b)$.

- $S_Y(a, b) = (-a, b)$.

- $S_0(a, b,) = (-a, -b)$.

Junior Certificate Examination 2004

Paper 2, Q5

5. (a) Write down the co-ordinates of the point a.

    Solution $a = (-2, 3)$

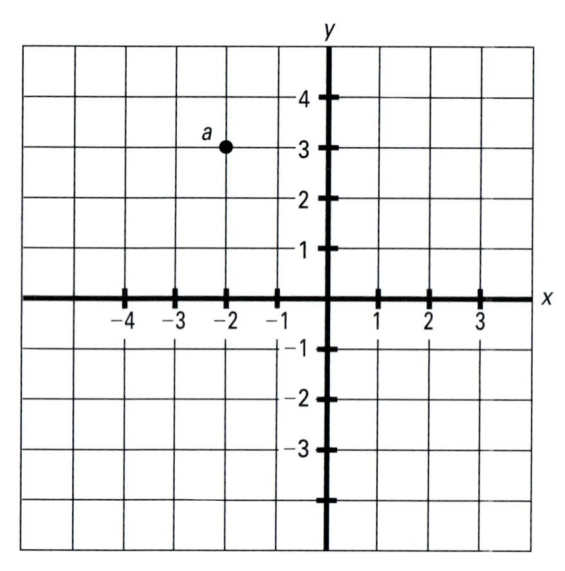

(b) p is the point $(1, 3)$ and q is the point $(3, 5)$. Find each of the following:

    i.   The midpoint of $[pq]$.

    ii.   The slope of pq.

Solution i. Let $(x_1, y_1) = (1, 3)$
Let $(x_2, y_2) = (3, 5)$

$$\text{The midpoint of } [pq] = \left(\frac{x_1 + x_2}{2}, \frac{y_1 + y_2}{2}\right)$$
$$= \left(\frac{1 + 3}{2}, \frac{3 + 5}{2}\right)$$
$$= \left(\frac{4}{2}, \frac{8}{2}\right)$$
$$= (2, 4)$$

Solution ii. Let $(x_1, y_1) = (1, 3)$
Let $(x_2, y_2) = (3, 5)$

$$\text{Slope } m = \frac{y_2 - y_1}{x_2 - x_1}$$
$$\Rightarrow m = \frac{5 - 3}{3 - 1}$$
$$\Rightarrow m = \frac{2}{2}$$
$$\Rightarrow m = 1$$

iii. The equation of the line pq.

Solution Let $(x_1, y_1) = (1, 3)$

$m = 1$

So, $y - y_1 = m(x - x_1)$

$\Rightarrow y - 3 = 1(x - 1)$

$\Rightarrow y - 3 = x - 1$

$\Rightarrow -x + y - 2 = 0$

$\Rightarrow x - y + 2 = 0$

(c) *i.* L is the line $3x - 2y - 12 = 0$. L cuts the x-axis at the point c. Find the co-ordinates of the point c.

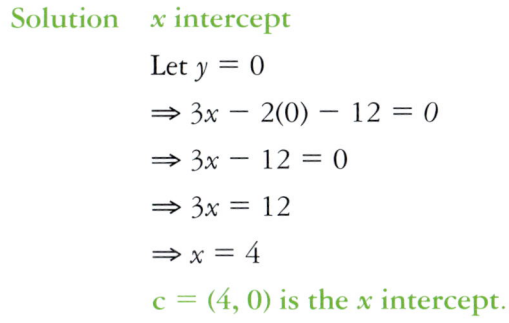

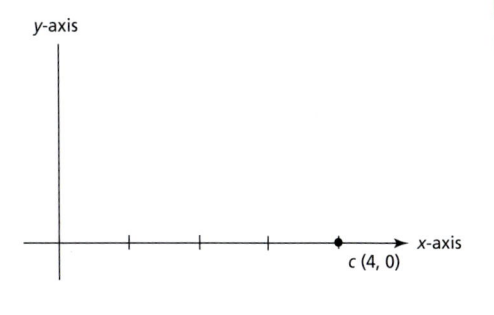

Solution x intercept

Let $y = 0$

$\Rightarrow 3x - 2(0) - 12 = 0$

$\Rightarrow 3x - 12 = 0$

$\Rightarrow 3x = 12$

$\Rightarrow x = 4$

$c = (4, 0)$ is the x intercept.

ii. The point $(k, 6)$ is on the line $3x - 2y - 12 = 0$. Find the value of k.

Solution Left-hand side: $3k - 2(6) - 12$ Right-hand side $= 0$

$= 3k - 12 - 12$

$= 3k - 24$ Let $3k - 24 = 0$

$\Rightarrow 3k = 24$

$\Rightarrow k = 8$

Formulae

Midpoint of a line segment: $\left(\dfrac{x_1 + x_2}{2}, \dfrac{y_1 + y_2}{2}\right)$

Slope of a line: $m = \dfrac{y_2 - y_1}{x_2 - x_1}$

Equation of a line $y - y_1 = m(x - x_1)$

Junior Certificate Examination 2005

Paper 2, Q5

5. (a) a is the point $(1, 2)$.

   b is the point $(-3, -2)$.

   Plot the points a and b.

   Solution

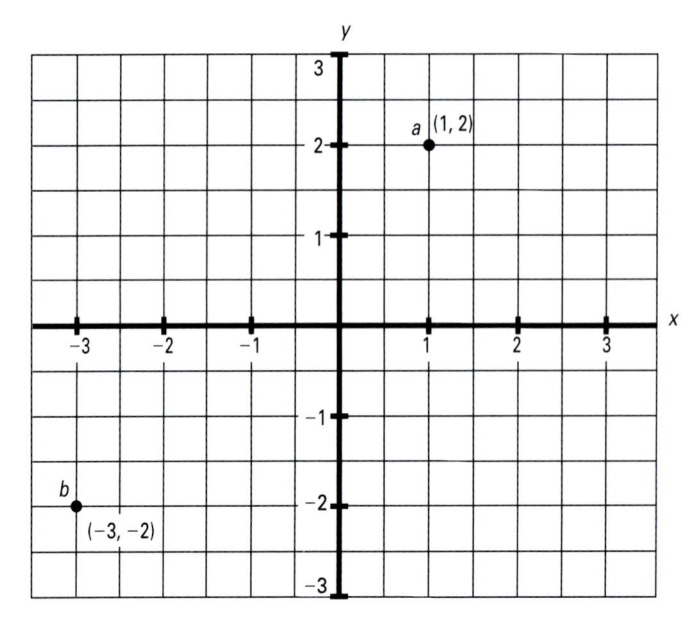

   (b) p is the point $(2, 1)$ and q is the point $(4, 3)$. Find each of the following:

   i. The length of $[pq]$.

   Solution $|pq| = \sqrt{(4-2)^2 + (3-1)^2}$
   $|pq| = \sqrt{2^2 + 2^2}$
   $= \sqrt{4 + 4}$
   $= \sqrt{8}$

   ii. The slope of pq.

   Solution   Slope $m = \dfrac{y_2 - y_1}{x_2 - x_1} = \dfrac{3-1}{4-2} = \dfrac{2}{2} = 1$

   iii. The equation of the line pq.

   Solution $y - y_1 = m(x - x_1)$
   $\Rightarrow y - 1 = 1(x - 2)$
   $\Rightarrow y - 1 = x - 2$
   $\Rightarrow 0 = x - y - 1$
   $\Rightarrow x - y - 1 = 0$

(c) L is the line $2x + 3y - 10 = 0$.

   i. L cuts the x-axis at the point c.

       By letting $y = 0$, find the co-ordinates of the point c.

       Solution   Let $y = 0$

$$\Rightarrow 2x - 10 = 0$$
$$\Rightarrow 2x = 10$$
$$\Rightarrow x = 5$$

Point $c = (5, 0)$

   ii. Show that the point $(8, -2)$ is on the line $L: 2x + 3y - 10 = 0$.

       Solution   Is $2(8) + 3(-2) - 10 = 0$?

Is $16 - 6 - 10 = 0$?

Is $16 - 16 = 0$?

Yes $\Rightarrow (8, -2)$ is on L.

   iii. The point $(k, 6)$ is on the line L. Find the value of k.

       Solution $2k + 3(6) - 10 = 0$

$$\Rightarrow 2k + 18 - 10 = 0$$
$$\Rightarrow 2k + 8 = 0$$
$$\Rightarrow 2k = -8$$
$$\Rightarrow k = -4$$

Formulae

Length of a line segment: $\sqrt{(x_2 - x_1)^2 + (y_2 - y_1)^2}$

Slope of a line: $m = \dfrac{y_2 - y_1}{x_2 - x_1}$

Equation of a line: $y - y_1 = m(x - x_1)$

CHAPTER 10
Trigonometry

Learning Objectives

- How to calculate the third side of a right-angled triangle when given two sides.
- Understand and learn the trigonometric ratios.
- Understand the use of the calculator in finding the sine, cosine and tangent of an angle.
- Understand how to calculate an angle in a right-angled triangle using the inverse sine, cosine and tangent functions on the calculator.
- Understand how to solve right-angled triangles.
- Be able to solve triangles that contain angles of elevation or angles of depression.

Right-angled triangles

A right-angled triangle has one angle of 90°. The other two angles combined give 90° because all three angles add up to 180°. In a right-angled triangle, the side opposite the 90° angle is called the **hypotenuse**. It is always the longest side. Pythagoras' Theorem states that the hypotenuse squared equals the sum of the squares on the two shorter sides.

So, provided we are given two out of the three sides, we can calculate the third side.

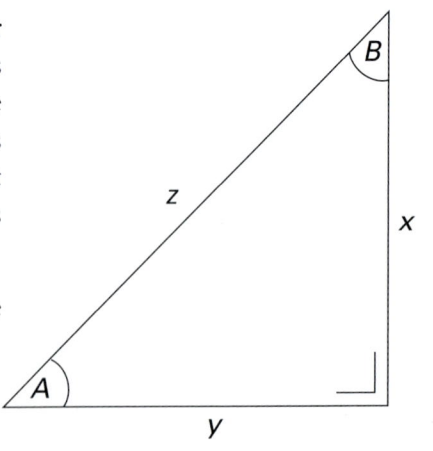

- $A + B = 90°$
- $x^2 + y^2 = z^2$

Example 1

Calculate the length of the hypotenuse in a right-angled triangle where the other two sides measure 3 cm and 4 cm.

Solution Draw diagram. Let $x = 4$ and $y = 3$. Calculate z.

Formula $z^2 = x^2 + y^2$
$z^2 = 4^2 + 3^2$
$z^2 = 16 + 9$
$z^2 = 25$
$z = 5$ cm
Length of hypotenuse = **5 cm**

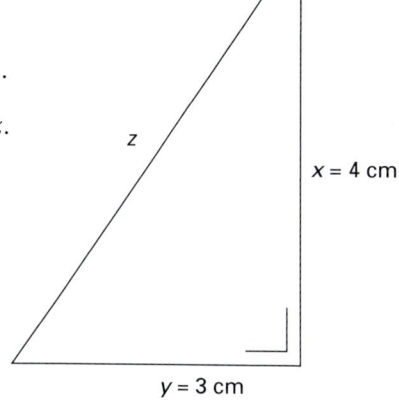

Example 2

In a right-angled triangle, the hypotenuse has a length of 13 cm. One of the shorter sides has a length of 12 cm. **Find** the length of the third side.

Solution Draw diagram. Let $z = 13$ cm and $y = 12$ cm. We want to find x.

Formula: $z^2 = x^2 + y^2$
$\Rightarrow 13^2 = x^2 + 12^2$
$\Rightarrow 169 = x^2 + 144$
$\Rightarrow x^2 = 25$
$\Rightarrow x = 5$
Length of third side is **5 cm**.

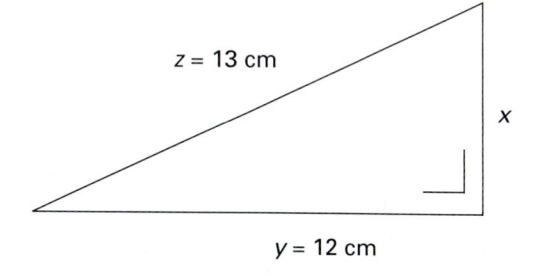

Top Tips

- The hypotenuse must be kept isolated on the left-hand side at the start.
- Sometimes the length of the unknown third side turns out not to be a whole number.
- Leave it either in $\sqrt{}$ form **or** use your calculator to give the answer to the required number of decimal places.

Example 3

In a right-angled triangle, the hypotenuse has a length of 7 cm, and one of the shorter sides has a length of 3 cm. **Find** the length of the third side (*a*) in $\sqrt{}$ form (*b*) correct to two decimal places.

Solution   Draw diagram. Let $x = 3$ cm and $z = 7$ cm. Let $y =$ unknown third side.

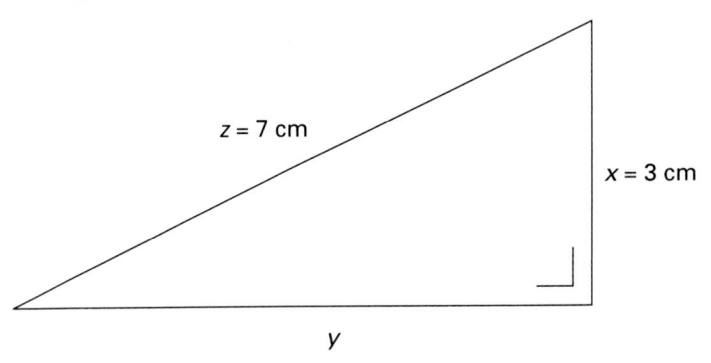

$z = 7$ cm

$x = 3$ cm

y

Formula $z^2 = x^2 + y^2$ Note that the hypotenuse is isolated.

$\Rightarrow 7^2 = 3^2 + y^2$

$\Rightarrow 49 = 9 + y^2$

$\Rightarrow y^2 = 40$ (*a*) $y = \sqrt{40}$ This is Surd form.

$\Rightarrow y = \sqrt{40}$ (*b*) $y \approx 6.32$ Done on a calculator.

$\boxed{\sqrt{}}\boxed{4}\boxed{0}\boxed{=}$

Top Tips

The symbol $\approx$ means 'is approximately equal to'.

Sides of a right-angled triangle

When we are dealing with the angle A, the names of the sides are as shown in the diagram.

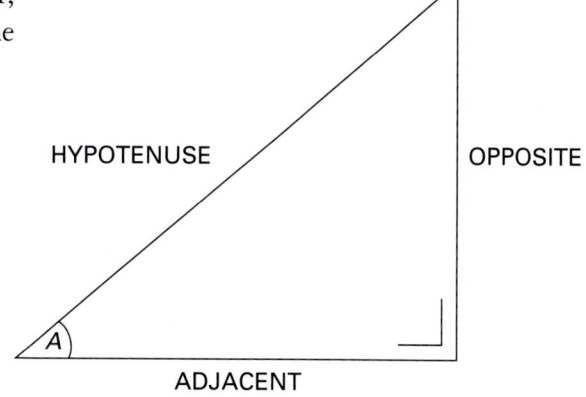

When we are dealing with the angle B, the opposite and adjacent sides are reversed.

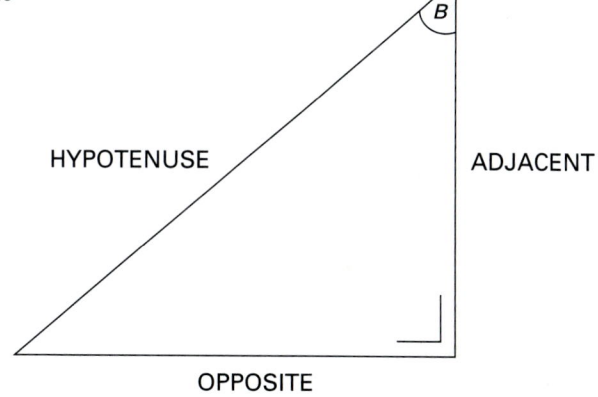

Trigonometric ratios

In the diagram, we specify angle A. This fixes the opposite and adjacent as shown.

Definitions

Sine $A = \dfrac{\text{opposite}}{\text{hypotenuse}}$

Cosine $A = \dfrac{\text{adjacent}}{\text{hypotenuse}}$

Tangent $A = \dfrac{\text{opposite}}{\text{adjacent}}$

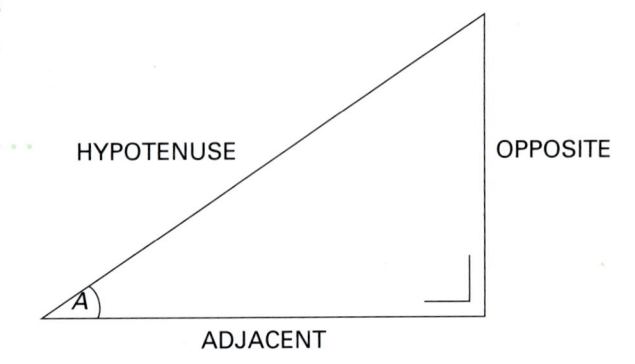

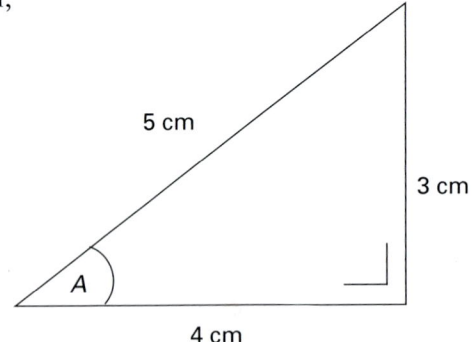

- These definitions must be memorised. Memory Aid: **O**h **H**ell, **A**nother **H**our **O**f **A**lgebra.

- These trigonometric functions are usually shortened to $\sin A$, $\cos A$, $\tan A$.

Example 1

In the diagram, **write down** the value of (*a*) $\sin A$ (*b*) $\cos A$ (*c*) $\tan A$ as fractions.

Solution From the position of angle A we see that
|opposite| = 3 cm, |adjacent| = 4 cm,
|hypotenuse| = 5 cm.

So, $\sin A = \dfrac{\text{opposite}}{\text{hypotenuse}} = \dfrac{3}{5}$

$\cos A = \dfrac{\text{adjacent}}{\text{hypotenuse}} = \dfrac{4}{5}$

$\tan A = \dfrac{\text{opposite}}{\text{adjacent}} = \dfrac{3}{4}$

Example 2

In the diagram, **evaluate** the length of the hypotenuse and hence **write down** as fractions the values of (*a*) sinA (*b*) cosA (*c*) tanA.

Solution Let z = hypotenuse length.
Pythagoras' Theorem: $z^2 = 8^2 + 15^2$
$\Rightarrow z^2 = 64 + 225$
$\Rightarrow z^2 = 289$
$\Rightarrow z = \sqrt{289}$
$\Rightarrow z = 17$

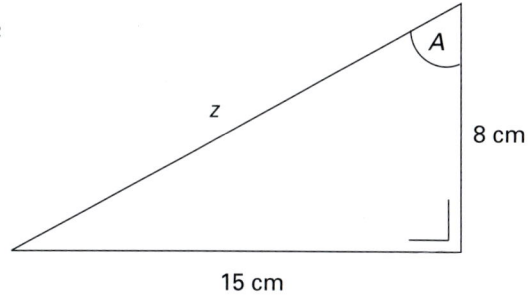

Updated diagram:

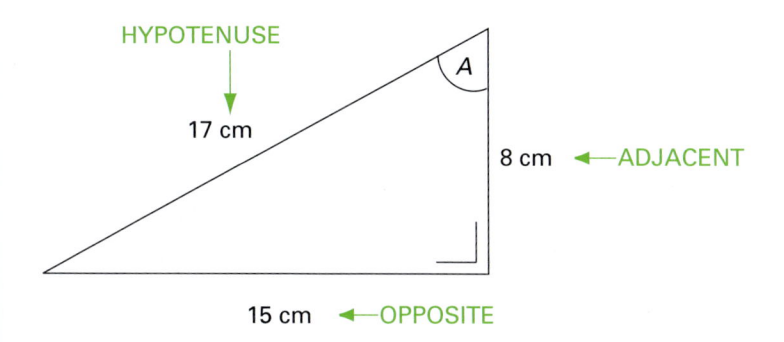

HYPOTENUSE
17 cm
8 cm ← ADJACENT
15 cm ← OPPOSITE

(*a*) $\sin A = \dfrac{\text{opposite}}{\text{hypotenuse}} = \dfrac{15}{17}$

(*b*) $\cos A = \dfrac{\text{adjacent}}{\text{hypotenuse}} = \dfrac{8}{17}$

(*c*) $\tan A = \dfrac{\text{opposite}}{\text{adjacent}} = \dfrac{15}{8}$

Self-test 1

1. In the following diagrams, write down (*a*) sin$A$ (*b*) cos$A$ (*c*) tan$A$ (*d*) sin$B$ (*e*) cos$B$ (*f*) tan$B$.

i.

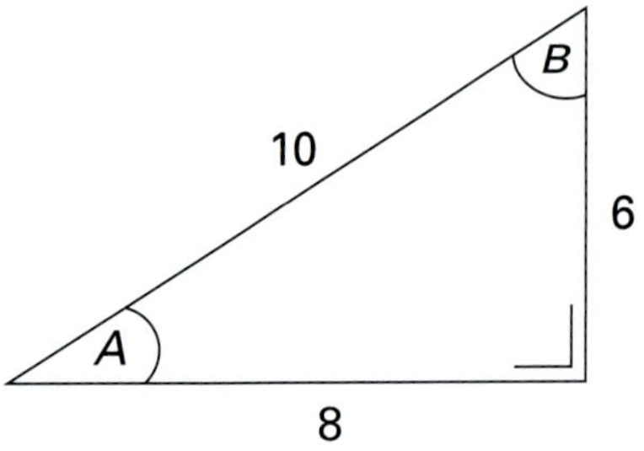

ii.

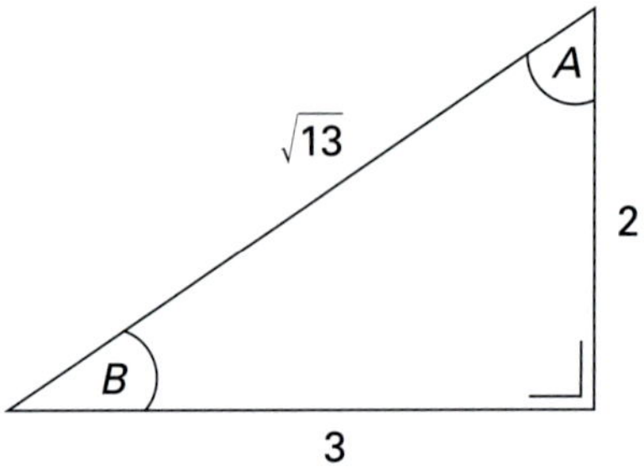

iii.

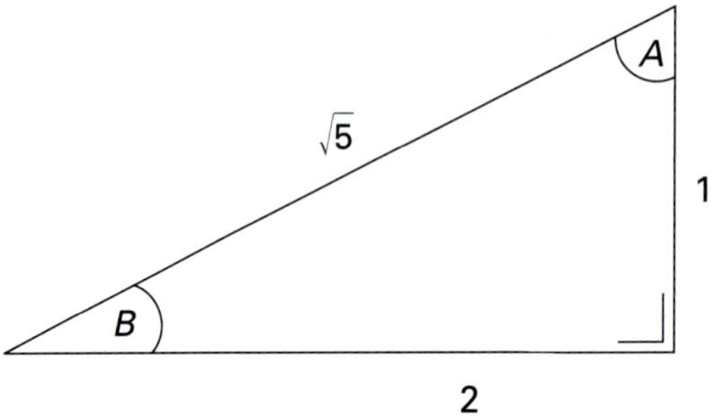

2. In the following diagrams, evaluate the missing side. You may leave your answer in Surd form where necessary. Then write down the trigonometric ratios (*a*) sin$A$ (*b*) cos$A$ (*c*) tan$A$ (*d*) sin$B$ (*e*) cos$B$ (*f*) tan$B$.

i.

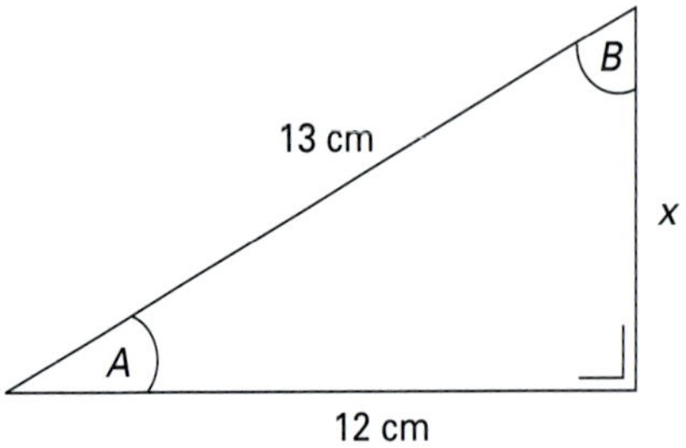

ii.

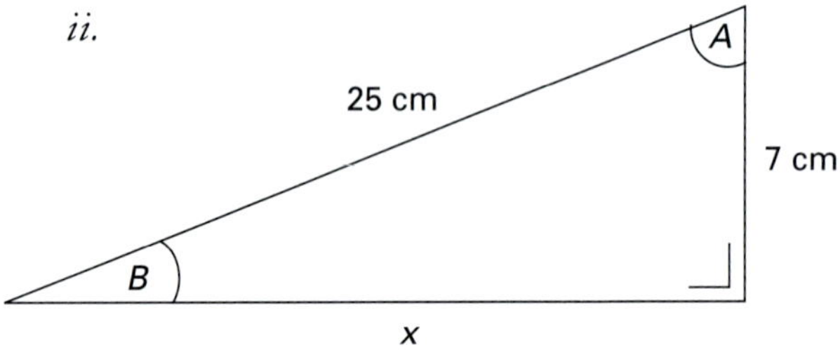

iii.

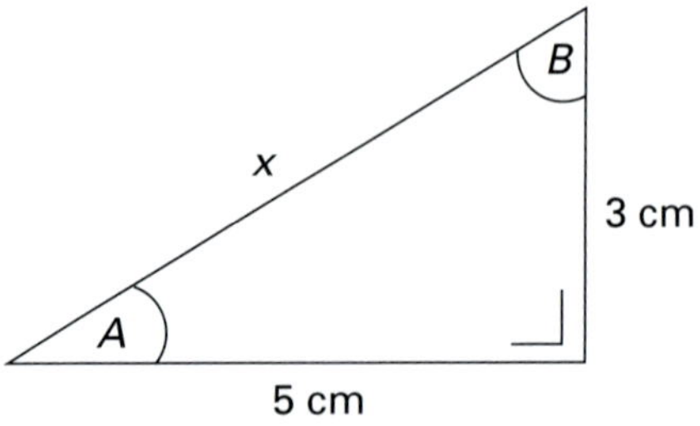

Use of calculator

When using the sine, cosine and tangent keys on the calculator, ensure that the DEG or D symbol appears on the screen. Press the DRG button to achieve this.

Example 1

Use your calculator to **find** (*a*) sin 73° (*b*) cos 47° (*c*) tan 25° correct to four decimal places.

Solution (*a*) Check that DEG appears on the screen. Press the following keys on the calculator:

$\boxed{\text{SIN}}\ \boxed{7}\ \boxed{3}\ \boxed{=}$

This gives 0.956304756 on the screen.

≈ 0.9563 correct to four decimal places.

(*b*) Press the following keys on the calculator: [DEG MODE]: $\boxed{\text{COS}}\ \boxed{4}\ \boxed{7}\ \boxed{=}$

This gives 0.68199836 on the screen.

≈ 0.6820 correct to four decimal places.

(*c*) Press the following keys on the calculator: $\boxed{\text{TAN}}\ \boxed{2}\ \boxed{5}\ \boxed{=}$

This gives 0.466307658 on the screen.

≈ 0.4663 correct to four decimal places.

Example 2

Find angles A and B in this triangle.

Solution Calculate A first.

Opposite = 3 cm

Hypotenuse = 6 cm.

Ensure calculator is in DEG mode.

So, $\sin A = \frac{3}{6}$

$\Rightarrow \sin A = 0.5$

$\Rightarrow A = \sin^{-1} 0.5$

$\Rightarrow A = 30°$

Finally, $B = 60°$ because $A + B = 90°$.

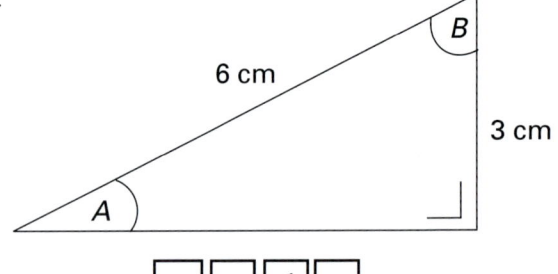

Calculator: $\boxed{3}\ \boxed{\div}\ \boxed{6}\ \boxed{=}$

Calculator: $\boxed{\text{INV}}\ \boxed{\text{SIN}}\ \boxed{0}\ \boxed{\cdot}\ \boxed{5}\ \boxed{=}$

Updated diagram:

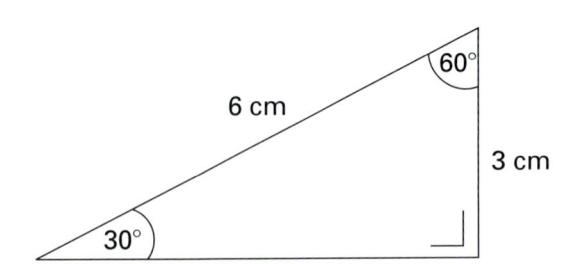

Example 3

Find to the nearest degree the measure of the two acute angles in the right-angled triangle whose two shorter sides are 3 cm and 4 cm.

Solution Draw diagram.

Position A in the bottom left corner.

Opposite = 3 cm

Adjacent = 4 cm

So, $\tan A = \frac{3}{4}$

$\Rightarrow \tan A = 0.75$

$\Rightarrow A = \tan^{-1} 0.75$

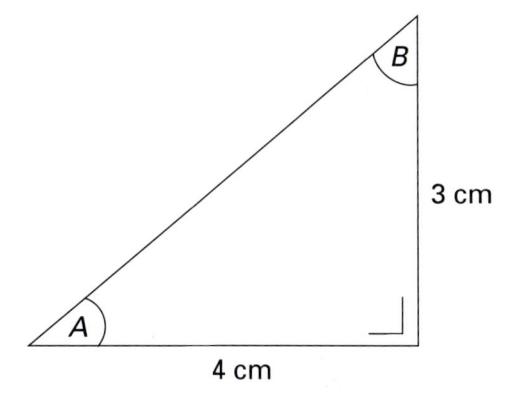

Use calculator:

| INV | TAN | 0 | . | 7 | 5 | = |

This gives 36.86989765 on the screen when the calculator is in DEG mode. It is sufficient to give the answer correct to the nearest degree.

So, $A \approx 37°$

Finally, $B = 90° - 37°$

$B = 53°$

Updated diagram:

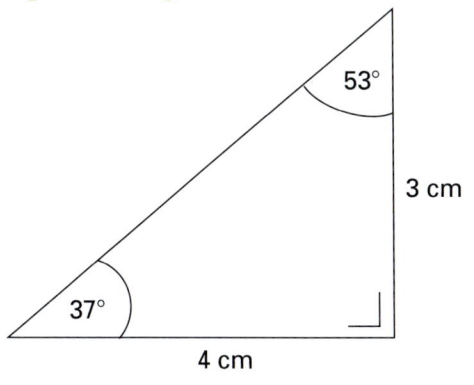

Solving right-angled triangles

When we solve a right-angled triangle, it is necessary to calculate the three unknown quantities from the three quantities we are given.

Example 1

We are given a triangle pqr in which $|\angle pqr| = 90°$, $|\angle qpr| = 40°$, $|pr| = 10$ cm.

Find (a) $|pq|$ (b) $|rq|$ (c) $|\angle prq|$.

Top Tips

- $\angle pqr$ is the angle at q.
- $\angle qpr$ is the angle at p.

Solution Draw diagram.

In dealing with the 40° angle, $[pq]$ is the **adjacent**, $[rq]$ is the **opposite**.

(a) $\cos 40° = \dfrac{|pq|}{10}$

$\Rightarrow 0.7660 = \dfrac{|pq|}{10}$

$\Rightarrow |pq| = 10(0.7660)$

$\Rightarrow |pq| = 7.66$ cm

(b) $\sin 40° = \dfrac{|rq|}{10}$

$\Rightarrow 0.6428 = \dfrac{|rq|}{10}$

$\Rightarrow |rq| = 10(0.6428)$

$\Rightarrow |rq| = 6.428$

(c) Finally, $|\angle prq| = 50°$

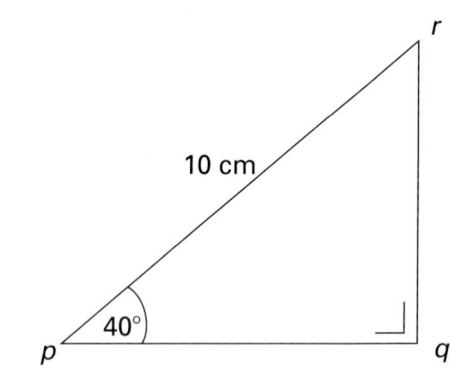

Updated diagram:

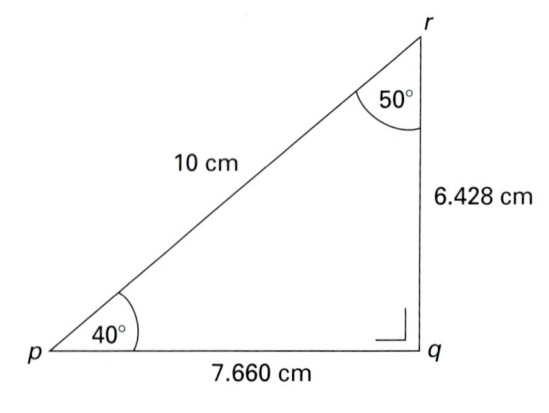

This triangle is now fully solved because we know all three sides and all three angles.

Example 2

Solve the triangle *abc* where $|\angle abc| = 90°$, $|\angle bac| = 55°$ and $|ab| = 18$ cm.

Solution Draw diagram.

We must find (*a*) $|\angle acb|$ (*b*) $|bc|$ (*c*) $|ac|$.

(*a*) $|\angle acb| = 90° - 55° = 35°$

(*b*) Use 55° angle.

   Opposite $= [bc]$

   |Adjacent| $= 18$ cm

   So, $\tan 55° = \dfrac{|bc|}{18}$

   $\Rightarrow 1.4281 = \dfrac{|bc|}{18}$

   $\Rightarrow |bc| = 18(1.4281)$

   $\Rightarrow |bc| = 25.7058$

   $\Rightarrow |bc| \approx 25.71$ correct to two decimal places

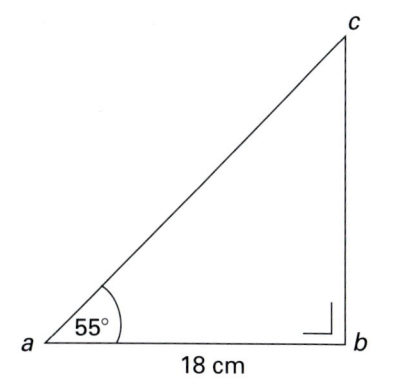

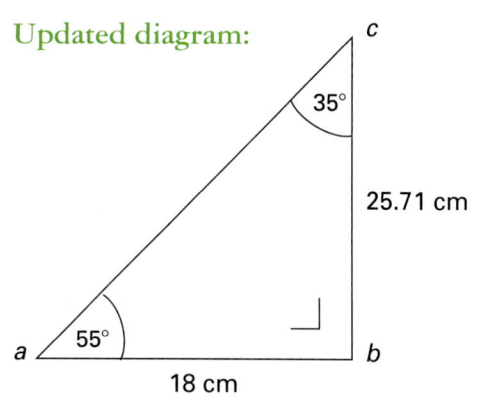

Updated diagram:

(*c*) Finally, we find $|ac|$. This is the hypotenuse of the triangle *abc*.

   |hypotenuse|² = |opposite|² + |adjacent|²

   $|ac|^2 = 25.71^2 + 18^2$ $\boxed{2}\boxed{5}\boxed{.}\boxed{7}\boxed{1}\boxed{x^2}\boxed{+}\boxed{1}\boxed{8}\boxed{x^2}\boxed{=}$

   $|ac|^2 = 661.0041 + 324$

   $|ac|^2 = 985.0041$

   $|ac| = \sqrt{985.0041}$ $\boxed{\sqrt{}}\boxed{9}\boxed{8}\boxed{5}\boxed{.}\boxed{0}\boxed{0}\boxed{4}\boxed{1}\boxed{=}$

   $|ac| = 31.38477497$

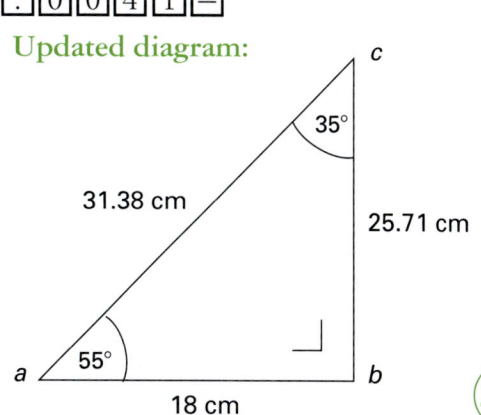

   $|ac| \approx 31.38$ cm correct to two decimal places

Updated diagram:

Self-test 2

1. **Find** correct to the nearest degree the angles A and B in the following diagrams.

   (a)

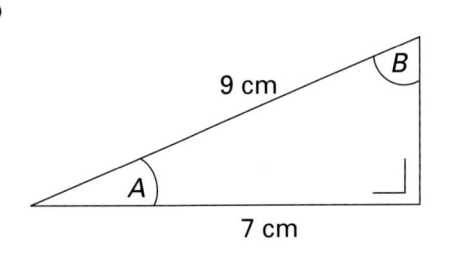

   (b)

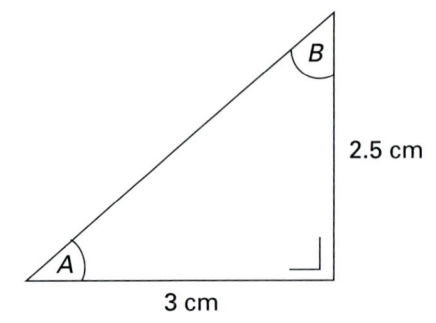

   (c)

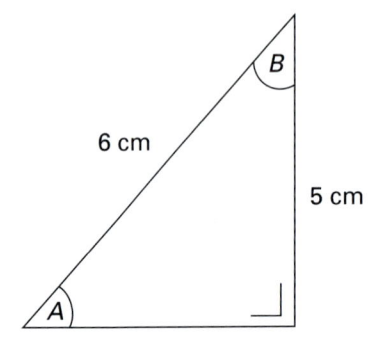

2. In the triangle xyz, $|\angle xzy| = 90°$, $|\angle xyz| = 50°$, $|xy| = 7$ cm. **Calculate** (a) $|\angle yxz|$ (b) $|xz|$ (c) $|yz|$ correct to two decimal places.

3. In the triangle pqr, $|\angle pqr| = 90°$, $|\angle qpr| = 34°$, $|pr| = 30$ cm. **Calculate** (a) $|\angle prq|$ (b) $|pq|$ (c) $|qr|$ correct to two decimal places.

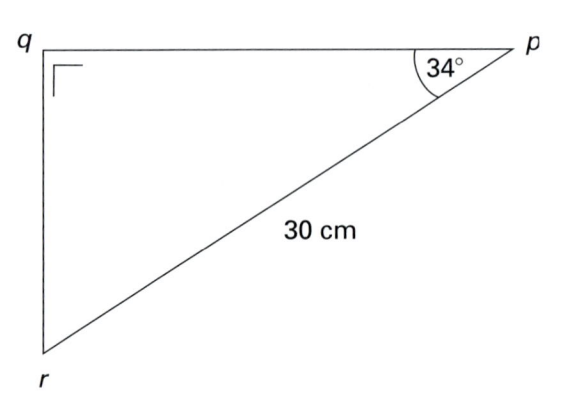

4. A vertical flagpole [pq] is 12 m high. It is supported by a cable [qr] as shown. If $|\angle qrp| = 30°$, find (a) $|\angle pqr|$ (b) $|pr|$, i.e. distance from foot of flagpole to cable (c) $|qr|$, i.e. length of cable.

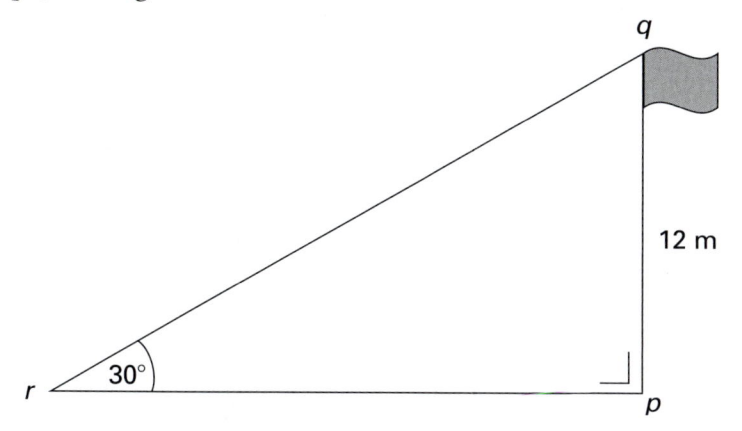

Angles of elevation and depression

- The angle of **elevation** is the angle which the line of vision makes with the horizontal when looking **upwards**.

- The angle of **depression** is the angle which the line of vision makes with the horizontal when looking **downwards**.

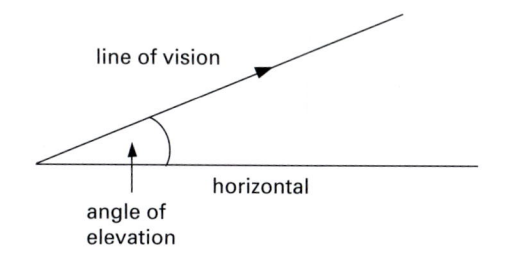

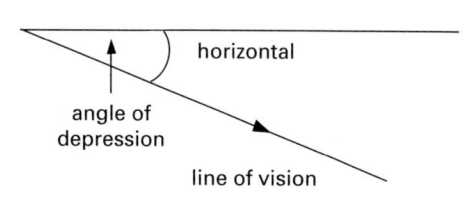

Example 1

When the angle of elevation of the sun is 37°, a building casts a shadow of length 15 m. Calculate the height of the building, correct to 3 decimal places.

Solution Draw diagram, including building and shadow. Position the angle of elevation in bottom left corner.

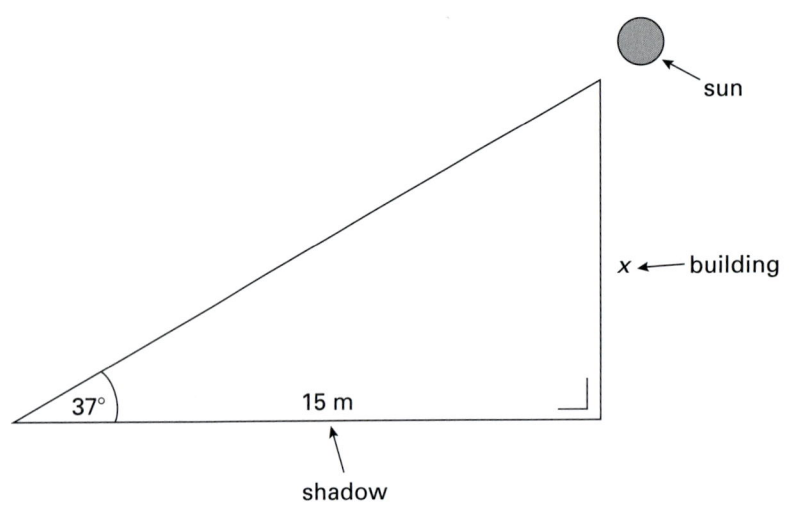

We want to find the height of the building x (opposite). We know the shadow length is 15 m (adjacent).

So, $\tan 37° = \frac{x}{15}$ Calculator: TAN 3 7 =

$\Rightarrow 0.75355405 = \frac{x}{15}$

$\Rightarrow x = 15(0.75355405)$

$\Rightarrow x \approx 11.303$ m

Example 2

From the top of a cliff, the angle of depression of a boat at sea is 28°. If the boat is 400 m from the foot of the cliff, **what is** the height of the cliff? Give your answer correct to two decimal places.

Solution   Draw diagram.

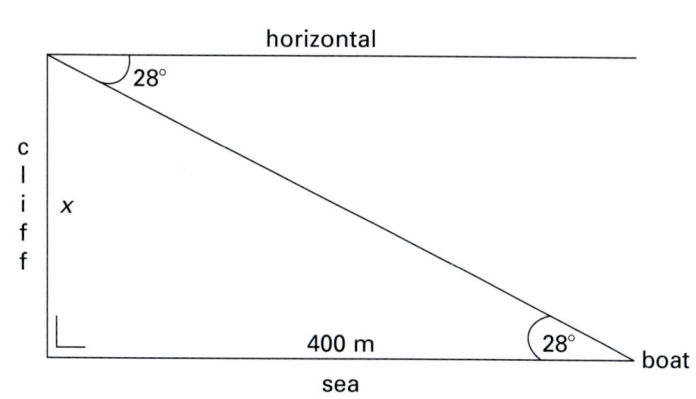

The 28° angle of depression can be transferred down to the angle where the boat is located, because these angles are **alternate**. See diagram.

Height of cliff = |opposite| = x
Distance from boat to foot of cliff = |adjacent| = 400 m
So, $\tan 28° = \dfrac{x}{400}$

$\Rightarrow 0.531709432 = \dfrac{x}{400}$

$\Rightarrow x = 400(0.531709432)$
$\Rightarrow x \approx 212.68$ m
Height of cliff = 212.68 m

Example 3

A vertical building 8 m high casts a shadow three times its height on horizontal ground.

(*a*) **Find** the length of the shadow.

(*b*) **Find** B, the angle of elevation of the sun, correct to the nearest degree.

Solution   (*a*) Length of shadow = 24 m

(*b*) $\tan B = \dfrac{8}{24}$

$\Rightarrow \tan B = 0.3333\ldots$

$\Rightarrow \quad B = \tan^{-1} 0.333\ldots$

$\Rightarrow \quad B \approx 18°$

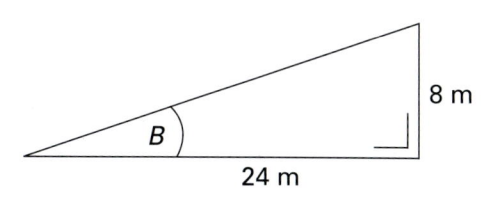

Self-test 3

1. **What is** the angle of elevation of the sun if a tree 10 m high casts a shadow 13 m long? Give your answer correct to the nearest degree.

2. From the top of a building, the angle of depression of a car in the street is 50°. If the car is parked 20 m from the foot of the building, **calculate** the height of the building correct to two decimal places.

3. An observer who is 30 m from the base of a TV mast on level ground makes an angle of elevation of 43° with the top of the mast. **Calculate** the height of the mast correct to the nearest metre.

4. An observer on top of a vertical cliff makes a 36° angle of depression when viewing a boat at sea. The straight line distance from the observer to the boat is 200 m. **Calculate** the height of the cliff correct to the nearest metre.

Self-test answers

Self-test 1

1. *i.* (a) $\sin A = \dfrac{6}{10} = \dfrac{3}{5}$ *ii.* (a) $\sin A = \dfrac{3}{13}$ *iii.* (a) $\sin A = \dfrac{2}{\sqrt{5}}$

   (b) $\cos A = \dfrac{8}{10} = \dfrac{4}{5}$ (b) $\cos A = \dfrac{2}{\sqrt{13}}$ (b) $\cos A = \dfrac{1}{\sqrt{5}}$

   (c) $\tan A = \dfrac{6}{8} = \dfrac{3}{4}$ (c) $\tan A = \dfrac{3}{2}$ (c) $\tan A = \dfrac{2}{1} = 2$

   (d) $\sin B = \dfrac{8}{10} = \dfrac{4}{5}$ (d) $\sin B = \dfrac{2}{\sqrt{13}}$ (d) $\sin B = \dfrac{1}{\sqrt{5}}$

   (e) $\cos B = \dfrac{6}{10} = \dfrac{3}{5}$ (e) $\cos B = \dfrac{3}{\sqrt{13}}$ (e) $\cos B = \dfrac{2}{\sqrt{5}}$

   (f) $\tan B = \dfrac{8}{6} = \dfrac{4}{3}$ (f) $\tan B = \dfrac{2}{3}$ (f) $\tan B = \dfrac{1}{2}$

2. *i.* $x = 5$ *ii.* $x = 24$ *iii.* $x = \sqrt{34}$

   (a) $\sin A = \dfrac{5}{13}$ (a) $\sin A = \dfrac{24}{25}$ (a) $\sin A = \dfrac{3}{\sqrt{34}}$

   (b) $\cos A = \dfrac{12}{13}$ (b) $\cos A = \dfrac{7}{25}$ (b) $\cos A = \dfrac{5}{\sqrt{34}}$

   (c) $\tan A = \dfrac{5}{12}$ (c) $\tan A = \dfrac{24}{7}$ (c) $\tan A = \dfrac{3}{5}$

   (d) $\sin B = \dfrac{12}{13}$ (d) $\sin B = \dfrac{7}{25}$ (d) $\sin B = \dfrac{5}{\sqrt{34}}$

   (e) $\cos B = \dfrac{5}{13}$ (e) $\cos B = \dfrac{24}{25}$ (e) $\cos B = \dfrac{3}{\sqrt{34}}$

   (f) $\tan B = \dfrac{12}{5}$ (f) $\tan B = \dfrac{7}{24}$ (f) $\tan B = \dfrac{5}{3}$

Self-test 2

1. (a) A = 39°; B = 51°   2. (a) 40°   3. (a) 56°   4. (a) 60°
   (b) A = 40°; B = 50°   (b) 5.36 cm   (b) 24.87 cm   (b) 20.78 cm
   (c) A = 56°; B = 34°   (c) 4.50 cm   (c) 16.78 cm   (c) 24.00 cm

Self-test 3

1. 38°
2. 23.84 m
3. 28 m
4. 118 m

Key Points

- In a right-angled triangle, the square on the hypotenuse equals the sum of the squares of the two shorter sides.

- $\sin A = \dfrac{\text{opposite}}{\text{hypotenuse}}$; $\cos A = \dfrac{\text{adjacent}}{\text{hypotenuse}}$; $\tan A = \dfrac{\text{opposite}}{\text{adjacent}}$.

- Three items of information out of six are required in order to fully solve a triangle.

- The angle of elevation is the angle which the line of vision makes with the horizontal when looking upwards.

- The angle of depression is the angle which the line of vision makes with the horizontal when looking downwards.

Junior Certificate Examination 2004

Paper 2, Q6

6. (a) The right-angled triangle abc has measurements as shown.

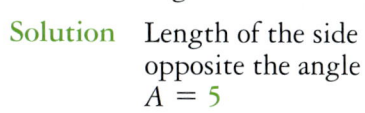

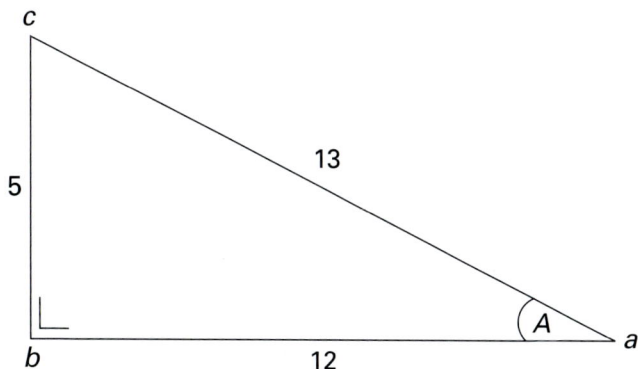

   i. Write down the length of the side opposite the angle A.

   Solution Length of the side opposite the angle $A = 5$

   ii. Write down the value of $\sin A$ as a fraction.

   Solution $\sin A = \dfrac{5}{13}$,

   i.e. $\dfrac{\text{opposite}}{\text{hypotenuse}}$

   (b) In the right-angled triangle pqr, $|pq| = 10$ and $|qr| = 4$.

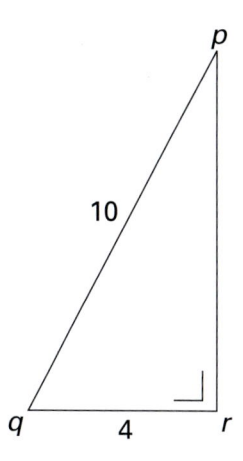

   i. Find the value of $\cos |\angle pqr|$.

   Solution $\cos |\angle pqr| = \dfrac{4}{10} = \dfrac{2}{5}$

   ii. Hence find the measure of $\angle pqr$, correct to the nearest degree.

   Solution $\cos \angle pqr = \dfrac{4}{10}$

   $\Rightarrow \cos |\angle pqr| = 0.4$

   $\Rightarrow |\angle pqr| = \cos^{-1} 0.4$

   $\Rightarrow |\angle pqr| \approx 66°$

   (c) An aeroplane leaves the ground at an angle of 20° to the runway. Its speed is 28 m/sec.

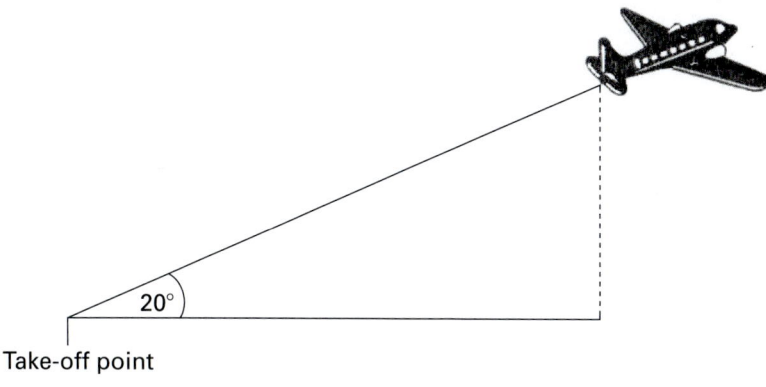

i. How far does the aeroplane travel in the first 30 seconds?

   Solution   28 m × 30

   = 840 m

ii. What is its height above the ground after the first 30 seconds? Write your answer to the nearest metre.

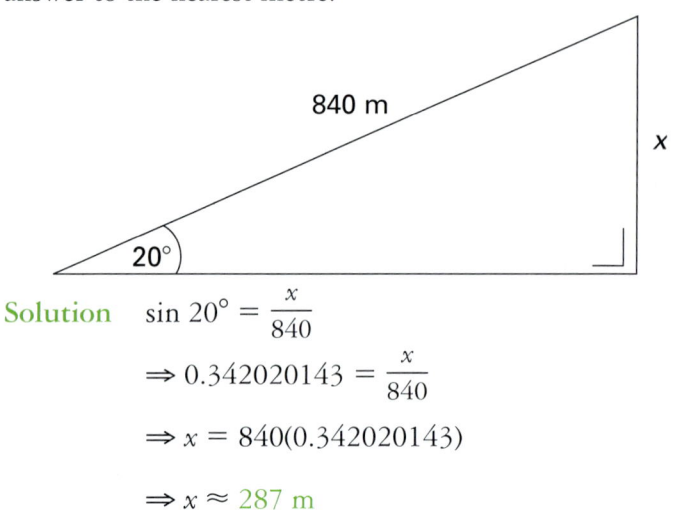

Solution $\sin 20° = \dfrac{x}{840}$

$\Rightarrow 0.342020143 = \dfrac{x}{840}$

$\Rightarrow x = 840(0.342020143)$

$\Rightarrow x \approx 287$ m

Junior Certificate 2005

Paper 2, Q6

6. (a) The right-angled triangle *abc* has measurements as shown.

   i. Write down the length of the side adjacent to the angle *A*.

   Solution   Length of the side adjacent to the angle *A* = 15

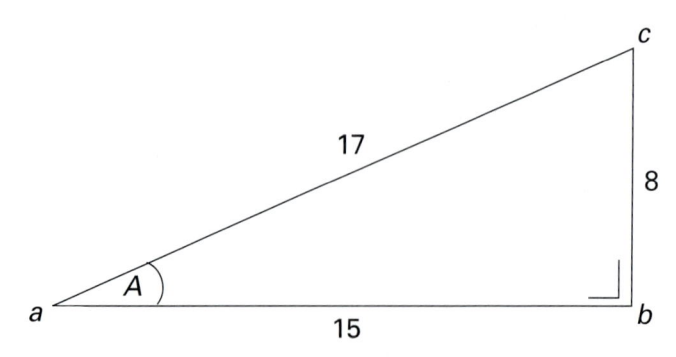

   ii. Write down the value of cos*A*, as a fraction.

   Solution $\cos A = \dfrac{15}{17}$

(b) In the right-angled triangle pqr, $|pq| = 12$ and $|\angle pqr| = 37°$. Let $x = |pr|$.

   i. Using the diagram, write down the value of $\sin 37°$, as a fraction.

   Solution $\sin 37° = \dfrac{x}{12}$

   ii. Using your calculator, write down the value of $\sin 37°$, correct to one decimal place.

   Solution $\sin 37° \approx 0.6$

   iii. Hence find x, the value of $|pr|$.

   Solution $\dfrac{x}{12} = 0.6$
   $x = 7.2$

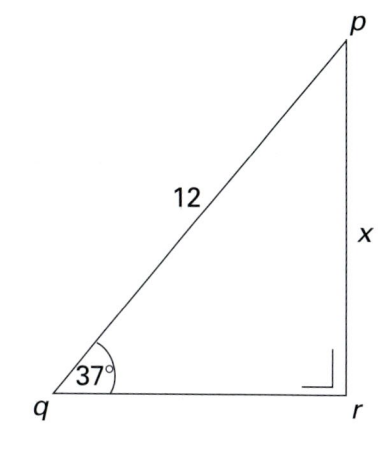

(c) Ciara wished to measure the width of a river. She was at point a on the riverbank, directly opposite b on the other bank. Ciara walked from a to c, along the riverbank, at an average speed of 1.5 m/s. It took Ciara 30 seconds to reach c. She then measured $\angle acb$ and found it to be $25°$.

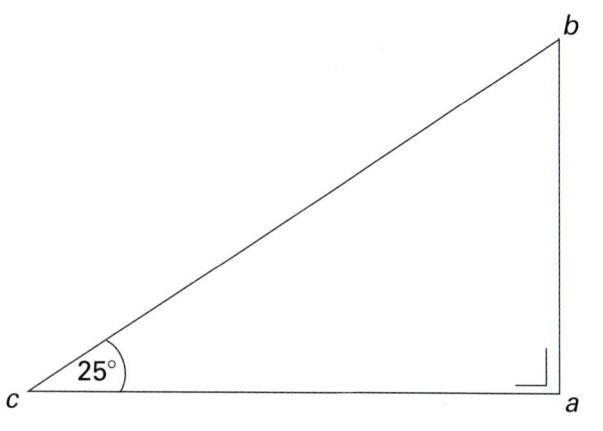

   i. Calculate $|ac|$, the distance walked by Ciara.

   Solution $|ac| = 1.5 \times 30$
   $= 45$ m

   ii. Hence, calculate $|ab|$, the width of the river. Give your answer correct to the nearest metre.

   Solution $\tan 25° = \dfrac{|ab|}{45}$

   $0.4663 = \dfrac{|ab|}{45}$
   $|ab| = 0.4663 \times 45$
   $|ab| = 20.9835$
   $|ab| \approx 21$ m

CHAPTER 11
Statistics

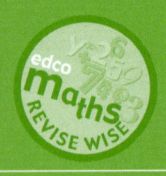

Learning Objectives

- Interpret a bar chart.
- Construct a bar chart given information in a table.
- Interpret a trend graph.
- Construct a trend graph given information in a table.
- Interpret a pie chart.
- Construct a pie chart from information given in tabular form.
- Calculate the mean (average) from a short list of numbers.
- Logically tabulate data given a long list of random numbers (frequency table).
- Find the mean from the tabulated data.
- Determine the mode either from a list or from a frequency table.

Bar charts

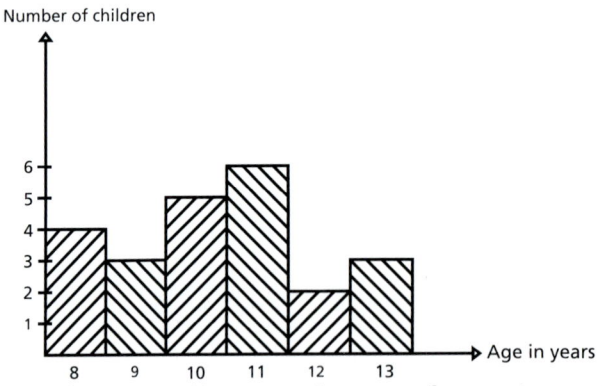

In the diagram, a vertical bar chart illustrates the ages of a certain number of children in a primary school. The heights of the bars show the numbers of children in each category. We can summarise the six pieces of information in a **frequency table.**

Age in years	8	9	10	11	12	13
No. of children in school	4	3	5	6	2	3

CHAPTER 11: STATISTICS

Top Tips

- The horizontal axis corresponds to the first row in the frequency table.
- The vertical axis corresponds to the second row in the frequency table.
- Both axes must be clearly labelled.
- Adding the numbers in the second row gives the total number of children in the school: $4 + 3 + 5 + 6 + 2 + 3 = 23$.

Example 1

Draw a vertical bar chart to illustrate the information in the following frequency table.

Shoe size (European measures)	40	41	42	43	44	45
Number of people	3	4	8	10	9	6

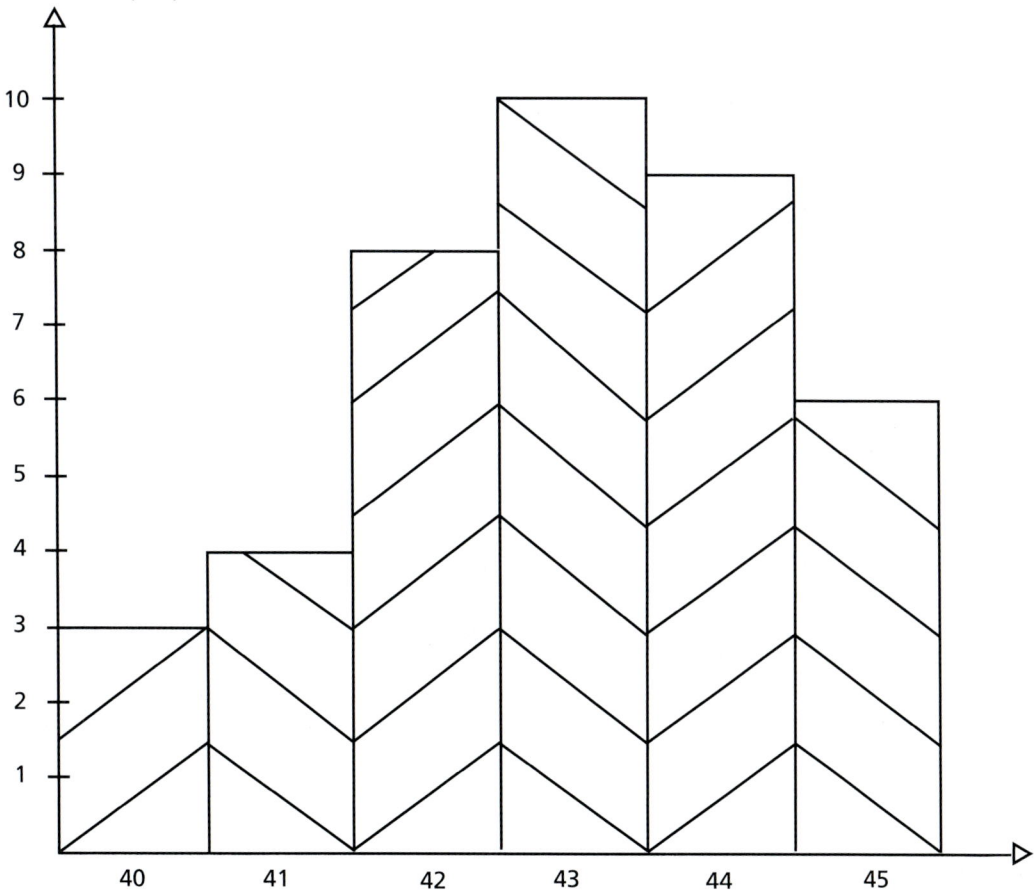

Solution

Top Tips

- Shoe size is labelled on the horizontal axis.
- Number of people is labelled on the vertical axis.
- All six bar widths are equal (2 cm in this case).
- Shoe sizes are written under the bars.
- Equal intervals of 1 cm on vertical axis.

Trend graphs

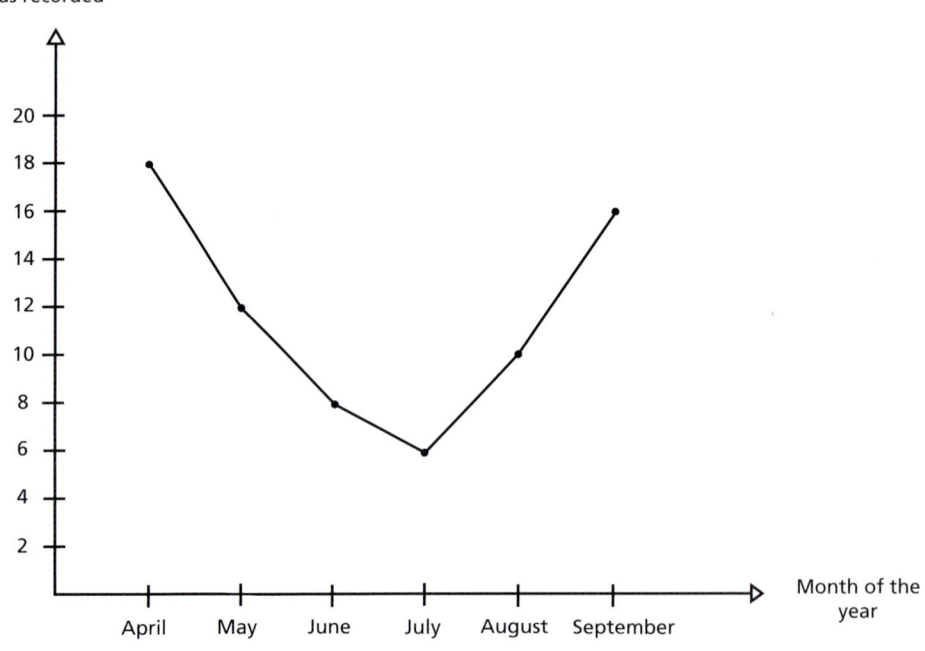

The diagram shows an example of a trend graph, illustrating the number of days on which rainfall was recorded in a certain month over a period of six months between April and September. The information can be summarised on a frequency table.

Month	Apr	May	Jun	Jul	Aug	Sept
Number of days with rain	18	12	8	6	10	16

CHAPTER 11: STATISTICS

> **Top Tips**
>
> - The total number of days with rain can be calculated by adding the numbers in the second row: $18 + 12 + 8 + 6 + 10 + 16 = 70$ days.
>
> - In general, trend graphs have periods of time (days, months, years, etc.) **equally spaced** on the horizontal axis.
>
> - The time on the horizontal axis corresponds to the first row on the frequency table.
>
> - The 'days with rain' are **equally spaced** on the vertical axis.

Example 1

The frequency table shows the number of mobile phones sold by a shop over a seven-year period between 1998 and 2004.

Year	1998	1999	2000	2001	2002	2003	2004
No. of mobile phones sold	100	150	200	300	350	500	450

Draw a trend graph to illustrate the information. How many mobile phones in total were sold in the seven years?

Solution

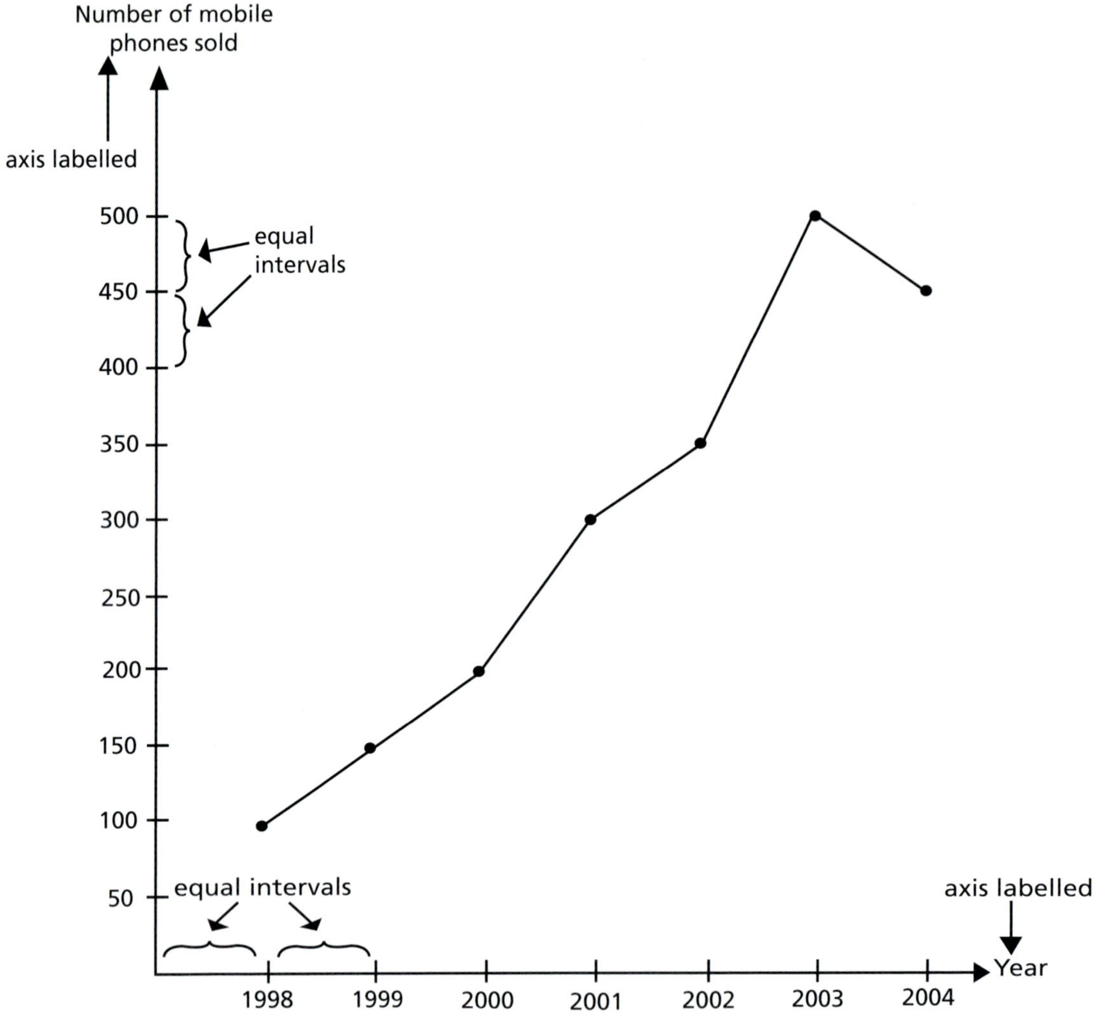

Number of mobile phones sold
axis labelled
500
450
400
350
300
250
200
150
100
50
equal intervals
equal intervals
axis labelled
Year
1998
1999
2000
2001
2002
2003
2004

Top Tips

- There were 2050 mobile phones sold in total over the seven years (100 + 150 + 200 + 300 + 350 + 500 + 450).
- The years are shown clearly at 1.5 cm intervals along the horizontal axis.
- The horizontal axis is clearly labelled 'Year'.
- Because the numbers involved are large, we choose 50-unit intervals along the vertical axis, 1 cm apart.
- The seven points are plotted and are joined by line segments from left to right, taking care not to omit any points.

Self-test 1

1. (a) **Fill out** the frequency table from the information on the bar chart.
   (b) **How many** students took the test?

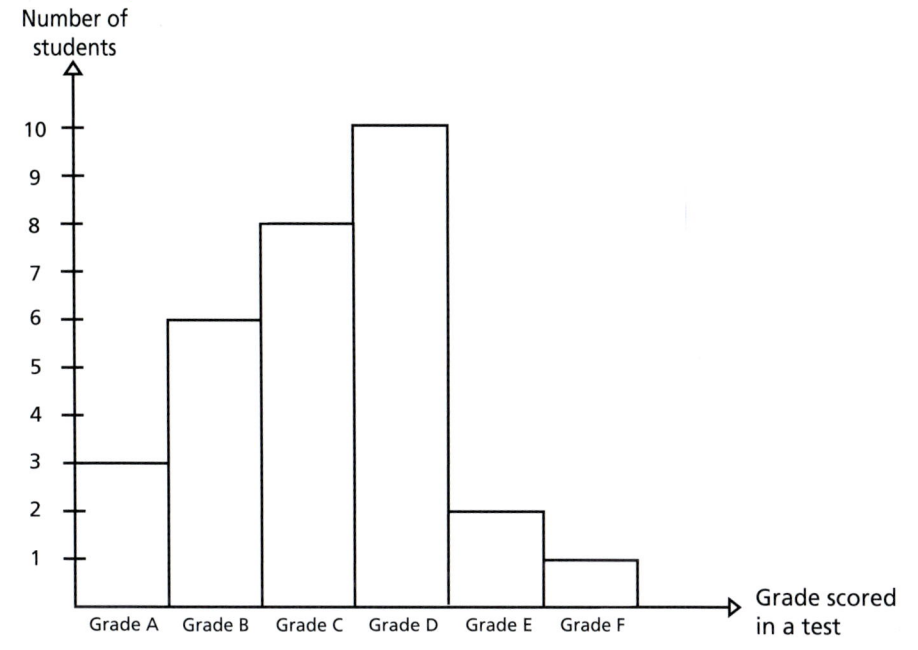

Grade scored	A	B	C	D	E	F
Number of students						

2. **Draw** a bar chart based on the information in this frequency table, which shows the number of goals scored in 30 matches.

Goals scored	0	1	2	3	4
Number of matches	7	9	8	4	2

   (a) **How many** matches could have been draws?
   (b) **How many** matches were definitely draws?

3. The trend graph shows the temperature in °C for a period of twelve hours in two-hourly intervals.

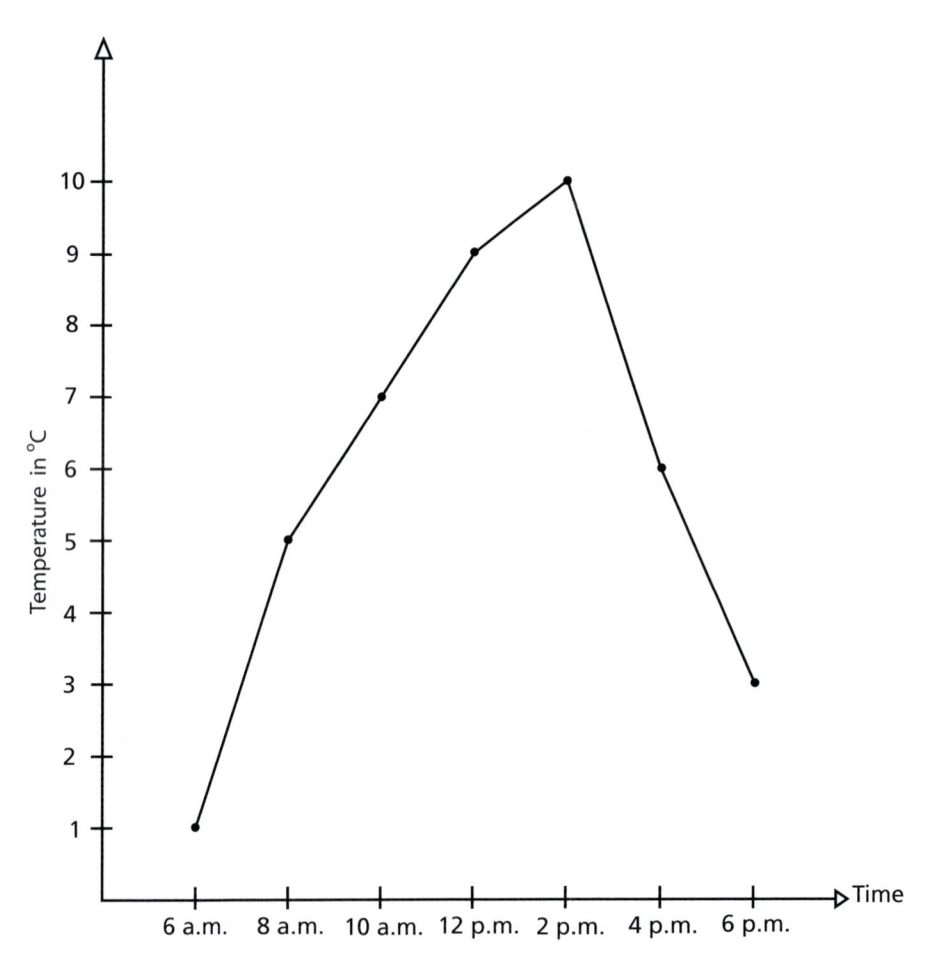

(a) **Fill in** the frequency table based on the information in the trend graph.

Time	6 a.m.	8 a.m.	10 a.m.	12 p.m.	2 p.m.	4 p.m.	6 p.m.
Temperature (°C)							

(b) **What time** is the highest temperature recorded at?

(c) **What is** the highest recorded temperature?

4. The frequency table shows the amount of money spent by a student over a seven-day period between Monday and Sunday.

Day of the week	Monday	Tuesday	Wednesday	Thursday	Friday	Saturday	Sunday
Amount spent	€10	€15	€15	€20	€30	€35	€20

(a) **Draw** a trend graph to illustrate this information.

(b) **What was** the student's total spending for the week?

Pie charts

Equipment needed: Compass, protractor, ruler.

- A pie chart is a circle divided up into sectors of different sizes.
- The size of the sector is dependent upon the quantity being represented.
- The entire circle has 360° at its centre. A half share has 180°. A quarter share has 90° and so on.

Example 1

120 people are asked to choose their favourite colour from red, blue, green or yellow. The results are shown on the following table.

Favourite colour	Red	Blue	Green	Yellow
Number of people	20	50	40	10

Draw a pie chart to illustrate the information.

Solution
- 120 people is represented by 360°.
- 1 person is represented by 3°, i.e. $\frac{360}{120}$.
- Red category: 20 people is represented by 60° (3° × 20).
- Blue category: 50 people is represented by 150° (3° × 50).
- Green category: 40 people is represented by 120° (3° × 40).
- Yellow category: 10 people is represented by 30° (3° × 10).
- Radius = 3 cm

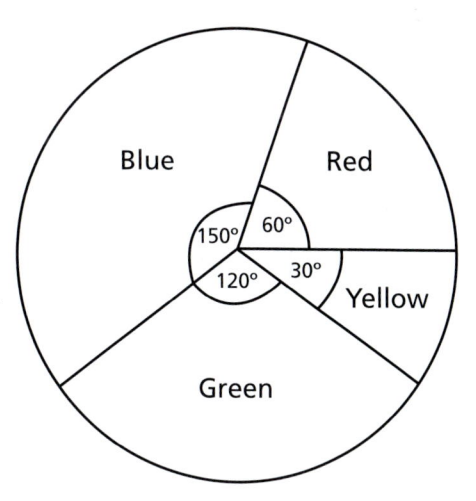

Top Tips

- The circle needs to be a reasonable size in order to write the information in the sectors.
- A horizontal radius should be drawn to use as a base for the first angle.
- Angles and categories must be written into sectors.

Example 2

In a particular six-week billing period, a person makes 200 telephone calls. The pie chart shows the proportion of different types of call made.

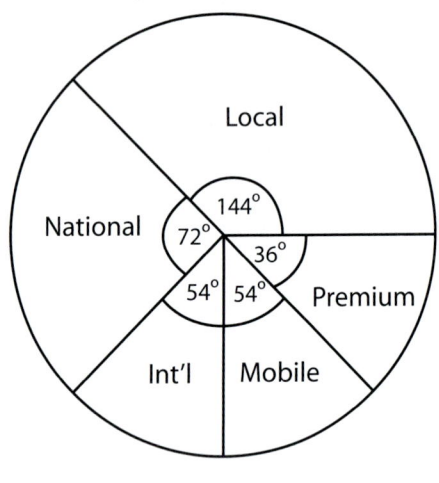

(a) **Draw** a frequency table to find out how many calls are in each category.

(b) **What percentage** of the calls were international?

(c) **What percentage** of the calls were local?

Solution (a) Calculations

$\dfrac{144}{360} \times 200 = 80$ local calls $\qquad$ $\dfrac{54}{360} \times 200 = 30$ mobile calls

$\dfrac{72}{360} \times 200 = 40$ national calls $\qquad$ $\dfrac{36}{360} \times 200 = 20$ premium calls

$\dfrac{54}{360} \times 200 = 30$ international calls

Type of call	Local	National	International	Mobile	Premium
Number of calls	80	40	30	30	20

(b) Percentage of international calls $= \dfrac{30}{200} \times \dfrac{100}{1} = 15\%$

(c) Percentage of local calls $= \dfrac{80}{200} \times \dfrac{100}{1} = 40\%$

Self-test 2

1. 180 people were surveyed about their favourite sport. The results are shown on the frequency table. **Draw** a pie chart to illustrate this information.

Favourite sport	Gaelic Football	Soccer	Hurling	Rugby	Athletics
Number of people	60	50	30	25	15

2. This pie chart represents 90 people. The sectors show where they travelled on holiday last summer. **Draw** a frequency table to show the number of people who travelled to each destination based on the angles in the sectors. (Note that you must work out the angle in the 'France' sector.)

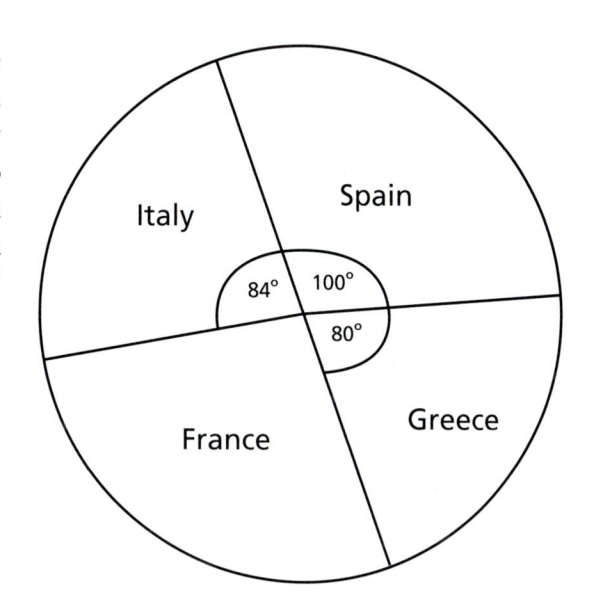

Mean and mode

- To get the **mean** (average) of a list of numbers, you must add the numbers and divide by the number of numbers in the list.

- The **mode** is the number in a list of numbers which occurs most frequently.

Example 1

Find the mean and mode of the list of numbers: 4, 3, 7, 6, 4, 5, 3, 4, 8, 6.

Solution   Mean = $\frac{4 + 3 + 7 + 6 + 4 + 5 + 3 + 4 + 8 + 6}{10} = \frac{50}{10} = 5$.

Mode = 4, because this is the number which occurs most frequently.

Top Tips

- When a list of numbers is long, it is helpful to make a frequency table before calculating the mean, particularly if the numbers in the list recur.

Example 2

In an apartment block containing 40 apartments, it was found that the number of people living in each apartment was as follows:

1,	3,	2,	4,	5,	3,	2,	1,	1,	5
2,	2,	3,	1,	1,	4,	1,	3,	1,	2
1,	3,	4,	2,	4,	3,	2,	1,	3,	1
5,	4,	1,	3,	1,	2,	5,	4,	1,	3

(a) **Draw** a frequency table to represent this information. (b) **Find** the mean number of people per apartment. (c) **Find** the modal number of people per apartment.

Solution (a)

No. of people per apartment	1	2	3	4	5
No. of apartments	13	8	9	6	4

(b) Mean number of people per apartment = $\dfrac{\text{total number of people}}{\text{number of apartments}}$

$= \dfrac{13 + 16 + 27 + 24 + 20}{40}$ ← Multiply first row by second row and add

$= \dfrac{100}{40}$

$= 2.5$ people

(c) Mode = 1 person because this number appears 13 times (the most frequent number in the list).

Example 3

A car maintenance garage serviced 50 cars in a certain week. The engine size of each car was recorded. The results in litres were as follows:

1.0, 1.2, 1.4, 2.0, 1.2, 1.0, 2.4, 2.2, 1.2, 1.4
1.8, 1.0, 1.4, 1.2, 1.0, 1.6, 2.2, 1.4, 1.8, 1.6
1.4, 2.0, 1.0, 1.6, 1.8, 1.0, 1.6, 1.2, 1.4, 1.0
1.2, 1.6, 1.4, 1.2, 1.0, 1.4, 1.2, 1.0, 1.6, 1.2
1.6, 1.4, 1.8, 1.0, 1.6, 1.0, 1.4, 1.2, 1.0, 1.2

(a) **Represent** the information on a frequency distribution table.
(b) **Calculate** the mean (average) engine size.
(c) **What is** the modal engine size?
(d) **What percentage** of the cars had an engine size of 1.6 litres or less?

Solution (a)

Engine size (litres)	1.0	1.2	1.4	1.6	1.8	2.0	2.2	2.4
Number of cars	12	11	10	8	4	2	2	1

(b) Mean engine size per car = $\dfrac{\text{total engine size of all the cars combined}}{\text{number of cars}}$

$= \dfrac{12 + 13.2 + 14 + 12.8 + 7.2 + 4.0 + 4.4 + 2.4}{50}$

$= \dfrac{70}{50} = 1.4l$

(c) Modal engine size = $1.0l$ because there were 12 of these cars.

(d) Percentage of cars whose engine size was $1.6l$ or less = $\dfrac{41}{\underset{1}{50}} \times \dfrac{\overset{2}{100}}{1} = 82\%$

Example 4

The table shows the number of hours of sunshine recorded at a weather station over a period of four weeks.

Week	Week 1	Week 2	Week 3	Week 4
No. of hours of sunshine	20	25	17	14

(a) **Find** the average number of hours of sunshine per week.

(b) If the number of hours for Week 5 is included, the average number of hours of sunshine per week increases to 21 hours. **How many** hours of sunshine were there in Week 5?

Solution (a) Average number of sunshine hours per week:

$$\bar{x} = \frac{20 + 25 + 17 + 14}{4} = \frac{76}{4} = 19 \text{ hours}$$

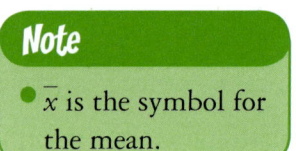

Note
- $\bar{x}$ is the symbol for the mean.

(b) If the average for the five weeks is 21 hours per week, then the total amount of sunshine must have been 105 hours (21 × 5).

But there were 76 hours in the first four weeks, so Week 5 must have had (105 − 76 hours) = **29 hours**.

Self-test 3

1. **Find** the mean and the mode of each of the following lists.
   (a) 2, 5, 4, 9, 5,
   (b) 3, 6, 4, 6, 6, 11
   (c) 0.3, 0.8, 0.5, 0.6, 0.6, 0.6, 0.1

2. The mean of five numbers is 16. When one extra number is added, the mean increases to 17. **Find** the sixth number.

3. The ages of 22 players on a soccer pitch are recorded randomly, as follows.

Team 1	14	15	16	14	15	16	16	13	14	15	17
Team 2	18	16	17	15	15	14	14	16	17	18	16

(a) **Draw** a frequency distribution table for Team 1. What is the mean age for Team 1?
(b) **Draw** a frequency distribution table for Team 2. What is the mean age for Team 2?
(c) **Draw** a frequency distribution table for both teams. What is the mean age of the 22 players? What is the mode?

Self-test answers

Self-test 1

1. (a) A = 3; B = 6; C = 8; D = 10; E = 2; F = 1.
   (b) 30 students
2. (a) 17
   (b) 7
3. (a) 1°, 5°, 7°, 9°, 10°, 6°, 3°
   (b) 2 p.m.
   (c) 10°
4. (b) €145

Self-test 2

2. Spain = 25 people
   France = 24 people
   Italy = 21 people
   Greece = 20 people

Self-test 3

1. (a) mean = 5; mode = 5
   (b) mean = 6; mode = 6
   (c) mean = 0.5; mode = 0.6
2. 22
3. (a) mean = 15
   (b) mean = 16
   (c) mean = $15\frac{1}{2}$, mode = 16

Key Points

- Vertical and horizontal axes must be labelled in bar charts. The bars must all be the same width.

- In trend graphs, the time period appears at equal intervals on the horizontal axis. Vertical and horizontal axes must be clearly labelled.

- In pie charts, the angle must be written in the sector. The category corresponding to the angle must be written in the sector.

- The mean (average) of a list of numbers is obtained by adding the numbers and dividing by the total number of numbers.

- The mode of a list of numbers is the number which arises most frequently.

- When a list of numbers is big, make a frequency table first before evaluating the mean.

Junior Certificate Examination 2004

Paper 2, Q3

3. (a) Find the mode of the numbers 10, 8, 12, 5, 10, 12, 10, 18.

   Solution   Mode = 10

   (b) All students in a certain class sat a test. The grades that they obtained in the test are shown in the following bar chart.

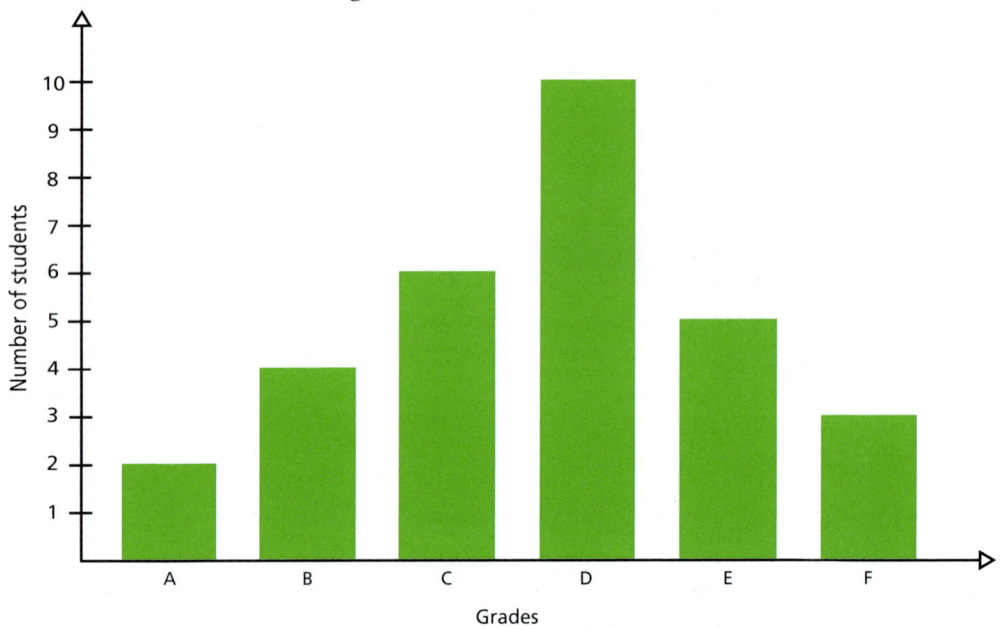

   i. How many students were in the class?

   Solution $2 + 4 + 6 + 10 + 5 + 3 = 30$

   ii. How many students achieved a grade lower than a grade D?

   Solution   8 got E or F.

   iii. Express the number of students who achieved a grade A or a grade B as a percentage of the total number of students in the class.

   Solution $\dfrac{6}{30} \times \dfrac{100}{1} \%$

   $= 20\%$

(c) The table shows the number of CDs sold per day in a shop from Monday to Friday of a particular week.

Day	Monday	Tuesday	Wednesday	Thursday	Friday
No. of CDs sold	25	20	50	35	50

i. Draw a trend graph of the data, putting the days on the horizontal axis.

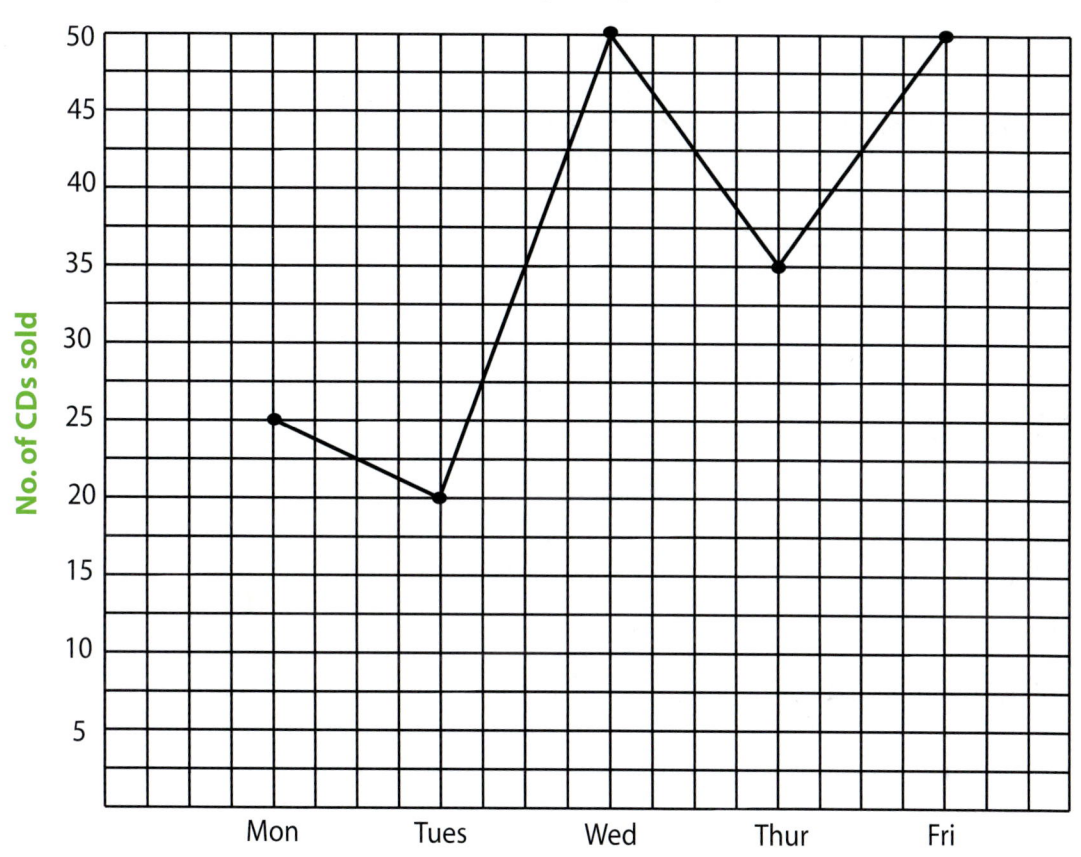

ii. Calculate the mean number of CDs sold per day from Monday to Friday.

Solution Mean $= \dfrac{25 + 20 + 50 + 35 + 50}{5}$

$= \dfrac{180}{5} = 36$ discs

iii. The shop was also open on the Saturday of that particular week. The mean number of CDs sold per day from Monday to Saturday was 40. Calculate the number of CDs sold on that Saturday.

Solution Total for 6 days $= 40 \times 6$
$= 240$
Number sold on Saturday $= 240 - 180$
$= 60$ discs

Junior Certificate Examination 2005

Paper 2, Q3

3. (a) Find the mean of the numbers: 4, 6, 7, 12, 16.

   Solution   Mean $= \dfrac{4 + 6 + 7 + 12 + 16}{5} = \dfrac{45}{5} = 9$

   (b) The trend graph below shows the rainfall in mm for the first six months of last year. Use the trend graph to answer the following questions.

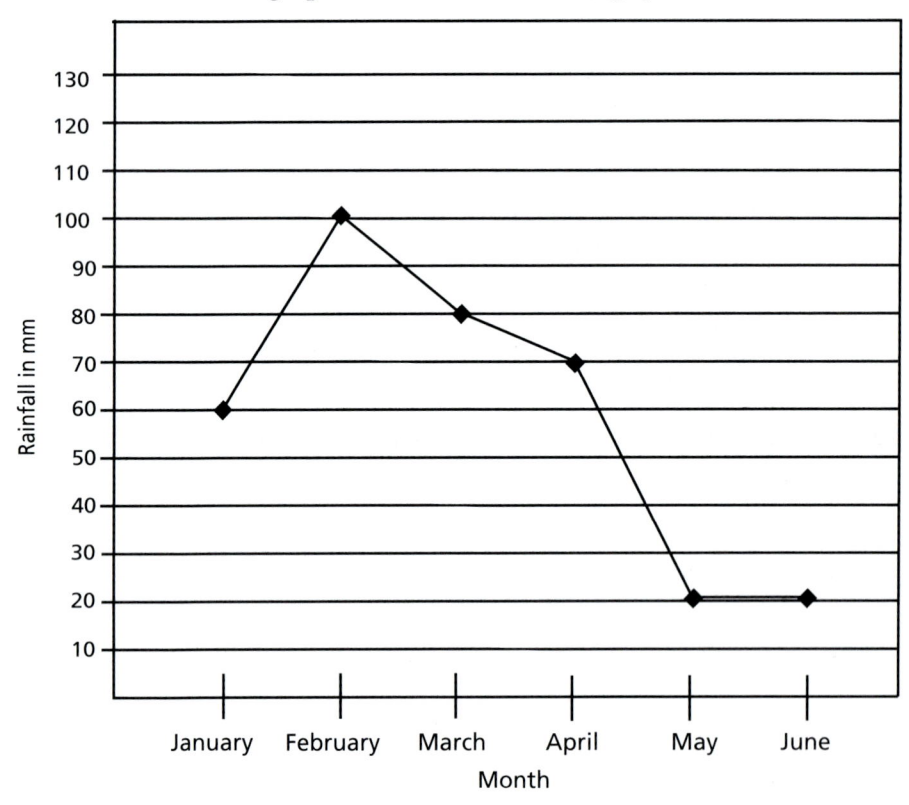

   i. Which of the given months had the highest rainfall?

   Solution   February

   ii. What was the total rainfall, in mm, for the given six months?

   Solution $60 + 100 + 80 + 70 + 20 + 20 = 350$ mm

   iii. What percentage of the total rainfall for the given six months fell in the month of April?

   Solution   % of rain in April $= \dfrac{70}{350} \times \dfrac{100}{1} = 20\%$

(c) A survey was taken of 40 students who owned mobile phones to find out the number of text messages that they sent on a particular day. The table shows the results of the survey.

Number of text messages	0	1	2	3	4	5
Number of students	3	5	7	5	14	6

i. Draw a bar chart of the data.

Solution

ii. What was the modal number of text messages sent on that day?

Solution Mode = 4 text messages

iii. Calculate the mean number of text messages sent on that day.

Solution $\bar{x} = \dfrac{(0 \times 3) + (1 \times 5) + (2 \times 7) + (3 \times 5) + (4 \times 14) + (5 \times 6)}{3 + 5 + 7 + 5 + 14 + 6}$

$\Rightarrow \bar{x} = \dfrac{0 + 5 + 14 + 15 + 56 + 30}{40}$

$\Rightarrow \bar{x} = \dfrac{120}{40}$

$\Rightarrow \bar{x} = 3$ text messages

Glossary

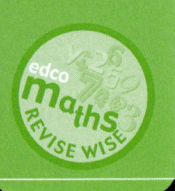

acute angle	An angle measuring less than 90°.
alternate angles	Equal angles on opposite sides of a transversal.
angle of depression	When looking downwards, this is the angle which the line of vision makes with the horizontal.
angle of elevation	When looking upwards, this is the angle which the line of vision makes with the horizontal.
annual interest	Interest for one year.
axial symmetry	Mirror image in a line.
axis of symmetry	Line that divides a shape into two equal parts.
bar chart	The heights of the bars in a bar chart show the frequency of the event in question.
binomial	An expression made up of two terms.
bisect	To divide a line segment or angle into two equal quantities.
brackets	simple/curve ( ), chain { }, square/block [ ].
central symmetry	Mirror image in a point.
circumcircle	A circle drawn through each of the three vertices of a triangle.
coefficient	A number that stands in front of a variable.
compass	An instrument for drawing arcs of circles and complete circles.
complement	All the elements that are not in a set.
composite number	A number with three or more divisors, e.g. 4, 6, 8, 9, 10.
compound interest	Interest for two or more years.
congruent	Shapes are congruent if they are identical in every way. All lengths equal, all angles equal.
constant	Any number.
corresponding angles	Equal angles on the same side of a transversal.

GLOSSARY

domain	Set of all first components of a relation.
equilateral triangle	A triangle with all three sides equal in measure and all three angles equal to 60°.
estimation	Approximation.
frequency	The number of times a particular event occurs.
function	A set of couples, but no couples have the same first component.
HCF	Highest common factor.
horizontal axis	The x-axis.
hypotenuse	The longest side in a right-angled triangle.
incircle	A circle drawn inside a triangle which touches each line segment at one point only.
income tax	Tax on a person's income.
index/indices	The 'power' that a number or variable is raised to.
intersection	All the elements common to two or more sets, counting each element once.
isosceles triangle	A triangle with two sides and two angles equal in measure.
LCM	Lowest common multiple.
line segment	The infinite set of points between the two endpoints given.
maximum point	Highest point on a curve/parabola.
mean	Another word for the average.
minimum point	Lowest point on a curve/parabola.
mode	The piece of information in a list which appears most often.
multiple	The multiple of a number is either the number itself or a larger number into which the original number divides evenly, e.g. 5, 10, 15, 20 are all multiples of 5.
N	Set of natural numbers, i.e. positive whole numbers, including zero.
null set	Empty set.
obtuse angle	An angle measuring more than 90° but less than 180°.
parallel lines	Lines which have the same slope and therefore never intersect.
parallelogram	A four-sided figure where opposite sides are equal in length and opposite angles are equal in measure.

perpendicular lines	Lines which meet at 90°.
pie chart	A circle divided into sectors of different sizes. The size of the sector is dependent upon the quantity being represented.
prime number	A number with two and only two divisors, e.g. 2, 3, 5, 7, 11.
protractor	An instrument for measuring the size of angles.
Pythagoras' Theorem	In a right-angled triangle, the square on the hypotenuse equals the sum of the squares on the other two sides.
R	Set of real numbers, i.e. any number on the number line.
range	Set of all second components of a relation.
ratio	A comparison of two or more numbers.
reflex angle	An angle measuring more than 180° but less than 360°.
relation set	A set of couples.
right angle	An angle measuring 90°.
right-angled triangle	A triangle in which one of the three angles is 90°.
scientific notation	A convenient method of writing numbers that are very large or very small.
set difference	All the elements in one set that are not in another set.
set	A collection of well-defined objects.
slope of a line	This is the vertical distance travelled divided by the horizontal distance travelled.
SRCOP	Standard rate (of tax) cut-off point.
standard form	Scientific notation.
straight angle	An angle measuring 180°.
subset	A set inside of a set.
surd	Numbers using the square root sign, e.g. $\sqrt{2}$, $\sqrt{5}$.
tax credit	Tax refund.
translation	This transformation moves a shape a certain distance in a certain direction.
transversal	A line intersecting two or more parallel lines.

trend graph	A set of points joined together from left to right by line segments. The upward or downward direction of the line segments gives the trend over a time period.
triangle	A two-dimensional shape with three vertices joined by three line segments.
trinomial	An expression made up of three terms.
trisect	To divide a line segment into three equal lengths.
union	All the elements in two or more sets, counting each element once.
universal set	All the elements under discussion.
variable	Any letter.
VAT	Value added tax.
Venn diagram	A graph for illustrating sets.
vertex	An extreme point in any shape.
vertical axis	The y-axis.
x intercept	The point where a line cuts the x-axis.
y intercept	The point where a line cuts the y-axis.
Z	Set of integers, i.e. positive and negative whole numbers, including zero.

Study Plan

REVISE WISE STUDY PLAN

Date				
Time				
Section to be revised				

Date				
Time				
Section to be revised				

Date				
Time				
Section to be revised				

Date				
Time				
Section to be revised				

Date				
Time				
Section to be revised				

Date				
Time				
Section to be revised				

Night before exam

Sections to be revised